HISTORY OF
ÍRELAND

HISTORY OF
ÍRELAND

Desmond McGuire

Exeter Books

NEW YORK

A Bison Book

Page 1: The lion symbol of
the Evangelist Mark from
the *Book of Armagh,* a
manuscript of the New
Testament written at
Armagh at the dictation of
Abbot Torbach who died in
808.

Pages 2-3: 'The O'Connell
Centenary Celebrations.' A
painting by Charles Russell
depicting a parade in Dublin
in 1875 to commemorate
Daniel O'Connell's birth.

This page: 'The Grand
Square, Trinity College,
Dublin', 1820.

CONTENTS

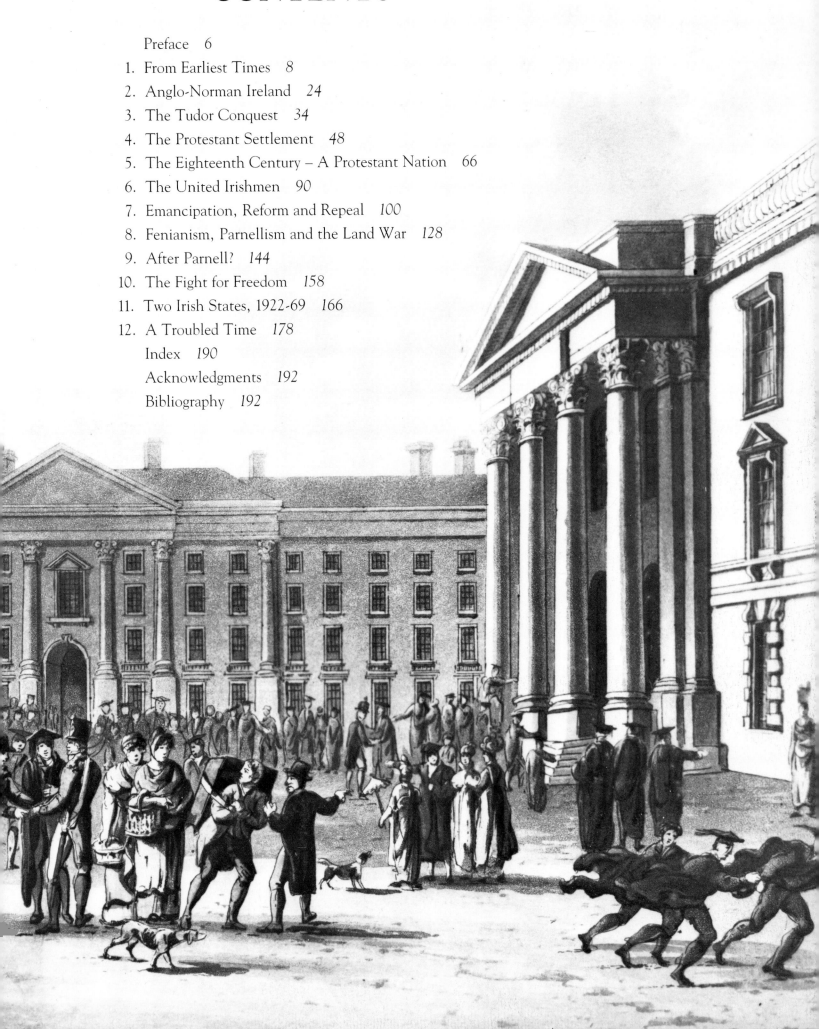

PREFACE

There is no single history of Ireland. There are merely a multiplicity of potential narratives about different aspects of the life lived by people on the island of Ireland over time. If there is any unity in such a story it is provided by place or people or by both. Geographical boundaries often but not always denote national boundaries. This notion of a nation is however a modern one. This history attempts to summarize certain aspects of the life lived on the island of Ireland. But there is no agreed canon of 'what happened.' Since things happen all the time the historian merely chooses to relate those happenings that seem to him to be significant. Every generation finds different aspects of the past interesting. There are, however, certain agreed events that seem at all times to be significant. Thus certain events always seem to be important in every generation. The coming of Christianity is agreed to be important though historians who have researched the fifth and sixth centuries now say that the transformation that it wrought was neither so immediate nor so absolute as was formerly thought. Thus historians often find that when they study an event or a 'happening' in detail it is often more complex and more surprising in its course than a swift analysis would suggest.

The purpose of writing a history like this is not to suggest that there is some agreed story of what happened in Ireland in the past but to provide some basic agreed core events around which the reader can see some shadow of the life lived on the island at different times. This history says certain things but the most useful way to read it is with the knowledge of what it does not say. Thus in describing the story of the rebellion of 1798 there is no mention of how a Wexford peasant felt when he went out with his pike to fight, there is no sense of the magistrate's feelings as he sentenced a man to death, no understanding of how Wolfe Tone felt as he cut his throat to avoid a humiliating execution. A history of this length is merely the bones of a story. It can be fleshed out if the reader remembers all that lies outside it, or if it leads him to read more detailed and scholarly work.

A great interest in Irish history over the past twenty years has produced countless detailed works by historians. They have studied the nature of the Tudor conquest, the meaning of the Penal Laws, the evolution of Irish nationalism, the persistence of patterns and wakes that the Catholic Church sought to root out, the improvement of living conditions after the famine. Some of this work has been characterized as revisionist but in effect it has merely redeemed certain aspects of the past from obscurity and re-examined formerly accepted pieties in their historical context. The maxim that historians ought not to consider periods of time but to examine problems is a valid one. Here there is an attempt to consider respective periods in terms of the problem that seems most central to contemporaries. History is above all about understanding how and why things happen, or how or why people think in certain ways. If it is not that then it is merely a litany of occurrences.

I have assumed that many people reading a short history of Ireland are concerned to discover the basis of the present political problems of Northern Ireland. For this reason the core concerns of this book are political. The recent events in Northern Ireland are neither incomprehensible nor recalcitrant to anyone who understands the history of Ireland. The central political reality in the politics of Ireland for many centuries, but particularly from the passing of the Act of Union in 1800, has been the British connection. Thus here the story of the nineteenth century is presented as one of the evolution of the political response to that Union throughout the century. Clearly that is not *all* that happened in the island in the period. In many respects it may have been at most times irrelevant to the preoccupations and concerns of the lives of ordinary people. It is, however, a story that became relevant to the lives of ordinary people through the success of Irish political nationalism in the twentieth century and the creation of an independent Irish state. It was also relevant to those who lived in the newly-constituted state of Northern Ireland which was constructed in response to the demands of Irish nationalism in the rest of the country. It has been said that boundaries once erected harden into permanence. In Ireland it seems equally true that the lives of most people have been affected by political decisions. Such decisions have at different times altered the political structures within which the lives of most people are lived and as such permeate society. It is for that reason that this is primarily a political history. For those interested in other aspects of the life lived in Ireland over time there are some suggestions for further reading in the bibliography.

Right: Ireland, showing the administrative divisions in both North and South.

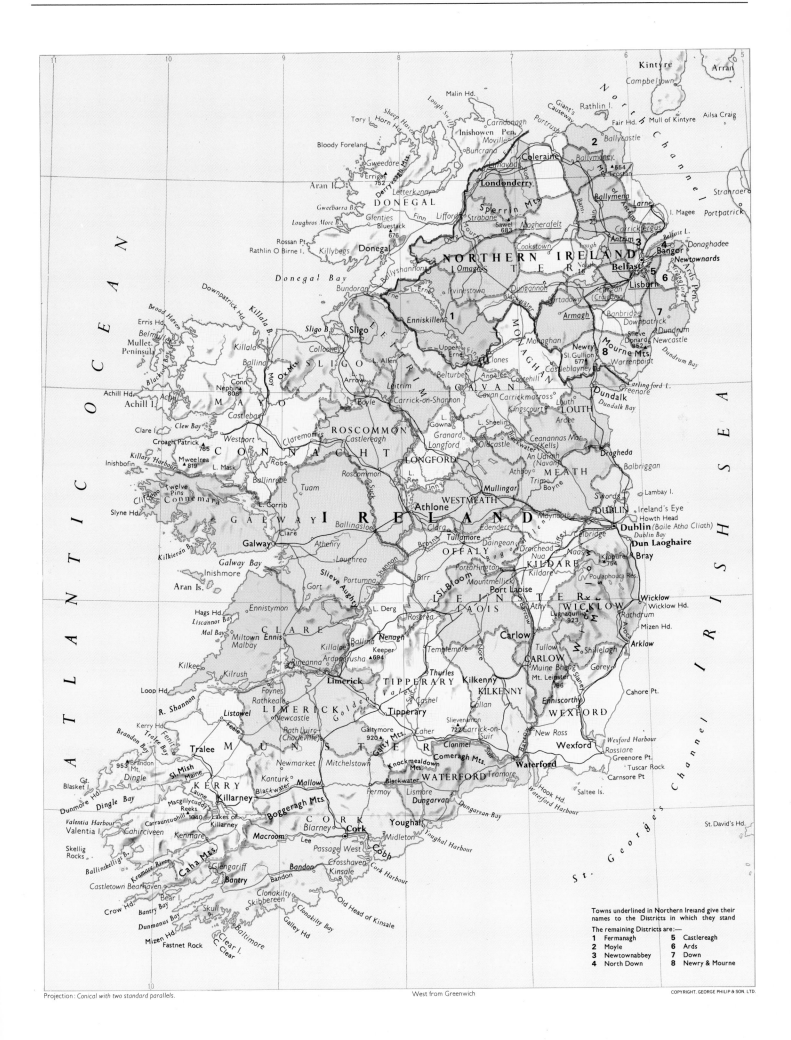

Towns underlined in Northern Ireland give their names to the Districts in which they stand

The remaining Districts are:—

1	Fermanagh	5	Castlereagh
2	Moyle	6	Ards
3	Newtownabbey	7	Down
4	North Down	8	Newry & Mourne

Projection: Conical with two standard parallels.

West from Greenwich

COPYRIGHT. GEORGE PHILIP & SON. LTD.

CHAPTER 1

FROM EARLIEST TIMES

KNOWLEDGE of the earliest inhabitants of Ireland is vague and uncertain; the little information that we have is derived from physical artifacts and organic remains scattered through the contemporary Irish landscape. That even this evidence is fragile is demonstrated by the fact that since the first systematic recording of archaeological sites in the Ordnance Survey maps of 1833-35 over one third of the sites listed have been destroyed. Those most affected by such vandalism are the Celtic ring forts of the later Iron Age.

The earliest inhabitants of the island were hunter-gatherers, but from about 3500 BC they gradually absorbed successive groups of farmers and, by acquiring their skills, they cleared and settled the land. But for the period before the New Stone Age – which is marked by the appearance of polished stone tools which are testaments to cultivation – the evidence for lifestyle, population or indeed culture in even its simplest sense is inconclusive.

It is from the years after 3500 BC that we begin to have concrete if ambiguous physical objects through which some idea of the life lived can be dimly seen. The most powerful and evocative of these are the megaliths – huge stone formations, of which there are over a thousand examples strewn across the Irish landscape. Contrary to the myths and sagas, in which they are explained as the random scatterings of warring giants or gods, all these stone sites had a special significance for the people who created them. These arrangements of large stones are similar to those found at Stonehenge and other parts of southwest England, but they are also to be seen in southwest Wales and areas of Scotland. The size of the sites, the size of the stones used and the complexity of

Previous pages: Poulnabrone Dolmen, The Burren, County Clare.

Below: The Giant's Causeway, County Antrim. The causeway features in legend as a bridge to Scotland, in reality it is an ancient lava formation.

Left: Fourknocks passage grave, County Meath. Such graves are most commonly found in the Boyne Valley in Meath and are believed to have been constructed mainly in 2500-2000 BC.

their arrangement vary from place to place. The similarities between sites, however, outweigh individual discrepancies and imply a shared cultural meaning. Whether that meaning relates to religious sacrifice, burial, power of a secular kind, or divine appeasement is, however, unlikely ever to be known with certainty.

Some formations are, however, unambiguous in purpose. These include the court cairns or burial chambers like those found on the furthest extremity of the Dingle Peninsula at Slea Head. These burial places are crude but complex. Rect-angular stonebuilt burial chambers are fronted by a sunken court, flanked by erect boulders. While they are certainly primarily burial places it is significant that their location often appears to be defensive or at least prominent. These stone structures changed in meaning and purpose over time, since they were erected over a period of more than 2000 years.

The most magnificent human achievements of the late Stone Age in Ireland are the austere and sophisticated passage graves set into the ground of the rich alluvial plains of the Boyne Valley at

Below: A stone circle near Killarney, County Kerry.

Above: The great tumulus above the passage grave at Dowth, one of the largest and best known of the type. Containing many thousands of tons of stone, such graves are testimony to a highly organised society.

Knowth, Dowth and Newgrange. These are remarkable not merely because in size and scale they dwarf all others, or because of the sophistication of the engineering skills that were required for their construction, but because they are part of a series of passage graves that seem to be strung in a line across the center of Ireland from the Boyne Valley, through the hills of Lough Crew, west to the Bricklieve Mountains in County Sligo and beyond to the precarious elevation of Knocknaree. While most of these passage graves are characterized by their elevation and consequent visibility for miles through the otherwise flat interior of the island, the Boyne group of graves lies low and concealed in its meandering course. Within the graves' complex interiors are ornamented stones, the island's earliest examples of human decoration. In this mysterious iconography of concentric whorls, intricate patternings and abstract repetitions we see a glimpse of an ordered world or at least of an aspiration toward a controlled movement beyond the natural and haphazard. In Newgrange the passage grave contains an aperture through which the sun, just after it rises at midwinter, shines and throws its light down a passage to illuminate the farthest extremity of the end chamber.

By the year 2000 BC the population of Ireland probably numbered about 100,000 to 200,000. From European research, and it must be remembered that it is unlikely that Irish developments were greatly out of step with the rest of northern Europe, it seems that this scattered population lived mainly on the high ground over the treacherously wooded lowlands. The homes of the inhabitants were rectangular structures of wooden laths culled from the hard woods of the lowlands, arranged in settlements of five or six houses. Living on cultivated crops, domesticated cattle, game and gathered food these people present a picture of scattered insecurity in a less than temperate climate.

But when we look at the ritual associated with the construction of even the simplest court cairns, quite apart from the sophistication of the great passage graves, we realise that these first settlers – of whose language we know nothing, for whom literacy did not exist – cannot merely be dismissed as crude and simple creatures concerned with little beyond survival. The construction of their finest monuments demanded the presence of large numbers of workers over considerable periods of time. Their very diligence demanded organization and, almost by definition, hierarchy. The monuments themselves, whether testaments to the exaltation of gods or men, display a consciousness of concerns beyond the transient and ephemeral. The number of washed cremated bones reveals the extent to which some unit of social organization beyond the scattered community controlled and ordered life. And of the art we can say little, except that these non-representational, abstract beginnings were to survive and dominate the Irish tradition for many centuries.

There is no sharp disjunction between the late Stone Age and the early Bronze and Iron Ages. Such divisions merely serve to aid the archaeologist or historian to order his own view of how the lives of populations change over time. It is possible to see a world of stone remains which gives way to one of metal objects, but in fact the skills of metalwork filtered in slowly over time and reached parts of the island more swiftly than others. There was no instant cessation of the buildings we describe as Stone Age, just as there was no 'turnover' of population in which one people gave way to another. As Professor Liam de Paor has written, it is perhaps best to see population as a stew which constantly absorbs new elements. So too with the notion of 'Ages': more skills, implements or technical developments are added to a base of knowledge, but there are no sharp disjunctions except as seen by posterity.

The acquisition of new skills and the knowledge of new materials – copper from the earliest mines at Mount Gabriel in West Cork, gold from the Wicklow Hills – were stimulated by contact with Britain and the Continent. Former histories often speak of the so-called Beaker people arriv-

Above: Carved standing stone at Reask, County Kerry.

Left: Interior of the great chamber of the passage grave at New Grange, County Meath. The chamber is corbel vaulted to a height of over twenty feet.

Right: Sunlight illuminates the intricate carvings on the east lintel of a passage grave at Loughcrew, County Meath.

Far right: Staique Fort, County Kerry, a formidable defensive work with walls up to 13 feet thick.

ing in Ireland in the early Bronze Age. Instead we now think of a style in pottery and metalwork which developed near the Danube and penetrated Ireland through travel and trade or the migration of a small number of skilled craftsmen. Northern Europe at this time was linked by travel and trade. In a burial chamber at Tara lies the body of a youth buried in about 2000 BC. Around his neck he wears a lace of beads. These are of copper from Ireland, of amber from Jutland or the Baltic, jet from Yorkshire and faience of uncertain origin. Around 1200 BC there was a period of rapid and turbulent change in which Ireland and all of northern Europe was embroiled. It is in this period that some of the most stunning early metalwork is produced, such as the gold lunula found at Mangerton in Kerry.

Instead of the coming of the Celts in the early Iron Age, that is to say about 1000 BC, it is more accurate to speak about Celticization. Who the Celts were is debatable. That the word 'Celtic' had a historical significance is undeniable. If the notion of selfconscious selfdefinition is taken to be central to being 'a people' then there were no Celts, at least not until the romantic movement of the late eighteenth and early nineteenth century invented them. But there is a style of art, dating from this period, described since its rediscovery in the late nineteenth century as La Tène or Celtic. There is a group of Indo-European languages described as Celtic. And more importantly there were peoples living across Northern Europe who were called Celts by the

Right: Golden lunula found at New Ross, Westmeath, dating from about 1800 BC. This type of flat collar, so called because of its crescent-moon shape, seems to have been a particularly Irish style since far more have been found in Ireland than elsewhere.

Second right: Gold plated lead pendant, 700 BC.

Below: Psalm 56 'Misere mei Deus' from the 'Cathach' or Battler as the Psalter supposedly written by St Columba is called. Written in the early part of the 7th century, before the Irish mission to Northumbria the 'Cathach' is unaffected by English style. The Irish hand is clearly developed but the vocabulary of decorative motifs is exclusively La Tène.

Right: St John's Crucifixion Plaque, late seventh century Roscommon, one of the earliest representations in Irish art of the crucifixion. Probably originally designed as a book cover, the representation of Christ resembles the slightly earlier figure on the Carndonagh Cross in Donegal.

Roman influence did reach the southeast through migrations to and returns from Pembrokeshire, and the culture of the dominant group of the southeast, the *Déisi* is the first that reveals the existence of a form of writing, a sharp alphabet carved into *Ogham* stones. These people saw themselves as being descended from a common ancestor *Eógan* and were known as the *Eóganacht*. In the midlands the *Ui Niall*, or descendants of Niall, gradually usurped at least partial control from the *Laigin*. Thus, though the early laws of Celtic or Gaelic society, the Brehon Laws, made the lordship of a tribe an elected office, or as it emerged over time a concession to superior might, the basic kinship structure of which these patrilineal names give evidence was the primary matrix of social structure. The assumption of a name was often merely an acknowledgment of allegiance or vasselage rather than a recognition of blood. The *rí* or king was originally a sacred person though his sacredness was conferred by office rather than implicit in his person or descent. Tribal law and custom was the province of the highest class among those of learning who were collectively termed the *oes dana*. The *filí* or the poets were the trained memory of the community, preserving genealogies later written down in apparently ceaseless litanies, knowing the vast lore of place so important in a society that resisted movement. The *Connachta* who dominated the west were the final 'high' *tuath* group but there were hundreds of others less noble, and parallelling their inner stratifications there existed other separate *tuaths* almost totally unfree or subservient.

Pope Celestine consecrated Pelladius, a deacon of the Gaulish church, in 431 and sent him to be the first bishop of the Irish Christians. In popular memory, however, the bishop has no role and the Christianization of Ireland is represented as the single divine purpose of Patrick, a romanized Briton captured by Irish pirates and brought to live in slavery on the slopes of Slemish in County Down. The legend states that on freeing himself he decided to devote his life to the task of bringing Christ to the Irish. There are two documents attributed to this Patrick, one a relatively minor letter addressed to a British chief who had seized Christian slaves from the Irish coast, the other a *Confessio* in the manner, of St Augustine. These are the only documents to survive from fifth century Ireland, although in the seventh century further writings attributed to to Patrick were used by ecclesiastics to defend the distinct church that he had founded and centered at Armagh from being absorbed into the rigid conventions that had developed in European and British Christianity.

Ireland was unique in being the only western European country, with the exception of the Viking north, to which Christianity came without Roman conquest. The account of Patrick in his *Confessio* suggests that he wished to concentrate his mission in the interior and west of the island where Roman influence was largely nonexistent, despite the fact that we associate him primarily with the north. It is clear that the absence of a Roman conquest, and the maintenance of native structures in all areas, affected the nature of the Irish Christian Church. Because of the absence of a Roman centralized organization Irish Christianity was directly absorbed on to the Celtic pagan base. Or, put another way, it was backed by no formal secular or doctrinal power. The Irish Church developed in a world at the very margins of Christendom and for many years no external authority formally marked off the old gods from the new. In the sagas there is a nostalgia for the lost romance of the pre-Christian world. In the post-Christian saga, the Fianna cycle, Oisin seems touched by a sense of lost wonder. Lir's lonely daughters, slumbering as swans for hundreds of years awaken to the forlorn peal of a Christian church bell, one that marks the passage of their old familiar world. But though there is a sense of nostalgia and loss there is no sense of a

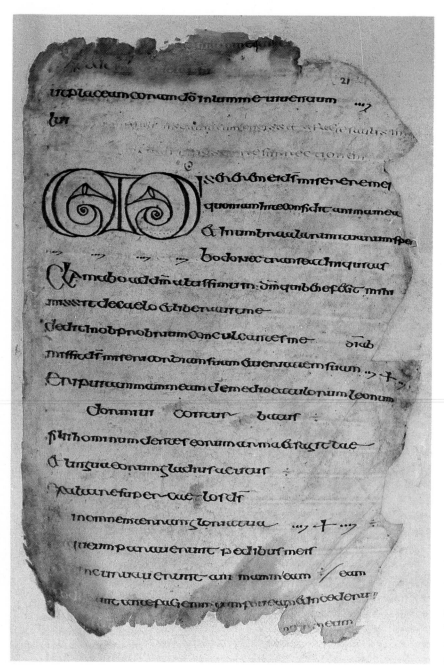

Above: The early Christian Tara brooch is in a design that was originally Roman. It is the richest example of Celtic jewelry still preserved. Found in a wooden box near the mouth of the River Boyne with a number of other pieces it was in all probability abandoned loot.

brutal transition from pagan to Christian. Pagan goddesses like Gobnait, to whom the bees were sacred, blended effortlessly into their new roles as Christian saints. Old pagan harvest festivals – Bealtaine, Samhan, Lughnasa – gave way in similar fashion to saints' days which just happened to fall on precisely those dates, in the Irish if not the Roman calendar. New native saints like Brigid of Kildare demonstrated their Christian sainthood in the conventions of old pagan womanly nobleness. Anomalies of polygamy, or the question of children born out of wedlock, continued to be the rule rather than the exception and found their moral and legal resolution in the Brehon Laws rather than in church doctrine. Most significantly, however, despite the structuring of certain dioceses and a network of bishoprics the Irish Church became primarily a monastic church, never properly assuming the centralized, geographically ordered network which the Roman Church, modelled on the structure of the Roman Empire, wished to impose.

Through trade with England Christianity had been felt along the eastern coastal strip for many years before it came to the island as a whole.

Whether that relates to the fact that the earliest evidence of literacy – the *Ogham* stones – are found there is debatable. Such literacy may be merely Roman. As Christianity spread to small groups of converts so did Roman dress and hairstyles, Roman law and, above all, literacy in the Latin language. The church's clerics were a new class of learned men, rivalling the *filí.* Their monasteries and churches, originally situated on marginal waste ground, gradually merged into the patrimonies of the old chiefs. The *filí,* anxious to retain their status, rapidly acquired the new skills of literacy, though whether their mnemonic culture of litanies, lists and genealogies was transformed to mark the conceptual leap between orality and literacy is debatable.

A new class of scribes grew up, often rising from the lower orders of the hierarchic Celtic world condemned to unchanging servitude under the old order. They initiated a native tradition, which drew upon Anglo-Saxon styles to illuminate the sacred manuscripts which they copied. Scribbled in the margins of even the most magnificent of these are commentaries, witticisms and asides in Old Irish. The classic sketch of the monk scribe is provided by one of these notes:

> Me and Pangur Ban my cat
> What a nice task we are at
> Hunting mice is his delight
> Hunting words I sit all night

Christianity and the Roman learning which it brought was a dynamic force. The introduction of Roman designs in brooches and jewelry, the use of precious stones in chalices, merging with the native tradition, produced objects and manuscripts of unrivalled magnificence.

St Finian of Clonard is thought to be the great mentor and molder of the Irish monastic tradi-

Right: Cross of Patrick and Columba, Kells, Meath. During the eighth century the construction of high stone crosses in the precincts of monasteries continued. During the later eighth and ninth centuries such crosses became more ornate, complex and sophisticated in style.

Second right: One of several grave slats in the grounds of the monastery at Clonmacnoise, County Offaly. The stone dates from the 10th-12th centuries and the inscription reads 'Pray for Thuthal the Mason.'

tion. His rule or penitential survives. Contrary to Roman orthodoxy, the form of monastic life favored by the Irish was that which most closely approximated to that tradition of pagan gathering which focused around the bones of the dead. Around such church reliquaries the Irish monks constructed their simple cells, some beehive-shaped, as on the Dingle Peninsula south of Slea Head, others more erratically ordered like the buildings on Skellig Michael off the most south-westerly point of Kerry. The great monastery of Clonmacnoise, erected by monks who came not from the great *tuath* backgrounds, and the monastery of Glendalough share one common feature – the solitary monk in his cell. This view of human isolation is found in the harsh monasteries scattered on the island retreats of the Mediterranean and the arid coastal limbos of North Africa and Greece. It is not typical of the continent of Europe, though it characterized those monasteries founded by Irish monks in the sixth and seventh centuries of which Iona, founded by Columba on the western isles of Scotland, is the most notable. Columba was a member of an important branch of the *Uí Néill*, and his commitment to Christianity may be seen as marking a marriage between the old order and the new – a demonstration of how Christianity was stamped and redefined by the indigenous culture of the island. Adomnan's life of Columba conveys not merely this sense of meeting, but also the complexity of the life of the monastery. The great monasteries of Ireland as opposed to the tiny scattered mud-walled retreats and oratories which dotted the countryside, through their protected relationships with the more powerful *tuatha*, the richness of their trading, their role as places of refuge, cultural centers and places of production gradually evolved into incipient walled towns. In the late sixth century Irish monks pouring from these centers, in pursuit of even harsher penance and exile went to the continent of Europe. In Bobbio (now in Switzerland), to name but one monastery, manuscripts and texts in the Irish style were produced, but the increased centralization and starkness of European monasticism was at variance with the individualistic Irish model. During the late eighth century, within the Irish monasteries at home, there was a reform movement, that of the *Céli Dé*, or God's clients, which took its impetus from a resistance to the Roman movement on the continent.

Thus, Irish Christianity existed in close communion with the old system of jostling *tuaths* in a society that was still essentially Iron Age. The dynamism of its arrival gave way to absorbtion into a society where change, insofar as it occurred, was a matter of the shifting ascendancies of successive groups.

From the fjords of western Norway bands of raiders forayed forth in the last years of the eighth century. Driven by hope of booty they attacked the coasts of northeastern England and eastern Ireland . Later they changed their strategy to colonization. Yet these colonizers came in no organized fashion, nor did they have specific strategies in mind. They were seen as barbarous anti-Christian hordes determined to wreak havoc on the priceless artworks of the monasteries. Their initial attacks on Ireland were on the north and northeastern coasts, a spillover from their Scottish raids, in one of the most notable of which they sacked and pillaged the monastery of Iona. Throughout the ninth century they sporadically raided the north of Ireland, causing occasional and localized alarm. This changed gradually, and by the middle of the century they were in possession of more detailed knowledge of the country. While the poverty and harshness of their own environment had at first led them to venture on sea raids for goods and booty, over time their aims changed to a desire of land. They continued to pillage the monasteries because they were the centers of wealth and power. Viewed as places of protection and refuge it was within their walls that people fled in the face of threat or danger. Given their status as bureaucratic and adminstrative centers, they clearly stood out as prime targets for the plunderer.

The intensity of inter-dynastic rivalries had not lessened over time. If anything, they had increased and in an environment of perpetual feuding there was ample scope for the outsider. The political unity of Britain, insofar as it existed, was the consequence of conquest, a response of outsiders seeing it as a unit. Ireland had no such experience and every local chief or king saw himself as loyal to his land, to the romance of his position and as responsive to the threats to that position posed by his neighboring peers. Not to win was to lose; the struggle was endless. The Vikings, therefore, met no united opposition. Not merely that, they were positively welcomed

Below: Monks' beehive shaped stone huts, Slea Head, County Kerry.

Right: A page from the most magnificent of the illuminated manuscripts, the Book of Kells.

Far right: The Little Skellig seen from the larger Skellig Michael, the site of one of the remote island monastic settlements of the early Christian church. Situated in the Atlantic, off the west coast of Kerry, it remained inhabited by ascetic monks until the 12th century. The remains of six beehive shaped monks cells survive as do a small church and an oratory.

Below: Glendalough. The church, round tower and monks' cells still stand in the monastic settlement of Glendalough. Situated in a valley of two lakes, from which it derives its name, Glendalough was an important crossroads of routes through the Wicklow mountains. By about 800 Glendalough was a flourishing monastic community, more like a hubbing town than a bleak retreat in the fashion of Skellig Michael.

as their superior weapons were seen as potential tools with which to beat an old enemy. It would be false to suggest that they were not resisted but true to say that they were assimilated as yet another group among the existing competitors. But land gained by them was by definition lost to others and in this they were strenuously resisted. They settled in pockets along the east coast, in precarious proximity to the sea. It was around Dublin Bay that they maintained their tightest grip. Excavations of Viking Dublin reveal that they settled there and continued to raid the rest of Europe from that new base. In the early tenth century Vikings from these European bases came and established towns in the southeast and west – on the Wicklow coast, in Wexford – named, as so many of their settlements were, in their own tongue – Cork and Limerick.

The *Uí Néill* of the north did attempt to check the Vikings, but essentially as a part of their pursuit of dominance over all other groups. In the south the *Eóganacht* were under threat from their own vassals, the *Déisi*, and their new adversaries, the *Dál Cais*. Coming from a position of weakness the *Dál Cais* of Clare were unencumbered by the necessities of retention which weighed down the old power of the *Eóganachta*. They seized Cashel, the center of southern power, and successfully took on and destroyed the Viking center of Limerick. Their leader, known as Brian Boru, took on one dynasty after another. He brought all of the Viking towns under his tribute, though he did not destroy them, and proclaimed himself high king and chief overlord of all Ireland. Though he had defeated all those whom he had taken on, his power was more rhetorical than actual as he had no means of retaining it. Leinster revolted against him, in the company of the Dublin Vikings, and though he defeated them at Clontarf, it was a hollow victory marked by his own immediate death and the absence of a successor to consolidate his gains. If his victory changed anything, it was simply to ensure that the pursuit of dominance in the future would be no longer focused as in the past on regional hegemony. In the future the prize was to be dominance of all Ireland. In the absence of an agreed ideology of overall kingship such a triumph was merely an invitation to deposition.

While the Vikings never controlled power, in the native Irish sense of power, they did control, through their more highly developed material culture, power of another kind. The remains of Viking Dublin reveal their houses, streets, coins, trades and goods. Though these came from their trading bases in Britain they were nonetheless present. They were sought after by the provincial powers, and their trade changed the Irish hinterland. Viking taste and Viking gold and silver changed art and architecture. They were not the only force for change, however. Irish kings like Cormac MacCarthy independently dealt with the outside world. He brought in stonemasons to construct his magnificent chapel at the now re-gained *Eóganacht* center of Cashel, a chapel that rivalled in magnificence Sitric, the Viking king's splendid cathedral of Christ Church in Dublin. The classical campanile of Europe was adapted by native stone masons to the distinctively Irish form of round tower.

But the impact of the Vikings was limited. In the monasteries works like the *Book of the Dun Cow* were written by writers who turned from the celebration of the universal to a consideration of the island's heroic past. There was no native tradition of philosophic doubt, nor was there an incipient movement toward the individual or confessional within this monastic tradition. The physical isolation of the island, despite the dynamic intrusions of the Vikings, proved impregnable. Repetition and perfection of existing modes rather than the pursuit of the new was the society's hallmark. Put crudely, Ireland was on the road to nowhere, if one excepts the anomaly of Brendan's alleged voyage to the Isles of the Blessed. Travellers bring change, glimpses of other worlds. Dynamic cultural change takes place at the crossroads of men. This absence explains both the strengths and the weaknesses of Irish culture in the Viking period, perhaps in all periods. Deprived of a relative sense of self, it was a society strangely confident and selfpossessed. In notions of power, in buildings, in works of art, the perfection of the given, the rearrangement of static elements was the dominant reality. Outside forces that attempted to reorder or remold native beliefs or patterns, like the Cistercians who came to Mount Mellifont in the twelfth century, were resisted and eroded until they accommodated themselves to the existing ways. Likewise with the attempt to force the medieval Irish Church to conform to European norms. It was rejected out of hand, doubly so when the Vikings joined the battle on the side of their brothers in Britain. Even the Vikings themselves, though they built their cities, plied their trade and imposed their styles of art to a degree, were absorbed rather than followed. They failed to impose their language, though it flourished in towns. In parts of the west independent imitations of Viking development were effected by the

twelfth century king, Turloch O'Conor. The old monastic sites of Tuam and Cong were built up to a wealth that rivalled that of the Viking towns. The Irish chiefs began to construct their own protective dwellings in the Viking style, though most continued to live in the old fashion. By the end of the twelfth century the Vikings were living harmoniously, another element in the rotating wheel of the internal power lottery.

Left: A 13th century miniature wooden ship excavated from a Viking and medieval site, Wynetavern Street in Dublin.

Below: A Hiberno-Norse penny of Shitric III 989-1029, Norse ruler of Dublin.

Below: The Rock of Cashel, County Tipperary. A historic focus of secular power in the south, it was transformed as the center of the southern see of the church when Cormac MacCarthy, the local king completed a magnificent chapel on the ancient site in 1134.

CHAPTER 2

ANGLO-NORMAN IRELAND

Previous pages: King John's Castle, Carlingford, County Louth. The castle, despite its name was not in fact the king's. It was the power base and fortress of Hugh de Lacy in the twelfth century.

Below: A representation of Diarmait MacMurrough from the margins of a late edition of the account of Giraldis Cambrensis.

IN 1166 a typical dynastic feud, similar to many in the past was to change the structure of power irreversably. Diarmait MacMurrough, deposed king of Leinster, decided that in order to retrieve his kingdom and defeat his adversaries, the 'high king' Ruairi O'Conor of Connacht and O'Rourke of Breiffne, he required outside assistance. With the tacit approval of the Norman king of England, Henry II, he rounded up a band of Norman lords in pursuit of wealth and adventure. Over 10 years earlier the English pope Adrian had followed up the Roman reordering of the Irish Christian Church at Kells by authorizing the English king 'to proclaim the truths of the Christian religion to a rude and ignorant people.' This was a tribute to Rome's final success in taking over a church that had defied all conventions for over 400 years. Moreover it was a recognition of an inability to place the Church in Ireland under the See of Canterbury, an attempt at external control that had been utterly rejected by the reordered Irish bishops at the Synod of Kells. Essentially Adrian's *Laudabiliter* was an empty letter at the time of its promulgation, a sop to a defeated attempt to control and monitor the Irish Church. Diarmait's introduction of Norman power into Ireland was however to convert that empty religious formula into a potent weapon for the achievement of secular power.

The Norman barons who accompanied MacMurrough in his reconquest of Ferns were not complete strangers to Ireland. They had defeated the Welsh and taken over parts of the Welsh coast, particularly the area around Pembrokeshire. They were accustomed to trading with the Irish Viking coastal towns. The Norman forward parties were led by Robert FitzStephen, Maurice FitzGerald and later by Raymond le Gros. Successive landings, the first at Bannow Bay in Wexford preceded by archers and flanking cavalry in full coat of arms brought a complex medley of thrusting adventurers whom Henry was in due course to restrain and control.

These landings and consequent settlements were described by one of their own, Giraldis Cambrensis or Gerald the Welshman who also gave an analytical account of the native society unlike any found in the annals of the old literature. The annals of Inisfallen, of Ulster and Tigernach were produced in the monasteries under the patronage of the dynasties as works of validation or historiographical self-justification. They presented the past in litanized repetitions of the rise and fall of dynasties, unenlightened by analysis or explanation, and displayed an unwillingness to recognize the existence of the Ostmen or Vikings except by scathing references to their possession of territory purchased not by immemorial right but by the sword. This 'sword land,' as the Gaelic chiefs called it was treated as a mere temporary intrusion on a land seen to be on the point of reversion to the old ways, this after 200 years of Viking settlement. This history of the annals was often a representation of a desired rather than actual view of the past. Gerald's accounts had a propagandist base too – to prove to his own people and to posterity that conquest of the native powers was desirable and necessary from the perspective of civilization. While his fierce condemnations of the savagery and brutality of the old Irish way of life can be read with consequent skepticism, his accounts do provide an outsider's description of a society that the annalists never troubled to delineate, since they wrote for the initiated, and were absorbed by local detail.

Giraldis was born into the society of southeast Wales which produced the adventurers who came in with Diarmait. His account of the conquest is the only reliable contemporary one we have, with the exception of *The Song of Dermot and the Earl* which was written over 30 years later. Gerald's account is not that of an eyewitness though he claims that it is. In the *Expugnatio Hibernica* he recounts each stage of the conquest, but in the *Topographia* the observations of the outsider become clear. In the former he is telling the his-

tory of his own people in Ireland from the inside; in the latter he describes, unsympathetically, what lay before them.

Diarmait met the first expeditionary force and they proceeded to capture Wexford town from the Ostmen. Wexford initially resisted. In the words of Gerald:

When they [the inhabitants of Wexford] saw the lines of troops drawn up in an unfamiliar manner, and the squadron of knights resplendent with breastplates, swords and helmets gleaming, they adopted new tactics in the face of changed circumstances, burned entire suburbs, and immediately turned back and withdrew inside the walls.

Diarmait began in victory as he was to continue. He 'immediately assigned the city and all its lands' to FitzStephen and Maurice. To Hervey of Montmorency he assigned under grant the two cantreds 'which border on the sea and lie between the two cities of Wexford and Waterford.' The old sword land of the Ostmen was insignificant compared to the granting of land to the Norman barons, initiated by Diarmait in this single act. It was utterly to alter the structure of power in all but the remote fastnesses of the west and south where the Irish leaders were to live out a relentless resistance on the margins between two worlds.

Enlivened by victory Diarmiat proceeded against a host of his old enemies, subduing all before him with the aid of the new arrivals. Richard de Clare, earl of Strigoil, known as Strongbow, became Diarmait's most important and powerful Norman ally. To mark the depth of the new

alliance Diarmait gave his daughter Aoife in marriage to Strongbow at conquered Waterford. This ceremony was to maintain significance for the Irish for generations, finding its classic symbolic expression in the painting of the nineteenth century romantic artist MacLise. His view of the event, though sentimentalized is not inaccurate. The divisions between the past and the future are now clearly etched. The initiative has passed to the Normans. Giraldis describes within his own cultural framework the speech of Ruairi 'prince of Connacht and ruler of all Ireland' to the men who rallied against Diarmait and his allies:

Renowned and brave warriors, defenders of our fatherland and liberty , let us consider . . . See how that enemy of this country that despot over his own people and universal enemy, previously driven from his country, has now returned flanked by the arms of foreigners, to bring about our common ruin . . . So this man, himself our enemy has brought in a race most hostile to ours, a race which has long been eager to rule us all alike, Diarmait included, a race moreover which asserts that by the fates' decree they are entitled to jurisdiction over our island. So he has now made ready to spread his poison so widely that, after everyone else has been tainted by the general infection, he has not even spared himself, in order that no one at all may be spared. . . . Wherefor in defense of our fatherland and our freedom, and creating for ourself a renown which will long endure by making bold an assault, let us bring the matter to a successful conclusion, so that the death of a few many inspire fear among many, and because of the awful warning of their fate, foreign peoples may be forever deterred from such an execrable venture.'

Above: 'The Marriage of the Princess Aoife of Leinster with Richard de Clare, Earl of Pembroke' otherwise known as Strongbow, by Daniel MacLise.

Below: A Dublin-issued halfpenny of John, Lord of Ireland, *circa* 1177.

MacMurrough's successful campaigns eroded a forced submission which Ruairi O'Conor had extracted from him in an early march into Leinster before the full Norman contingent had arrived. Even had MacMurrough wished to disengage from the Normans, which he did not, matters developed rapidly beyond his control. The seizure of Waterford by Raymond le Gros; Strongbow's skill in keeping MacMurrough to the promise of his daughter's hand and the ensuing rights of succession to the kingdom of Leinster; and their joint seizure of the city of Dublin: all conspired to strengthen the new ties. Diarmait had learned a lesson about his allies, a lesson at which Ruairi's words hint. While the Normans were his allies they were more truly his mercenaries, mercenaries whose primary loyalty was to their own desire for land. When Prendergast de Roche had attempted to desert Diarmait at a time when the latter's forces were hopelessly outnumbered he had not hesitated to offer his services and those of his men to one of Diarmait's oldest enemies. Diarmait was bound to the FitzGeralds, the Barrys, the de Cogans and others by necessity and the desire for power and revenge. In his quest for revenge he succeeded, but the power he regained was his for a mere two years before his death in 1171. He had the dignity of death in his old fastness at Ferns but those that benefitted after him were Strongbow and lesser Norman lords who saw greater opportunities in Ireland than in the well-worked territory of the Welsh Marches.

Henry's attention had never been engaged by the Irish campaign. His concerns in Acquitane were absorbing and Ireland seemed at best a useful diversion for his more recalcitrant barons. In 1171 Henry was answerable to the pope for the death of Thomas à Becket at Canterbury. But the realization that Strongbow was assuming the role of king, albeit an Irish king, was to become a source of considerable anxiety. In theory Ireland was a game hardly worth the candle. To conquer it had seemed more trouble than it was worth. But the fact that certain of his own barons were entrenching themselves there and constructing an independent power base presented Henry with a simple choice – to halt the process or to take it over by placing the conquest in his name, the name of the Crown of England. Moreover, from happier days he had a charter of right in respect to such a decision in the form of *Laudibiliter.* Late in 1171 Henry came to Ireland. He negotiated with the Irish provincial rulers who complained of baronial infringements on ancient rights. They submitted to his overlordship in return for protection from the worst excesses of his knights. He failed to realize the extent to which such submissions in an Irish context were merely a prelude to repudiation. Since Irish and Norman concepts differed on almost all significant fundamentals – the concept of kingship, the relationship between lords, or *taoisigh,* and kings, the meaning of territory, the concept of land as inheritance, the reckoning of wealth and status, the nature of inheritance – to name but a few – the potential for misunderstanding was considerable. Feudal concepts were unknown in Ireland. The developing concept of chivalry was meaningless. The Irish had their own measures of honor, valor and integrity, but they were the moral standards of an utterly different culture.

Henry left the Irish convinced that they believed their land been granted by him in the feudal fashion in return for protection. Such a view of rights to land was of course meaningless to those who reckoned their wealth not in acres, but in cattle, and who saw acres as fastnesses rather than sources of potential wealth. Land came down by immemorial right without the need for royal intervention.

Henry now intervened to curb the power of Strongbow which he viewed as dangerous to his own interests. He granted the old fifth province of the midlands, *Midhe,* to Hugh de Lacy. He took the Ostman towns from under the control of Strongbow. Control of Dublin was granted by charter to Bristol, its chief trading partner. At a synod convened in Cashel he obtained the overlordship of the Irish church. It seems that both religious and secular powers in Ireland saw Henry as an honest broker between them and the barons who were becoming excessively powerful as a result of manifestly superior military skills in set battles. Ruairi was acknowledged by Henry as 'high king' in areas outside Norman control. The precise extent of these areas was open to question since in defiance of earlier agreements Henry persisted in issuing new land grants to newly arrived barons. The Irish assumption that they were negotiating on the basis of the number of barons already on the island was erroneous. Henry granted the lordship of Ireland to his youngest son John, as the least prestigious of his domains. But of his four sons John alone left heirs, ensuring that the lordship of Ireland was incorporated into the kingdom of England.

The Normans were assiduous colonizers. Buildings were their forte. Even today the country is scattered with motte-and-bailey earthworks, the remains of Norman strongholds of wood which they built on piled earthen mounds before graduating to the formidable stone castles which still linger on the countryside. They were constructive and hard-working. Above all they measured their progress in terms of their effect on the landscape. Their agricultural methods were new to Ireland and concerned with soil cultivation rather than the raising of cattle. Giraldis praised the lush richness of the country in his account but also commented on the lack of human imprint:

The soil is soft and watery, and even at the tops of high and steep mountains there are pools and swamps. The land is sandy rather than rocky. There are many woods and marshes; here and there there are some fine plains but in comparison with the woods they are indeed small. The country enjoys the freshness and mildness of spring almost all the year round. The grass is green in the fields in winter just the same as summer. Consequently, the meadows are not cut for fodder, and stalls are never built for the beasts. The land is fruitful and rich in its fertile soil and plentiful harvests. Crops abound in the fields, flocks on the mountains, wild animals in the woods. It is rich in honey and milk. Ireland exports cow hides, sheep skins and furs. Much wine is imported. But the island is richer in pasture than in crops, and in grass rather than in grain.

In commending the rule of Hugh de Lacy, Giraldis comments on the lengths to which de Lacy went to win the trust of the native Irish, the extent to which he kept his word to them, the perseverance with which he built castles 'and finally when they were hemmed in by the castles and gradually subdued he compelled them to obey the law.' Gerald is writing from hindsight, from a less than pleased perspective on the progress of the conquest after the visit of John. He is analyzing the mistakes that have been made, and the fashion in which they can be redeemed. He concludes the *Expugnatio* with a consideration of these matters, the most important part of his text, he explains. The visit of John, the future king was a mistake he claims, one of many. Firstly the Normans erred by going back on their word to their former Irish allies, by dispossessing them of their lands, and by placing lazy borderers in their place. This lost them many allies. When John came on a lavish trip to Ireland and landed at Waterford he was greeted by Irish nobles who came to pay homage. Instead of treating them with respect, the Normans 'tweaked the Irish about their beards,' worn long in the Irish fashion and treated them with contempt and derision. Outraged they proceeded to Limerick where they spoke to Ruairi O'Conor, among others, and advised against

Below: The ruins of the Cistercian Abbey at Inch, County Down, founded by John de Courcey after his campaign in Ulster. The building was completed in 1187.

Above: St Patrick's Cathedral in Dublin, built in the 1190s by John Comyn, Archbishop of Dublin.

Below: Doe Castle, County Donegal.

Meanwhile this was the state of affairs in Ireland: everywhere there was gloom, everywhere cries of despair; all roads became impassable; no-one was safe from the axes of the Irish; every day brought new reports of fresh disasters befalling our people. All this was happening outside the cities, and only within their walls was there some semblance of peace.

This described a temporary state of turmoil after John's visit, a time when it seemed the Normans were losing their grip.

This wily race must be feared far more for its guile than its capacity to fight, for its pretended quiescence than for its fiery passion, for its honeyed flattery than for its bitter abuse, for its venom than for its prowess in battle, for its treachery than for its readiness to attack, and for its feigned friendship than for its contemptible hostility.

Despite the failure of John's visit in 1185, the reality was that by the date of John's coronation in 1199 the Norman presence had altered the Irish landscape. The area of their greatest influence was the northeast, particularly Ulaid, roughly what is now Down and Antrim. They did extend into Tyrone but, especially west of the Bann, they were prevented from further expansion by O'Neill power. This was primarily the territory of de Courcey who Henry had seen as a check on the pretensions of Hugh de Lacy in Meath. De Courcey brought workers from Scotland to till his newly acquired acres and when, in 1179 de Lacy was decapitated at Durrow, de Courcey, as king's justiciar or representative in Ireland became manifestly pre-eminent. The other areas of Norman influence were almost all of what is now the province of Leinster with particular concentration in Meath, Kildare, Kilkenny, Wexford – where the cantreds of Bargey and Forth were to retain unassimilated 'Norman' peculiarities of manner, dress and speech right down until the nineteenth century – Waterford, particularly around Lismore and parts of north Tipperary. But Limerick, which had been gained from the Ostmen and then lost to the native Irish, was an enduring invitation to expansion west of Shannon and there were sporadic raids into the lands of the O'Briens of Clare. West Cork and North Kerry were equally inviting. The Normans had a manual of conquest, a blueprint of slow penetration carefully consolidated by a fortificatory network of linked castles which could come to one another's assistance in time of native uprising. They had precedents for their colonising. Some came directly from Normandy but in the main those who settled Ireland came from that relatively small kinship group that had conquered the harsh borderlands of Celtic north Wales.

The Normans' greatest fortificatory network was along the Shannon. The early agreement with the old high king Ruairi O'Conor was set aside, but subsequent arrangements with his heir Cathal Crobderg left the Shannon as the essential divide between Norman and Gaelic Ireland

trusting the Normans. Those who were on the brink of submitting to him instantly reconsidered.
For this race like every uncivilized people, has an inordinate desire to be treated honorably, while themselves not knowing what honor means.

though the de Burghs were later granted official if not actual control of Connacht. The Norman bases along the Shannon have in the main endured and the bulk of the towns of the south and west midlands today have origins in Norman settlement. The strength of the Normans' building skills is attested by the castles that still stand, some like Bunratty in preserved integrity, the majority standing as ruined walls in the streets of prosaic country towns. In Dublin they erected St Patrick's Cathedral as a rival center of magnificence to the adjacent Christ Church. As more towns were granted the power to mint money, John ordered that a secure treasury be constructed in Dublin. Dublin Castle, which was built for this purpose, endured not merely as a fastness of mammon but as the seat of power in Ireland for eight centuries. In representing John's desire to control finance it also served as a monument to his attempt bureaucratically to assimilate his Irish lordship into the rest of the kingdom. A more real focus for this urge was an attempt to root out the old Irish Brehon Law and replace it with the English common law. In this his administration was only partly successful. For the Norman barons, despite their ostensible control of the material surface, displayed, almost from the time of their arrival, a susceptibility to an undertow that was to mark all subsequent arrivals. It was the pull of place and culture made concrete by marriage alliances with the native Irish. Within two or three generations, though the names of

Normandy dominated Ireland east of Shannon, the actual holders of the name were usually the sons of Irish mothers and often the grandsons of Gaelic lords. Despite the initial Norman attempt to excoriate and in certain cases to exterminate the lowest among the native population, the realities of accommodation and expansion ensured a network of strategic intermarriage. More significantly the force of language, of customs, of dress and of local practise proved irresistible to the numerically inferior group of settlers. The taunt was that the Normans were 'more Irish than the

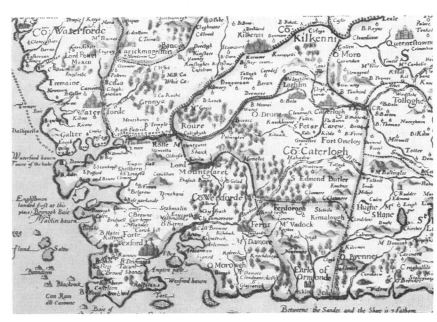

CHAPTER 3
THE TUDOR CONQUEST

DURING the Wars of the Roses Ireland, or rather Norman Ireland, was Yorkist. Richard, duke of York was lieutenant of Ireland in 1449. He had ties with many of the great Anglo-Norman families and pleased them by his awareness of how diminished was their power since its zenith in the early thirteenth century. The economy was weak. Changes in climate and the dramatic fall in population as a result of the ever-recurring Black Death conspired to increase native Irish confidence, and to undermine the ability of the colony to raise sufficient funds with which to launch a successful counterattack. The cows of the Gaelic chiefs grazed on formerly rich tillage land, and to many Normans it seemed as if nature and their own government conspired to claw back their achievements.

After the triumph of the Yorkist cause in the person of Edward IV, Ormond, the single notable supporter of the house of Lancaster, was executed. The earl of Desmond, in a self conscious display of loyalty, defeated Ormond's brother

Previous pages: Annabally Castle and medieval earthworks, County Galway.

Below: Cadaver effigy from the 15th century, Beaulieu, County Louth.

when he attempted to re-enter the country. In reward for this piece of egregious self-serving Edward made Desmond justiciar of Ireland. The colony had, however, gone over to Irish ways even more than had been realized and Edward was unable to tolerate the markedly 'Irish' way in which Desmond conducted his administration. He was rapidly replaced by Sir John Tiptoft who beheaded Desmond for unspecified acts of treason in dealing with the Irish enemy. This attack upon Desmond's family was the signal for a rising of protest among the native Irish, but more significantly among the colony. The FitzGeralds of Kildare availed themselves of the new turmoil to press their claims as the only remaining Anglo-Norman family of the first significance, with the exception of the de Burgos or Burkes who were embroiled in their own immediate concerns.

With Henry Tudor the Lancastrian cause was reasserted at Bosworth, but the resumption of power did not close the question of legitimacy. This was Henry VII's primary concern since it was the question on which the endurance of his dynasty depended. The collusion of Thomas Fitz-Gerald and the earl of Desmond (successor of the earl beheaded by Tiptoft) in respective plots to place first Lambert Simnel and then Perkin Warbeck on the throne of England was drastically to alter Henry's view of his Irish lords.

The Simnel plot went to the point at which he was crowned Edward VI in Dublin on 28 May 1487. The plots were, however, defeated. Desmonds and Kildares suffered – the latter having more to lose, suffered most. The Kildare Geraldines lost – at least temporarily – their role as the king's representative in Ireland.

Henry was now to look with new eyes on the Irish territory which had been held in name, if not under the writ of the English Crown for three centuries. Despite exports of hides, furs and other raw materials Ireland could no longer be viewed as an economic benefit to the English treasury. The descendants of the Welsh borderers had made their killing, but their wealth added little to the king's revenues.

The house of Kildare was not utterly reduced. They did hold the ostensible reins of power again for a few years, while Henry bided his time. On 12 September 1494 he appointed his son Henry as nominal lieutenant, but gave actual power to his old companion Sir Edward Poynings. Poynings killed off the Warbeck Plot, summoned a parliament at Drogheda and enacted a number of laws not dissimilar in intent to the Statutes of Kilkenny. There was however one significant difference. Instead of attempting to pull the colony out from entanglement with the native Irish as had then been the case, it was as if the Crown now viewed native and planter as part of one entity without internal differentiation. Henceforth it was the power of the colony that was to be restrained for the good of the Crown. Poyning's enactments did acknowledge the need to protect the colony but that concern was secondary to a desire to restrain it. The ninth act of the parliament, henceforth to be known as Poynings' Law was to govern the nature of the parliamentary relationship between the two islands to the close of the eighteenth century. It decreed that no parliament could be validly held in Ireland unless the lieutenant and the Irish Council of the king first informed the king under the Great Seal of Ireland why that parliament was being called and what acts were to be passed. It further decreed that only if the king then issued his approval under the Great Seal of England could that parliament be called. The intent and effect of the law was to ensure that there would be no independent parliamentary development that might seek to cut across the power of the Crown. It was a direct response to Geraldine control of the council and power over the calling of parliaments that had made them the actual rulers of Ireland.

Kildare, formerly attaindered for dubious loyalty and held in London, returned under the new dispensation to rule as the king's man. Gearoid Mór ruled in his own fashion, administering a heady brew of common and Brehon Law in a strange confusion, wearing English dress when occasion demanded but skirting dangerously close to the Gaelic margins in custom, family ties, mode of lordliness and familial culture. FitzGerald moved between both worlds, but he did not correspond to the accepted ideals of the Renaissance gentleman. He lived in style, but it was a rawer, rougher style than that found at English court or indeed in the homes of English lords.

In 1509 Henry VIII succeeded to the throne. Ten years later he recalled Gearoid Óg (Garret the Young to differentiate him from his father Garret the Great) on charges of misgovernment. *The Kildare Rental* which begins in the 1518 shows

Left: A Processional Cross, made for Cornelius O'Conor of Kerry in 1479. Found at Ballymacasey. Often known as the Ballylongford Cross.

just how great the wealth and power of the Fitz-Geralds was when Henry decided absolutely to curb it. In a section marked 'Duties upon Irishmen' are listed the names of those Gaelic lords who paid protection to the family. Significantly, many of these tributes are contingent upon Fitz-Gerald being Lord Deputy. In an agreement in Irish between FitzGerald and the MacRannals of Leitrim it is stipulated that a shilling from the rent in every quarter of land is to be paid to the earl on All Hallows every year 'in consideration of the earl's defending and assisting them against

Left: The estates of the Kildare Geraldines, from a map of Ireland by Baptista Boazio, 1599.

all men subject to his authority.' As James Lydon has pointed out in *Ireland in the Later Middle Ages* it is clear that the source of much of the wealth of the Kildare Geraldines and of the other great families in the time of their political ascendancy was derived from this entirely illegal levying of fees on lesser Gaelic lords for political protection. Such anomalies were not entirely unknown within the common law, but were the order of the day under the Brehon code. Hence the ease with which such sums were extracted from secondary magnates. The standing army which the Geraldines had raised by the creation of the Fraternity of Arms through the Dublin parliament of 1474 meant that they had in fact the resources to effect their pledges of protection. It was this power that Henry VIII was resolved to break in time. Gearoid Óg was not the man his father had been nor was his heir 'Silken Thomas'. More truly he was still a late medieval lord, while the Tudors were Renaissance princes moving inexorably to the changes brought about by Thomas Cromwell and his adjutants. In short, they were men of another age. In this context, perhaps Gerald MacShane's advice to the earl's son, reported to Cromwell in 1533 is less powerful than it might at first appear. He exhorts Thomas to be more like his father:

Thou fool, thou shall be the more esteemed in Ireland to take part against the king: for what hadst thou been if thy father had not done so? What was he set by until he crowned a king here; took Garth the king's captain prisoner; hanged his son; resisted Poynings and all deputies; killed them of Dublin upon Oxmantown Green; would suffer no man to rule here for the king but himself?

Gearoid Óg's dismissal in 1519 was primarily a

consequence of Wolsey's dislike of the Geraldines and of Irish intriguing in general. It was followed by a period during which Henry tried to rule Ireland without the intervening power of the Fitz-Geralds. Thomas Howard, earl of Surrey was appointed as lieutenant. Henry's dispatch to Surrey emphasized that he wanted his dominion brought to order by 'sober ways, politique drifts, and amiable persuasions.' Despite apparent successes in gaining submissions from Conn O'Neill and Hugh O'Donnell in Ulster and more doubtful ones from O'Carroll, O'More and O'Conor, and further contacts with Desmond, MacCarthy Mór and MacCarthy Réagh, it was found that the cost of conquering Ireland and ruling it without the assistance of the old internal power-brokers was formidable. Surrey sent a studied estimate of the cost of reconquest to Henry. An army of over 5000 men would be required whose billeting and financing would be a charge upon the English exchequer. To consolidate the reconquest castles and towns would be required to hold new lines. A new group of English settlers would be required. Surrey withdrew and in his stead Piers Roe Butler, a Butler of Ormond was appointed. Piers Butler was from a subsidiary Butler family, the main line having no male descendants. He was of that branch at Polestown who had defied the Statutes of Kilkenny and had continued to take Irish wives, the marriage between Sabina Kavanagh and James Bulter being for years a celebrated law case. Piers Roe was their son and he spent much of his early years attempting to prove the legitimacy of his parents' marriage. Thomas, the last earl of the original Buter line left two daughters, one of whom was the grandmother of Anne Boleyn. Piers Roe's assumption of the lieutenancy in 1522 was, however, to result in his official recognition as earl of Ormond and apparently to close the claims of the Boleyns through the female line. Gains were shortlived for Piers Roe politically. Within three years Kildare was back in control, now with the full support of the only other significant lords, the earls of Desmond. That accommodation too was to be brief.

In 1533 Henry married Anne Boleyn, setting aside his first wife Catherine of Aragon in defiance of the pope. More importantly he succeeded in alienating the emperor, Charles V, nephew of Catherine. In a series of complicated moves the two issues of the government of Ireland and the Reformation within the English Church became inextricably bound. It was also the final year of Kildare control in Ireland. The writing had been on the wall of over a decade. Gearoid Óg was no longer young and after being wounded in battle in 1532 in the words of Stanihurst, the Tudor historian, 'He never after enjoyed the use of his limbs nor delivered his words in good plight.'

After its breach with Rome, Thomas Cromwell extended the bureaucratic reordering of the Church to Ireland. He appointed the new Master of the Rolls, John Allen essentially to spy on Fitz-

Gerald's activities. A case was slowly built up culminating in the allegation that Kildare was removing the royal ordnance from Dublin Castle to his home at Maynooth. His son Silken Thomas, earl of Offally was left nominally in charge as Gearoid Óg was ordered yet again to London. Committed to the Tower on arrival, it was reported in Dublin that Kildare had been summarily executed. This was not the case, but believing it to be true Silken Thomas (so-called because of his love of fine clothes) proceeded to Dublin, flung the sword of state before the members of the council, and joined a highly heterogeneous rebellion composed of Geraldine supporters from the Pale and the Gaelic powers of Leinster. Only Butler of Ormond, (of the Boleyn family – since Henry had in due course taken back the earldom of Ormond from Piers Roe) stood by Cromwell in his sweeping blow against the Fitz-Geralds.

The Reformation was only indirectly the cause of the rebellion insofar as it had catalyzed Cromwell's organizational passion, but it was as yet too new a phenomenon to be responded to doctri-

Above: Henry VIII in 1536 by Holbein.

Above: Kilkenny Cathedral. Effigy of Piers Butler, 8th Earl of Ormond, died 1539. Butler is depicted in a style of armor still common in Ireland at the time but outdated elsewhere, perhaps a token of loyalty to Irish custom.

nally. Yet the European instability engendered by Henry's repudiation of the pope was a potential, if largely ephemeral, lever to the Irish in their discontents. In 1534 Cromwell received a letter from Cowley about Gearoid Óg's son Thomas which went as follows: 'The said earl's son, kinsmen and adherents do make their avouant and boast that they be on the pope's sect and band, and him they will serve against the king and all his partakers.' It was rumored that an imperial army of Charles V, invited by the earl of Desmond was on the point of coming to FitzGerald's defense. Gearoid Óg died in December 1534, having seen the power built up by this family over generations reduced to nothing. He was at least spared the spectacle of the execution of his son Thomas together with five of Thomas' uncles at Tyburn. It was less an act of thoughtless cruelty than a deliberate attempt to wipe out Kildare power in Ireland for all time. In effect its only immediate consequence was to consolidate the

Desmond-led rebellion in Munster against the forces of Lord Grey, the deputy who had replaced Kildare. Grey was a superb military commander and his assault on Desmond and his ancillary Gaelic lords of the Geraldine League was systematic and relentless. Grey held a parliament in 1536 which passed a declaration of royal supremacy and a denial of the pope's authority on the English model. A special commission was appointed by Henry, or more precisely by Cromwell, and presided over by Sir Anthony St Leger to supervise the dissolution of the monasteries, among other measures of Reform. The commissioners who arrived from England in 1537 were in the grip of Cromwellian efficiency, determined to reorder every bureaucracy in the land. The dissolution of the monasteries was not as in England a task sufficient unto itself. In Ireland it was linked to the putative, if halfhearted, reconquest, an unfortunate decision for the future progress of the new religion. Monasteries once vacated, particularly around the Pale, became military strongholds for Lord Grey's army, and their spoils and lands rewards for willing supporters.

Since the title lord of Ireland was that through which Henry ruled Ireland on the authority of the papal grant *Laudabiliter* it was apparent that some substitute was required. Henry decided to be henceforth king of Ireland, a declaration ratified by act of parliament in Dublin in 1541. The other anomaly which he wished to clarify was the basis on which Irish lands were held. A situation was required in which they would be held as in England 'of the king'. To this end St Leger devised a policy known as 'surrender and regrant'. In effect this meant that those who held land in an increasingly conquered Ireland had a choice. They could continue to live as outlaws and in due course be hunted down, or they could accept the king's generous offer and surrender their land to him on the understanding that he would then grant it back. It was then in effect granted at the king's pleasure, and that act could be revoked in the event of disloyalty or rebellion.

In theory this was straightforward but Irish law did not recognize the right of any individual ruler to surrender his land or indeed his title. Land was merely held in trust within the family from generation to generation, and in the absence of the legitimacy conferred by *Laudabiliter* the Irish saw no evidence of Henry's right. To many, the arrangement was repugnant, particularly in a period when their leading Anglo-Norman family had been killed, their lands laid waste by Grey's campaign, their monasteries and churches desecrated and their former buildings used to garrison the English forces. The nature of the links, both temporal and material, that yoked the Reformation to conquest in Ireland were scarcely calculated to bring the potential new converts into an imaginative sympathy with their new church. Nonetheless, 'surrender and regrant' was entered into, if largely in bad faith, because it was a more attractive alternative than living as an outlaw and waiting to be subdued.

The Norman families, who looked upon themselves as at least legally English, were outraged at the treatment they had received. Though they fought with the Gaelic chiefs as allies in the Geraldine League they did so for complex reasons. They certainly were not insensitive to their status as the English colony in Ireland, and were shocked that the new Tudor dispensation meant that they were no longer to run their own affairs as they had done for so long. Yet they had no innate hostility to the policy of 'surrender and regrant' which conformed with their land law, that is to say the common law. Nor were they by definition hostile to the Reformation. By the time of Henry's death in 1547 it was unclear how Ireland, and particularly Anglo-Norman Ireland would react to the Reformation.

Henry was succeeded by his young son, Edward VI. The boy king's regent appointed Sir Edward Bellingham to Ireland. Within a year Bellingham had supplanted the pre-eminence of St Leger by the ferocity with which he pursued the war. His aim was not merely to defend the Pale and establish an ostensible submission elsewhere. It was to extend the real area of control by further conquest and plantation of a new population loyal to England in the conquered lands. Fort Procter (later called Maryborough) and Daingean in Offaly were constituted as new outposts of the Pale. Edward's Catholic successor Mary, despite her attempts to turn back the clock on the Reformation by the most violent means in England, did not waver in the main aspects of Irish policy. In 1550 the Privy Council resolved to set up a frontier plantation under government auspices in Leix and Offaly.

It is important to recognize that the government of Ireland presented a problem to the Tudor monarchy long before the Reformation became an issue. From the early 1500s Henry VII was responding to pressures from a disgruntled center within the Pale, who resented the unchallenged hegemony of the FitzGeralds, to reimpose his authority on a country that was allegedly run as a network of minor fiefdoms emanating from the central powers of three large Anglo-Norman families. The reason for resentment of this state of affairs from within the Pale were complex. Partly that resentment derived from the sense that the colony was merely one in name. It also derived from the sense that the accommodation between the Anglo-Norman and Gaelic lords was far too intimate. Moreover it objected to the prevalence of Gaelic customs, not on grounds of barbarity, but rather on political grounds – that the assimilation of the Anglo-Norman lords outside the Pale into Gaelic culture contradicted the notion of the colony (which to an extent the Anglo-Norman presence had never been in reality), and hindered the maintenance of the English Crown in Ireland. There was also a moral argument couched in humanist terms which implied that it was the 'lower orders' who suffered

as a consequence of the neat accommodations of the Gaelic and Anglo-Norman lords. There was a degree of debate and discussion as to what precisely the aims of governmental policy in Ireland ought to be. Whether the Pale ought to be extended beyond the four counties around Dublin by subduing the Gaelic lords in Offaly to the west and Wicklow to the south, and whether this strengthened Pale with reassimilated Desmond, Ormond and Butler lands should be deemed to be the area of the king's dominion or commonweal. Whether, on the other hand, the Gaelic chiefs in the west and north should be invited into the king's dominion, as was in fact to happen in the policy of 'surrender and regrant'. The latter notion invoked a humanist ideal of re-education or forced acculturation, whereby the sons of the important Gaelic lords would be educated in the English way and facilitated in throwing off their old customs. This was the policy followed with the O'Neills of Ulster who surren-

Above: Bective Cistercian Abbey, County Meath. The photograph shows the huge tower built at the corner of the cloister in the 16th century, either by monks or their post-dissolution successors. After 1540 Bective was turned into a Tudor house to which the staircase belongs.

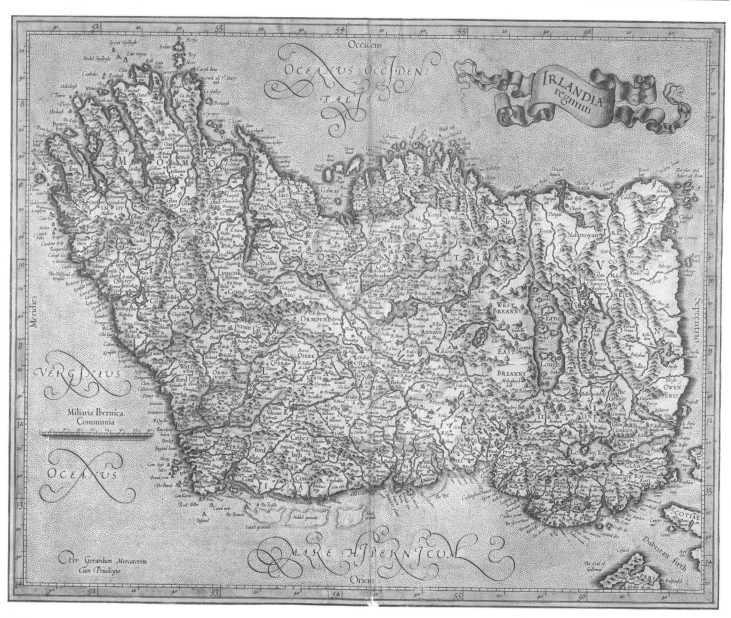

Above: Map of Ireland by Mercator, 1595-1600.

dered the Gaelic title The O'Neill for the earldom of Tyrone. The final option was forcibly to reconquer all of Ireland by military means, to transplant, or in some versions of the policy, utterly to drive out the native population and replace them with loyal Englishmen or, in the more moderate form to replace the overlords with loyal Englishmen and allow the lower classes to remain in place. None of these polices was ever singlemindedly adhered to, though elements from all of them were used in the course of the Tudor settlement of Ireland. At all times policy was constrained by the degree of priority London was to allow Ireland at any given time, and more importantly by the question of cost.

From the Irish point of view, however, policy seemed to present a different face. That the crushing of Kildare was incidental to Tudor policy in Ireland was never clear in an Irish context. That new considerations of bureaucratic efficiency in an English context lay at the heart of the regime of St Leger and the commissioners was even less clear. That the administrative reorganization contingent on the Reformation merely happened to coincide with longer held policies of administrative reform seemed simply

not credible. Hence in an Irish context Tudor efficiency presented a face of wilful disruption of formerly convenient accommodations. The imposition of all administrative reforms, but particularly religious ones, through the medium of commissions with Englishmen at their head, seemed to point in a direction wholly inimical to all of those who had formerly lived in relative freedom from outside interference. Up until the date of Elizabeth's accession to the throne, however, all positions were ambiguous and uncertain.

In the second decade of Elizabeth's reign Edward Tremayne, clerk of the Irish Privy Council, described the way of life that was no longer acceptable. In discussing the rule of Irish lords over areas almost the size of counties he said:

He attaineth into it rather by choice and election than succession. In which succession they observe to choose him of the kindred (which they call "septe") of such as have been used to rule them. Such are oneale, odonell, oreley, ocarroll, and such others. . . . When this great lord is thus in possession of his Country he is followed of all the warlike people of the same, viz., horsemen, gallowglasses and kerns [foot soldiers] and

The Gentleman of Ireland   The Gentlewoman of Ireland

The Civill Irish Woman   The Civill Irish man

The Wilde Irish man   The Wilde Irish Woman

of Tudor policy in Ireland is a topic on which historians do not agree, nor will they until more research has been done on the period. Relative assessments of changing policy from year to year are scarcely illuminating if they are based on obviously incomplete information.

The basic question of Elizabethan reordering was complicated by certain internal disputes in Gaelic Ireland. A succession dispute in the O'Neill patrimony which would have resolved itself in a traditional fashion had Tudor succession laws not constrained it, erupted into open rebellion against the queen under Shane O'Neill. The real issue was whether O'Neill was to be ruler in the Gaelic fashion or as the queen's earl. To simplify a highly complex sequence of events it is sufficient to note that by 1567 Elizabeth was ordering Sidney to ensure that this 'cankered, dangerous rebel' was 'utterly extirped.' Pursued by the Crown, warred against by the other northern lords, who resented his attempt to be lord of all Ulster, O'Neill threw himself on the mercy of his allies and relatives, the Scots settlers of Antrim, who rewarded his trust by killing him. Sidney secured his head and had it displayed on a pike on the wall of Dublin Castle as a warning to others. Yet Ulster still remained outside the Crown's control.

A new class of Englishman had settled in Ireland in the last days of Henry VIII's reign. Land

Left: Drawings of Irish costumes and types produced with a map of 'The Kingdome of Ireland' by Hondius Jodocus, 1616.

Below: Queen Elizabeth I, *circa* 1585-90, artist unknown.

with this multitude he useth the inferior people at his will and pleasure.

Elizabeth's reign began with such men in disorder and discontent. Sir Henry Sidney, her representative in Ireland, began his administration by recognizing the complex variations in problems affecting different regions. Thus, albeit for vastly different reasons, he returned to the localizing tendencies of the FitzGerald era, and began to administer through a system of locally constituted provincial presidencies. The precise motivation

Right: One of a series of woodcuts executed by John Derricke in the series called 'Images of Ireland.' This series provides us with the best visual information that we have on life in Elizabethan Ireland. Derricke accompanied Sir Henry Sidney as a propagandist for the conquest.

Right: Another of Derrick's images. Here the native Irish are even more clearly represented as barbarous and uncultivated. At the right of the picture are two figures in stages of self-exposure. The dress and demeanor of the Irish lords is more than usually dignified. On the other hand the proximity of the dog; the fact that dining is outdoor; that the cooking is done in an open pot within sight of the banqueters; and the proximity of those on the top left hand side of the etching who are clearly engaged in the dismemberment of a recently acquired animal for the next meal; all contribute to a view of the Irish as a people crying out for conquest and cultivation by the superior Elizabethan adventurers.

grants had rewarded military men as potentially lucrative acres were vacated by rebellion and insufficient 'regrantings.' St Leger's own son had a very substantial estate in the southwest and he was merely one of many. Then there were the rich lands of the decimated FitzGeralds, which were available for reallocation. The private war between the earls of Desmond and Ormond was an invitation to intervention and in 1565 both were summoned to London to answer to the queen. Desmond not unnaturally felt insecure since the Ormonds were after all closely related to Elizabeth and in 1567 Desmond was duly consigned to the Tower. James FitzMaurice Fitz-Gerald, Desmond's cousin led a rebellion in 1567 claiming to be acting in defense of 'the Catholic faith by God unto his church given and by the see of Rome hitherto prescribed to all Christian men.' This rebellion was ruthlessly crushed by Sidney and that victory was followed by a re-lentless quashing of all unrest in the province of Munster by Humphrey Gilbert. In France, to which he escaped in 1575, FitzMaurice plotted a more serious return attack. He developed contacts with some of the new alignments which emerged after the Council of Trent in 1563. The Counter Reformation is a loose description of the movement that arose as a result of decisions made to combat the new 'heresy of the north' at this council. It was a movement primarily doctrinal, but also military and political, co-ordinated under the powers of the Catholic kings and the papacy. In terms of the Counter Reformation Ireland was in certain respects a minor consideration, but it was sufficiently close to England to warrant military support from Spain, even if that support was less than wholehearted. In later years it was to be the doctrinal or missionary side of the Counter Reformation movement that was to become the most important in Ireland.

Left: A setback for the Queen's forces. Thomas, Earl of Ormond, Lieutenant General of her army in Ireland is taken prisoner by Irish forces under O'More, April 1600.

By 1579 Elizabeth had again allowed a more systematic kind of profiteering in land to develop in Ulster. This, however, involved the displacement of individuals who had been loyal to her during the rebellion of Shane O'Neill. It placed all security in land in jeopardy and encouraged an atmosphere of instability and disorder. Proposals for settlement came in the main from private individuals who clothed their self-interest in ostensible concern for the pacification of the queen's commonweal in Ireland. Sir Thomas Smith, secretary to the queen, drafted for the public good a plan which granted to him personally all of the lands of the O'Neills of Clandeboy. He was to hold this land as a tenant of the Crown, drive out all local lords and retain the working population. The incumbent lord drove the Smith party out. Elizabeth followed this defeat by granting most of Antrim to her favorite

Walter Devereux, earl of Essex. This too was a private enterprise under Crown protection. Although employing a force of over 1000 men, Essex too fled in failure.

Connacht and Munster had been subdued by Sir Nicholas Malby and Sir William Drury. The peace of Munster was again disrupted by the return of FitzMaurice FitzGerald with the blessing of Pope Gregory and an army of 700 men which landed at Smerwick on the Dingle Peninsula in 1579. The Desmonds and others responded to FitzMaurice's call for a defense of 'our country,' and though FitzMaurice himself was quickly killed the war dragged on. Endorsed by settlers like Edmund Spenser and Sir Walter Raleigh, who were part of the vanguard of adventurer settlers of West Cork, the crown forces waged a ruthless battle against the rebellion. The earl of Desmond was declared a traitor and an outlaw they spoke like ghosts crying out of their graves; they did eat the dead as carrion, happy where they could find them; yea and one another soon after inasmuch as the very carcasses they spared not to scrape out of their graves.

In 1585 the Dublin Parliament agreed to the confiscation of the entire Desmond estate. The earl himself had been killed in Kerry and his vast acres were now deemed free for settlement. Munster had been subdued and a loyal population was deemed necessary to maintain that subjugation. There were vested mercantilist interests in the development of such rich lands. Divided into large lots the province had absorbed the settlers by the late 1590s. The plantation was not a great success. The original plan to have a multiplicity of small estates was foiled by those who seized vast tracts. Securing younger sons to act as owners of vast estates was not a problem but finding yeoman farmers to follow them into the unknown wilds was. The new settlers – for their own convenience and initiation – retained the natives to work their land. Commercial realities dominated political strategy and the notion of the plantation as a secure civilian garrison to restrain Munster failed.

The final great campaign of Elizabeth's reign also ended in Munster. The English educated Hugh O'Neill, groomed as a Rennaissance earl, turned back to the leadership of his own people and launched a mission to resist Tudor power. In 1594 he was inaugurated in the Gaelic style as The O'Neill. He offered the crown of Ireland to the king of Spain and couched his rhetorical rallying cries in the language of the counter reformation. After years of successful resistance in Ulster he marched south to meet a Spanish support force under Don Juan d'Aguila at Kinsale in 1601. The story of his sophisticated and modernizing conduct of the war in Ulster is a consuming and complex one. But despite the ruin that he brought to Essex and others through his organization, the campaign to deadlock and besiege Ulster waged by Charles Blount, Lord Mountjoy, with the superior staying power of a state was bound ultimately to succeed. That was why O'Neill marched south to meet the Spanish forces, in an attempt to broaden and redefine the struggle. His exposed forces and those of Red Hugh O'Donnell were defeated by the English on Christmas Eve 1601 at Kinsale. The Spanish forces never even entered the fray. O'Neill returned north after his failed gamble and Sir John Carew, president of Munster returned that province to Tudor control. Only Ulster had stood out against Tudor power and its days were now clearly numbered.

O'Donnell, O'Neill's great ally, fled to the continent where O'Neill himself soon followed. Before Mountjoy and O'Neill had signed their peace at Mellifont, Elizabeth had died. 'The flight of the Earls' was a testament to the achievement of Tudor power in Ireland. The old order

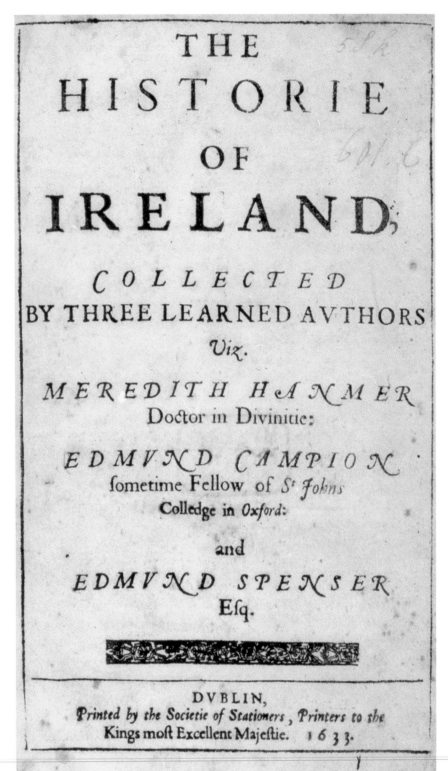

THE
HISTORIE
OF
IRELAND,

COLLECTED
BY THREE LEARNED AVTHORS
Viz.

MEREDITH HANMER
Doctor in Divinitie:

EDMVND CAMPION
fometime Fellow of *St Johns*
Colledge in *Oxford:*

and

EDMVND SPENSER
Efq.

DVBLIN,
Printed by the Societie of Stationers, Printers to the
Kings moſt Excellent Majeſtie. 1633.

Above: This history of Ireland was commissioned by Sir James Ware in the mid seventeenth century to sanction retrospectively the conquest of Ireland through the ostensibly impartial accounts of 'three learned authors.'

and he fled from his property to the fastnesses of the hinterland. His cry was that his battle was for the faith, and from within the Pale he received support from some Anglo-Norman allies, now described as the Old English to differentiate them from the new arrivals who were loyal Protestants almost to a man. The slaughter of the band of Spanish and Italians at Smerwick was merely a prelude to the first decimation of Munster in 1583. The scene is described by Spenser, whose home at Kilcolman was attacked:

Out of every corner of the woods and glens they came creeping forth upon their hands, for their legs would not bear them; they looked like anatomies of death;

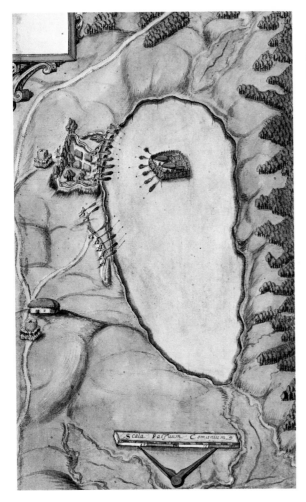

Left: Map of Armagh and a nearby fort by Bartlett executed in 1600 in the course of the Ulster campaign.

Second left: An attack on a *crannóg* (a traditional type of lake dwelling) from the same series.

that had existed at the time of Henry VII's accession was broken forever.

The later years of Elizabeth were notable for the extent of surveying and mapping that went on in every part of the country. Some of this was initially for military purposes, but the real dynamic came from the need to have accurate maps from which to parcel out land in the new plantations. The attaindered lands of O'Neill and O'Donnell joined the pool to be reallocated. These Ulster plantations continued to take place on a commercial footing on the precedent established in Munster. In Ulster the plantations under James I were to have an even more commercial and capitalist character. War charts made for Mountjoy demonstrate the Tudor achievement. The early ones show progress towards an English victory but with gaps. The later examples show the completed success.

Above: An Elizabeth I groat. Note how the design features an Irish harp.

Left: 'Tyrone's false submission afterwards rebelling,' from 'A thankful remembrance of God's mercie' by George Carleton, Bishop of Chichester. Published in 1630 this is a standard anti-Catholic tract of its period. Tyrone did submit to Essex as the picture shows but this was simply to gain time until the Spanish troops arrived. The background of the picture evokes the successful campaign which Charles Blount, Earl of Mountjoy waged when he replaced Essex as Lord Lieutenant.

CHAPTER 4

THE PROTESTANT SETTLEMENT

Previous pages: Cromwell at the siege of Drogheda. The fighting at Drogheda was not simply between English and Irish since the garrison commander and many of his officers were English Royalists. Nonetheless the massacre that ended the siege is usually remembered as an atrocity against the Irish.

Below: 'The Province of Ulster described,' by John Speed (1676). On the bottom left is Ennis Kelling or Enniskillen Fort, a symbol of the power to conquer the native Irish whose family names are written in over the areas that they still control.

ELIZABETH was succeeded by James I in 1603. On the surface his reign and that of his successor Charles I were tranquil in Ireland. But in the lives of ordinary people in areas where a plantation policy was being implemented the years from 1603 to 1641 were uncertain, insecure and disrupting. Moreover the apparent calm of the defeated was due to exhaustion and impotence and not to resignation.

The center of the plantation policy was Ulster where the lands of the defeated and exiled northern leaders were forfeited to the Crown and available for settlement. The direct role of the Crown in these plantations was minimal. Companies like the early Londonderry Company were not governmentally restrained, indeed such mercantilist developments were welcomed as useful adjuncts to Crown policy in Ireland. But on the other hand they were rarely the recipients of direct government assistance. While the concept of settlement as outlined by Machiavelli in *The Prince* ideally recommended the utter removal of the native population, the exigencies of moving into a new and hostile environment tended to make the ideal less than practical. Those who directed settlement were more concerned with economic success than the honor and glory of government, though both ends often seemed utterly compatible. In practice the native population was driven to the highlands and the margins of old territory, but they were not totally driven out for practical reasons. In the counties of Antrim and Down prolonged contact with Scotland over centuries, together with the pre-existing Scots population made absorbtion of the yeoman settlers from Scotland and the west easier. This was not true of the other Ulster counties where the main seventeenth century plantations were located. In the other parts of Ireland plantation was less systematic, though much of Leinster and the forfeited Desmond lands of Munster continued to be resettled. Here the native population was virtually undisturbed since their labor was necessary to ensure the economic success of the new ventures. Despite all of this it seems that in the first half of the seventeenth century three-fifths of the land remained in the hands of the Catholics of Ireland, whether Old Irish or Old English.

The Old English, as the Anglo-Normans, most of whom had remained Catholic, were called, continued to see themselves as the Crown's loyal servants in Ireland, though neither the London government nor the New English settlers saw them in this light. The traditional divide within Irish Catholicism between the native and the

Norman Church remained, but in English eyes they were all equally servants of Rome. Their professions of loyalty were met by an insistence on the incompatibility of loyalties to the English Crown and the pope of Rome. The fact that the papacy had made provision for Irish bishoprics through the mediating power of the rebellious O'Neill in exile enhanced the Crown view of all Irish Catholics as conspirators in a Counter Reformation papal plot. Further, the papacy administered the Irish Church in a fashion utterly unlike that employed in other Protestant kingdoms. Instead of having merely a missionary church, as in such countries, the Irish Church was structured as a full and complete hierarchy, directed from Rome but essentially a church in waiting. This was particularly ironic in view of the less than warm and harmonious nature of relations between the Irish Church and Rome over the centuries.

The official policy of the Catholic Church in Ireland as expressed by the primate of Ireland ruled that while the secular authority of James as king might be recognized, he was not a Christian king. His authority in the secular sphere was to be respected, provided that he ruled justly, that is, did not persecute Catholics. This was scarcely an acceptable accommodation for the English Crown. While the Old English did all in their power to express absolute loyalty to the limits of their religious capacity, the Old Irish persisted in relishing the divide and the discomfiture it caused to their loyal co-religionists.

The new settlers created a new infrastructure, building roads to link their settlements, particularly in the north; and in the provinces of Leinster and Munster constructing magnificent houses to reveal their new splendor. In Ulster the 'diamond' pattern of town or village dominated, and a system of shires and boroughs, tolls and gaming laws marked the new domestication. Government policy was confined to the question of raising monies from both the new settlers and the Old English – the latter's primary contribution was in the form of strictly pursued recusancy fines. To raise revenue for the king it was necessary that the Irish Parliament should sit, but equally important that the Old English Catholics did not dominate it. The management of this very delicate balancing operation was granted to Carew in 1611 and he ensured a slight Protestant majority in the parliament which he convened in 1613.

The reign of Charles I which began in 1625, was characterized in Ireland, by an unwillingness to rely on parliament almost equal to that which he displayed in England. In Ireland the policy was less blatant in view of the absolute infrequency of meetings even in normal times. Between 1543 and 1613 the Irish Parliament had met in all four times. Both communities were influenced subtly but firmly to give monies to the Crown, the Old English lest they be subjected to further recusancy fines, which their payments in effect were, the new settlers in response to the possible return of

power to Old English hands. Both were further constantly made aware of the potential insecurity of land titles. This delicate playing on respective fears was lucrative if unconducive to harmony within the island.

The first serious policy initiative since the appointment of Carew was made when Thomas, viscount Wentworth, later earl of Strafford was sent to Ireland in 1632 to assess its potential for the Crown. The system whereby funds were advanced by respective groups in return for 'graces' or favors (in effect the avoidance of penalties) seemed the natural course with which to persist. Wentworth was more ambitious and decided to call a parliament as a more effective policy, and one which was calculated to advance his practice of playing each side off against the centre. The dynamics of English politics did not directly impinge on Ireland, but Wentworth was Charles' man. His lack of sympathy for Presbyterianism was revealed by the speed with which he forced the oath of abjuration on the Scots Presbyterians of Ulster lest they follow in the footsteps of their Covenant-signing brothers in Scotland who began the process of defying Charles in 1638. The need to face the Scots was urged on Charles by Wentworth, and Ireland was to procure the money for the expedition. Not

Above: Richard Boyle, created First Earl of Cork by James I in 1620, as seen in a miniature by Isaac Oliver. Boyle was a successful and formidable adventurer, holding vast estates in the south west. His son was Robert Boyle, the famous scientist.

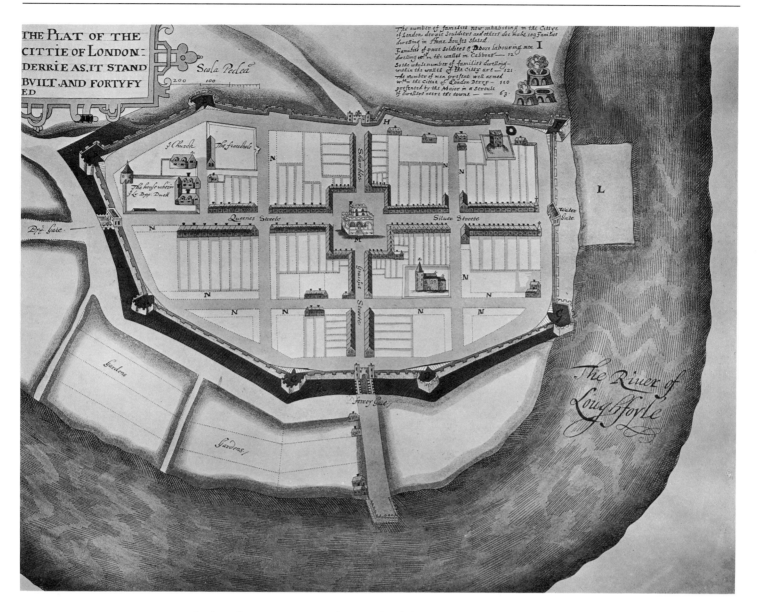

THE PLAT OF THE CITTIE OF LONDON=DERRIE AS.IT STAND BVILT.AND FORTYFY ED

Above: An inventory of the state of organization of the plantation city of Londonderry in 1622. On the top right hand corner the number of inhabitants is listed, as is their state of military preparedness, illustrating the siege mentality of the new settlers.

merely that, but it was rumored in England that it was proposed to raise a papist army for the purpose. Stirring up chaos in Ireland, and epitomizing to parliament all the worst about Charles I Strafford, as he now was, lost his head in 1641 at the King's warrant.

Chaos in England served as an invitation to the Old Irish who had lost everything to make an attack, and they attempted to structure a rebellion. As Conor Cruise O'Brien has quoted elsewhere the condition of the native Irish is best described by the words of Bishop David Rothe in 1617:

They have no wealth but flocks and herds, they have no trade but agriculture or pasture, they are unlearned men without help or protection. Yet though unarmed and they are so active in mind and body, that it is dangerous to drive them from their ancestral seats, to forbid them fire and water: thus driving the desperate to revenge and even the moderate to think of taking arms. They have been deprived of weapons, but are in a temper to fight with nails and heels, and tear the oppressors with their teeth . . . Since they see themselves excluded from all hopes of restitution or compensation and are so constituted that they would rather starve on husks at home than fare sumptuously

elsewhere, they will fight for their alters and hearths, and rather seek a bloody death near the sepulchres of their fathers than be buried as exiles in unknown earth.

The leaders of the rebellion in Ireland were Old Irish, but they received Old English support. Their loyalties were complex and difficult to unravel, though it is clear that certain of the leaders wanted to offer the Crown of Ireland to a foreign king. Many returned from armies abroad to direct the rebellion, especially from the Spanish army in Flanders. The leaders of the plot were Sir Phelim O'Neill in Ulster; Rory O'More from the midlands and Lord Conor Maguire of Fermanagh. In effect they seem to have identified their cause with that of Charles whom they believed to be sympathetic to the Catholic cause. Primarily they fought to avenge their dispossession and for the freedom of their faith. The earl of Ormond, the head of the king's army in Ireland received overtures from Catholic leaders offering to aid his recruiting drive for the expansion of the king's army. These initiatives were given short shrift by Ormond but do serve to show how unclearly the lines of conflict were drawn, Sir Phelim led the rebellion of 1641 in Ulster, proclaiming that they rose not against the king but in defense of their liberties. The 'high' military campaign to which the leaders aspired, involving the seizure of strategic buildings, was interpreted by the recently dispossessed smallholders in a quite different fashion. They viewed the call to arms as an opportunity to wreak a terrible revenge on those who had replaced them. All over the west and south of Ulster isolated plantation settlements were attacked and their occupants slaughtered. Hearing of the uprising, others fled in fear of their lives, a huge swollen procession of refugees converging on the fortified towns of Drogheda and Dublin. In the collective consciousness of northern Protestants this was to be the defining experience in their new land, one to which they were to return repeatedly in defining their attitudes to the 'papists.'

The leaders of the rebellion stood impotently on the sidelines, powerless to control what they had started, and terrified at its potential future consequences. The massacres were brutal and widespread. They were neither planned nor coordinated however. In the polemic of civil war in England they were to reach massive and utterly premeditated proportions. Not merely were the Old Irish leaders of the north seen to be at their root, so also were the Old English of the Pale. The massacres were represented as the co-ordinated responsibility of all the Catholics of Ireland, a perspective that allowed no distinction between arch-resister of revolt, and the poorest, most unlettered murderer of the hinterland. In fact, the imposition of responsibility on wealthy, educated and loyal Catholics was infinitely preferred by parliament since in the land forfeitures that

Above: The O'Conor Monument, Sligo Abbey, 1626.

Left: The ruins of Coppinger's Court, Cork, built in the early 17th century. A good example of a mansion built to be defended at a time when in England structures of domestic defense had largely been abandoned. Yet another illustration of the instability of the settlement and the insecurity of the settlers.

Above: An Oliver Cromwell crown of 1658.

Below: Tracts and illustrations like these greatly exaggerated the atrocities of the native Irish against the settlers in the rebellion of 1641. Accounts of Irish barbarity promulgated through such sources were very powerful in England and helped to create the climate of opinion in which any atrocity committed against the Irish was deemed to be justified. They also justified further land conquest. This particular etching is of events at Portadown in November 1641.

were to serve as punishment for such a rebellion the wealthy Catholics at least had something to forfeit.

That acts of barbarous cruelty were perpetrated is clear, that they were exaggerated beyond recognition seems to be accepted even by an historian as partisan as Lecky. But what actually happened was less important than what was said to have happened. For northern Protestants 1641 was a memory from which they could never escape, and for the English public – particularly for the Puritans – it was to confirm all previous views of the Catholic Irish as idolaters and barbarians who deserved no human quarter or civilized standards.

In March 1642 the Parliament of England passed an Adventurers Act to finance the reconquest of Ireland. This effectively meant that by pledging Irish lands against bonds the reconquest of Ireland would simultaneously gratify the policy of Parliament and the economic interest of individuals. In effect it was a loan to the English Parliament for the purpose of financing an army in Ireland which was to be repaid in the form of land confiscated at the conclusion of a successful campaign. Morally, however, the English did not see this land as parliamentary booty but righteously forfeited land, forfeited by the nature of the 1641 rebellion for which all Catholics were seen to be responsible. Similarly, as the war proceeded and the payment of Cromwellian soldiers became a problem it was enacted that those soldiers quartered in Ireland were to be paid in the form of debentures on Irish lands. In fact by the early 1650s more land in Ireland had been pledged in these fashions than could ever possibly be made available.

Up to the outbreak of Civil War in England in August 1642 the onus of suppressing the rebellion in Ireland had been on the King's shoulders, effected through Ormond, his commander in Ireland. When, however, the Civil War began there was a strange realignment of forces in Ireland. Ormond, on the King's behalf, attempted to negotiate with the Irish Catholic rebels who had now constituted themselves as an assembly in Kilkenny in 1642. In his attempt to quieten the rebels and bring them to submission, since the king after all maintained his claim to his Irish kingdom, Ormond was represented by London's Puritan parliament as fraternizing with the papists. This was of course used in an English context as yet another stick with which to beat King Charles.

Ormond was in an ambiguous position. Though a Protestant as a result of having been brought up as a ward of court, he was from the old Catholic Anglo-Norman family of the Butlers. The rebels with whom he negotiated were Old Irish led by Owen Roe O'Neill but there were also Old English, families of his own background and blood. His intimacy did give him certain advantages in that it enabled him to play on the divisions between the two groupings that were masked to outsiders by their shared participation in the alternative parliament or Confederation of Kilkenny. The Old English Catholics merely aspired to the free practice of their religion and the continued possession of their lands under the now deposed king. The Old Irish, on the other hand, had a far more triumphalist view of the reassertion of Catholic power, a position hardened and rendered more uncompromising by the arrival of the emisarry of Pope Innocent X, John Baptist Rinucinni, in 1645.

Protracted and complex negotiations reached no particular conclusions. The news of the trial of Charles in 1647 was however the final catalyst for the collapse of the Confederation of Kilkenny as the Old English, now oblivious to their former demands of the king, rallied to his side in opposition to the Puritan Parliament. Despite vastly differing motives, strategies and ambitions the Puritan Parliament failed to distinguish between different categories of papists and the aim of the Parliament's army in Ireland was to seize control from the Crown forces and suppress Catholic rebellion. Since the royalist cause was seen at crypto-Catholic in any case, differentiation was not a necessity.

In 1649 Rinuccini left Ireland having ensured that the full Confederation would not throw in their lot with the Royalists. Owen Roe O'Neill died and Oliver Cromwell came to Ireland to superintend reconquest personally. Ireland was a seething mess of confused alliances, subtle differentiations, half-waged campaigns and minimal control. Cromwell intended to root out ambiguity, punish rebels and instil fear and peace through a firm and irreversible conquest. Moreover a considerable amount of money had

Driuinge Men Women & children by hund: reds vpon Briges & casting them into Riuers, who drowned not were killd with poles & shot with muskets.

already been sunk in the Irish imbroglio; those who had advanced money under the Adventurers Act were impatient for repayment, and the Parliament's army in Ireland was hungry, unpaid and at a low ebb after almost seven years of aimless wins and losses.

Cromwell arrived in Dublin with a large army and directly proceeded to Drogheda where he carried out an exemplary massacre of the inhabitants with, he believed, moral impunity. It was, he claimed, a fitting punishment for the massacres of 1641 in Ulster, which he believed to have been premeditated and ordered by the Catholic leadership. The forces opposed to him were in disarray as the Old Irish bishops excommunicated all who rallied to the king's cause under Ormond. In their view there was little to choose between a Protestant king and a Puritan Parliament. Such remaining coherence as the Royalist cause had in Ireland was utterly shattered by Charles II's repudiation of the peace terms with the Catholics of Ireland which Ormond had so laboriously negotiated, and his further statement that under no circumstances would he grant terms to the Catholics of Ireland. Those whom he repudiated in this fashion felt some difficulty in continuing to fight for him. Cromwell marched unimpeded through a country where every mechanism of organized resistance had broken down.

After the brutal capture of Drogheda and Wexford Cromwell made it clear that he intended to give quarter in the terms outlined in the 'Declaration of the Lord Lieutenant of Ireland for the undeceiving of Deluded and Seduced people' promulgated after his landing at Ringsend. The con-

quest was not instantaneous but by the date of Cromwell's departure in 1650 the main lines of triumph had been drawn.

The prime aim after reconquest was to effect the settlements pledged in the original Adventurers Act. Much had changed since the original arrangement. Holders of bonds had resold them to others, there were at least three different reckonings of the arrangements made. Soldiers who were expecting to be paid in the form of Irish lands had no wish to spend the rest of their days in a country where they had endured misery, and many had already subsold what was being granted to them before receiving it. There was ample room for confusion, error and fraud in the reallocation of already allocated lands. Certain individuals proceeded summarily to seize what they believed to be their due, grossly overestimating what it in fact was. Old landowning families found themselves summarily driven out of their homes by individuals clinging to documents proclaiming forfeiture for treason. Not merely did individual third parties buy bonds, but groups of London merchants actually bought them in bulk as speculative ventures. It would be a mistake to see Ireland in this period as a recognized source of considerable wealth; in many cases the truth was that it seemed like the only possible means

Above: Portrait of Oliver Cromwell in about 1649, by Walker.

Left: From the Reverend Dr Southwell's *New Book of Martyrs*, subtitled in the original 'Representation of the principal scenes in the Bloody Irish Massacre in 1642 wherein 40,000 Protestants were inhumanly sacrificed by the papists.'

Right: Petition of Parliamentary soldiers in Ireland, 1647. Parliament had insufficient funds and the payment of their soldiers was not chief among their concerns. In Ireland officers in particular but also men were promised rewards in the form of conquered land after the successful conclusion of the Irish campaign. As the text of this petition reveals, however, for many soldiers immediate privation was the only reality.

The humble Petition of us the Parliaments poore Souldiers in the

Army of Ireland, whereof many are ſtarved already, and many dead for want of Chirurgions,

Sheweth,

THat we the poor diſtreſſed Souldiery under the Parliaments Service in Ireland, having heretofore ſerved the Parliament under the Lord Generall Eſſex, valiant Maſſey, and noble Sir William Waller, and the reſt, &c. did in all faithfulneſſe, hardſhip and deſperate ſervice as ever any, hazzard our lives and fortunes, and did according to order obey and disband then not ſo much as doubting of all our Arreares, and now have almoſt ſerved you two years in all integrity and faithfulneſſe both Winter and Summer, wet and dry, froſt and ſnow, having no other bedding then the bare ground for our beds, and the skies for our covering, and when dry in the day and night, no other ſigne to drink at but the Sun and Moone, and nothing but water, having no plenty, but cold backs, hungry bellies, and puddle water, and when ſore wounded, not a Surgeon to dreſſe us, or if a Surgeon, no cheſt, nor ſalve, nor oyntments; and for bread many times not a loafe of two pence under ſix pence, and rotten cheeſe ſent not fit for a dog, and for butter it went from London to Dover, and miſtook Dublin and went to Dunkirk, and for our new cloathes all made of the French faſhion, and being too little for any of us, were carried for France to cloath them, hardly hats to our heads but what our haire growes through, and neither hoſe or ſhooes, doublet or breeches, tearing our Snapſacks to patch a hole to hide our naked and ſtarved fleſh, and our ſwords naked for want of ſcabberds : Thus with our backs without cloaths, and our bellies without food, and not a penny to buy any thing, and the Kernes having burnt the corne and deſtroyed all fit for ſuccour, we forced to march bare legged and bare footed, having neither fire nor food, we periſh in miſery, and our Commanders being in a manner in the ſame caſe, having nothing but good words to pay us with, ſhewing us often your Orders upon Orders for our pay, plentifully promiſing but not performing; and thus wee dropping downe dead daily in our marching, and ſo feeble and ſo weak, being not able to fight or do any more ſervice without ſome ſupply, but all like to ſtarve and die in miſery, when all meanes is anticipated, and the Tax of 60000.l. wholly ingroſſed by your Army from us, and your Souldiery quartered in Kings houſes, and clad Gentile like, and fed in Free-quarter to the full, and lie in good beds, and take their pleaſure and eaſe in reſt and peace.

We humbly deſire our hungry bellies may once be filled, and our naked backs be cloathed, and our legs and feet be hoſed and ſhooed, and our Surgeons once more fitted, and all recruited with food to ſupply us once more, that we may go out again to finiſh that worke we have begun, and not to lie like Drones to eat up others meat, and we do not doubt, but with Gods bleſſing, to give you a happy account of the Conqueſt of the whole Land, and ſhall ever pray for a happy Parliament.

feb: 18 ·   DUBLIN: Printed by *W.B.* 164*8.* *1647.*

---

through which years of throwing good money after bad in the Parliamentary cause could be recouped, however unsatisfactorily.

An Act for Settling Ireland was passed by the English Parliament in August 1652. In theory it made all existing land in Ireland insecure and liable to forfeiture. In practice its aim was to remove land almost exclusively from the Catholics, who for reason of religion and rebellion were judged to deserve such a fate. It was emphasized that Catholics 'of the humbler sort' were deemed to be pardoned and left to work the land under

new owners. Certain scheduled groups were excluded from all pardon – Jesuits and priests involved in rebellion and officers who had fought against Parliament, in particular a list of named individuals in which Ormond held the chief position. All Catholic landowners not included in this category for whom forfeiture was summary were to surrender their estates without delay in return for which they would be granted land of one-third their present acreage west of the Shannon. Thus payment could be made to Parliament's emptors while simultaneously coralling the leadership of Ireland within an enclosed area.

The settlement could not in practice approximate to this level of absolute clinical efficiency. The forfeited land could be surveyed by an inquisition out of Chancery or Exchequer on precedents established by the Desmond Surveys. In effect, however, the alternative method employed by James I in Ulster was used, a survey by commission under the Great Seal. The surveys on which the settlement was based were the Gross Survey, the Civil Survey and the Down Survey carried out by Sir William Petty (so-called because it was written down). The Down Survey was completed in 13 months of 1651-52 and is in effect a Domesday book of seventeenth century Ireland. Accuracy in surveying was vital if the parcelling out of land was to be less than chaotic and Petty's achievement is remarkable. Petty estimated, probably underestimated, the population in 1652 to be about 850,000. He estimated that over 600,000 people had died in the decade of war since 1641.

The survey enabled an ostensible cloak of bureaucratic control to hang over the considerable chaos of such an exercise in transplantation and plantation. All Catholic landowners did not move west of the Shannon, though a very high percentage of them did. Complicated acts of fraud and bribery took place and Catholics who had money paid the new settlers to whom their land had been granted sums in excess of its value. Legally they were unprotected in such a transaction, if the grantee chose to re-present his claim. The majority of Catholics were not rich enough for such bargaining. They moved unless they were fortunate enough to slip through the net of officialdom. The Act for the Attainder of the Rebels of Ireland of 1657 bore witness to the fact that most confiscable land had been confiscated and more was required than the originally agreed 2.5 million acres. Existing agreed grants were honored by effecting a general devaluation. Not all of those granted lands in Ireland came there. In fact some of the larger merchant holders were informed that unless they proceeded to reside in their estates they would forfeit them, since the aim of plantation was to fortify and hold the conquered country. Those who did settle were in the main officers of the Cromwellian Army who bought up the stock of their soldiers.

The real alteration that the Cromwellian period brought about, apart from the obvious and manifest transfer of land from Catholic to Protestant hands and the strengthening of the New English in Ireland by the plantation of large numbers of Cromwellian settlers, was the final erosion of the legal and constitutional distinctions that differentiated the Old English from the Old Irish. The participation of the Old English in the rebellion of 1641 confirmed in English eyes their common cause with the Old Irish Catholics. Their protestations of loyalty to the Crown cut little ice in a Parliamentary administration for they were merely 'Irish papists' to the English.

The restoration of Charles II in 1660 was a source of hope and revival to all Irish Catholics. The Old English felt that Charles understood the distinction between religious and secular allegiance and would cease to rank them merely with the disloyal Irish. Their hope was for a restoration of their lands and a return to the toleration of their religion. In the latter aspiration they were satisfied at least in the first years of Charles' reign. The question of land was more complex. The Cromwellian settlers in Ireland proclaimed their loyalty to Charles with alacrity, advising him of their status as England's loyal garrison in Ireland. Tolerant though he was of Catholicism, Charles had no intention of alienating elements in the complex alliances that had brought about his restoration by presenting himself as the defender of Catholic demands for the return of their lands, a role that would place him in opposition to English power in Ireland as now constituted. True, certain notable Catholics who had been

Below: A later Cromwellian debenture on Irish lands given to provide payment for Parliamentary supporters. This one was issued in Dublin in 1658 and is probably a reissue of an earlier agreement. The sum in question is over seven hundred pounds which may have been paid in the form of land or in cash from the proceeds of sale.

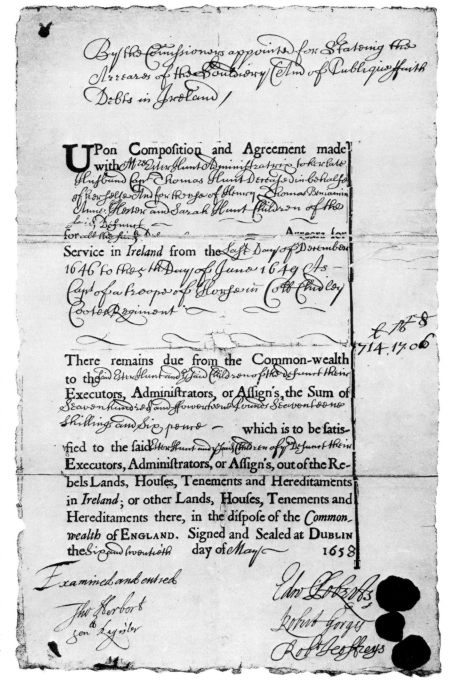

RD TYRCONNELL
ZORD LIEU.T
F IRELAND
OR JAMES 2.

prominent Royalists were returned their lands, but in a limited piecemeal fashion that entitled them to one third of the lands of the Cromwellian settlers. This redistribution was entirely haphazard and any gains were due not to superior claim but to superior connections. At the end of this redistribution with its attendant political and social unrest the amount of land in Catholic hands did not exceed one-fifth of the total. In 1641 the Catholic landowners' share had been about three-fifths.

The 1660s were years of reorganization in the Irish Catholic Church. Granted limited toleration the Church hierarchy determined to reconstitute and reorganize the Church in Ireland. The old divisions remained. The Old English looked to Rome and to the post-Counter-Reformation reforms within the Church. The Old Irish on the other hand continued to resent too close a degree of direct supervision from Rome. Anti-Catholicism in England reached a frenzied pitch in the early 1670s, reaching a climax in the 'popish plot' of 1678. In Ireland the aftermath of the 'popish plot' and the tensions within the Irish church oddly coalesced at the trial of the Archbishop of Armagh, Oliver Plunkett. Plunkett was of an Old English family from the Pale. He was arrested on manifestly trumped-up charges of planning the landing of a French army at Carlingford Loch for the purpose of overthrowing His Majesty's Government. Since the chances of making the charge stick in an Irish court with a familiar public were slim, the case was taken to London. Many of those who would have testified on Plunkett's behalf were afraid to come to England in

Above: James II. The ships in the background probably refer to James' exploits as an admiral in the English fleet before he became king.

the climate of emotional hysteria prevailing. Plunkett was in fact condemned to be hanged, drawn and quartered on the testimony of disgruntled friars of his own diocese who resented his organization and attempts to impose a Roman-style order on the Irish Church.

According to Petty, the Protestant population of Ireland almost doubled in the years from 1652 to 1672 from about 150,000 to about 300,000, of whom about 100,000 were Presbyterians concentrated in the northern counties. When James II succeeded his brother Charles in 1685 he perturbed this community by making Richard Talbot, the brother of the Catholic archbishop of Dublin, commander of the army in Ireland. He also made him earl of Tyrconnel. When he consolidated this position by also becoming lord lieutenant in 1687, placing Catholics in a variety of public offices from which they had hitherto been excluded, perturbation turned to serious unease. His further gesture, a re-examination of the land settlement, undertaken with the tacit agreement of James, placed the title to land of the majority of the new settlers in a position of technical insecurity and alienated them from James.

The Restoration years had been prosperous in Ireland. New men and new money poured into the country. Towns, roads and magnificent build-

Left: Preserved head of Oliver Plunkett, now St Oliver Plunkett, in Drogheda Church. Plunkett was executed for high treason, 1 July 1681.

Far left: Richard Talbot, earl of Tyrconnell, James II's viceroy in Ireland.

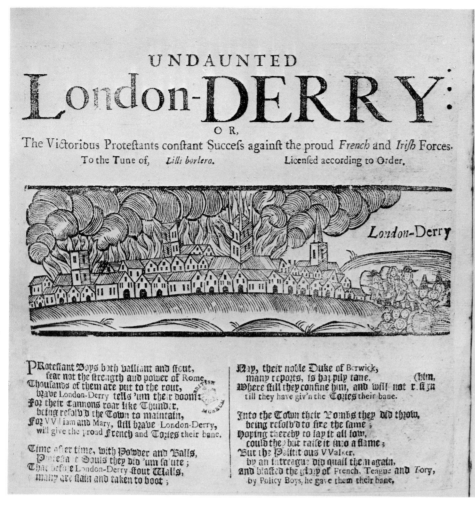

UNDAUNTED London-DERRY:
OR,

The Victorious Protestants constant Success against the proud *French* and *Irish* Forces.

To the Tune of, *Lilli borlera.*   Licensed according to Order.

London-Derry

PRotestant Boys both valliant and stout,
    fear not the strength and power of Rome,
Thousands of them are put to the rout,
    brave London-Derry tells 'um their doom;
For their Cannons roar like Thunder,
    being resolv'd the Town to maintain,
For VVilliam and Mary, still brave London-Derry,
    will give the proud French and Tories their bane.

Time after time, with Powder and Balls,
    Protestant Souls they did 'um salute;
That before London-Derry stout Walls,
    many are slain and taken to boot;

Nay, their noble Duke of Berwick,
    many reports, is happily tane.   (him,
Where still they confine him, and will not resign
    till they have giv'n the Tories their bane.

Into the Town their Bombs they did throw,
    being resolv'd to fire the same ;
Hoping thereby to lay it all low,
    could they but raise it into a flame ;
But the Papist ous VValker,
    by an intreague did quail them again,
and blasted the glory of French, Teague and Tory,
    by Policy Boys, he gave them their bane.

Thund'ring stones they laid on the Wall,
    ready against the Enemy came,
with which they bow'd the Tories to maul,
    when e'er they dare approach but the same:
And another sweet invention,
    the which in brief I reckon to name :
a sharp bloody slaughter, did soon follow after,
    amongst the proud French, and gave 'um their bane.

Stubble and Straw in parcels they laid,
    the which they straightways kindled with speed,
By this intreague the French was betray'd,
    thinking the Town was fir'd indeed :
Then they plac'd their scaling Ladders,
    and o'er the walls did scour amain,
Yet strait to their wonder they were cut in sunder,
    thus French-men and Tories met with their bane.

Suddenly then they open'd the Gate,
    sallying forth with Vigour and might;
And as the truth I here may relate,
    Protestant Boys did valliantly fight,
Taking many chief Commanders,
    while the sharp fray they thus did maintain,
With vigorous courses, they routed their Forces,
    and many poor Teagues did meet with their bane.

While with their blood the Cause they have seal'd,
    heaven upon their actions did frown,
Protestants took the spoil of the Field,
    Cannons full five they brought to the Town,
with a lusty large great Mortar,
    thus they return'd with honour and gain,
While Papists did scour from Protestants power,
    as fearing they all shou'd suffer their bane.

In a short time we hope to arrive,
    with a vast Army to Ireland,
And the affairs so well we'll contrive,
    that they shall ne'er have power to stand
'Gainst King William and Queen Mary,
    who in the Throne does flourish and reign,
We'll down with the faction, that make the distra-
    (ction,
and give the proud French and Tories their bane.
FINIS.

Printed for J. Deacon in Guiltspur-street.

Above: A song of victory from the Protestant Boys, celebrating the siege of Londonderry and the defeat of the Tories and the French.

ings grew up throughout the area east of the Shannon. The export trade in beef, butter, hides and grain flourished. There was undoubted wealth, revealed in the splendid buildings erected in Dublin in these years. There were threats to the new buildings and enclosed gardens by tories and rapparees, outlaws 'on their keeping' in the woods and uncultivated margins, but such threats were easily controlled by a population now large and secure enough to feel protected.

The policies of Tyrconnell and the birth of a Roman Catholic heir to the throne in June 1688 induced a feeling of utter insecurity among the settler community and the latter fact precipitated a strong reaction to James in England. The Irish dimension to the problem proved fatal to James' chances of retaining his throne when he moved an army largely composed of Irish Roman Catholics into the south of England as a deterrent to any putative uprising. It had the precise effect of provoking one. When James fled to France, Tyrconnell in Ireland raised an army on his behalf, and in a now familiar pattern Irish officers from the armies of Europe came home for another assault. Tyrconnell still held the reins of power in Ireland and set about reducing the power of the Protestants who all rallied to the cause of William and the Glorious Revolution. In March 1689 James, now in alliance with the Catholic Louis XIV of France in war against the Dutch, landed in Cork with an army of French, English and Scottish soldiers. An Irish army led by Tyrconnell met them.

At a parliament held in Dublin James paid the price for his Irish alliance by being obliged to revoke the land settlement of Cromwell. Elaborate legislation was passed by this parliament revoking the land settlement, providing compensation for those who had purchased land in good faith at one remove, proclaiming freedom of religion for all with, of course, a Catholic king. Thomas, earl of Wharton wrote a song mocking the former rule of Tyrconnell and epitomizing the contempt with which the settlers viewed the Catholic reassertion of power. The refrain is a mocking parody of the Catholic watchcry during the 1641 rebellion: 'An lile ba léir e, ba linne an la' (The lily prevailed, the day was ours.) This became, in the form of 'Lillibulero' the rallying song of the Williamite armies in Ireland. The final refrain captures the tone if not the lilting power:

> There was an old prophecy found in a bog,
> Our land would be ruled by an ass and a dog
> So now this old prophecy's coming to pass,
> James is the dog and Tyrconnell's the ass

Its fully cultural import is best savored by rendering 'th' as 'd' as in the original text.

James' campaign was financed by monies raised in the Irish Parliament in return for favors granted. The north of Ireland was the original focus for the war since it remained in Protestant hands. William sent money to Londonderry as the center of resistance. In April 1689 James marched on Derry in person to lead the siege of

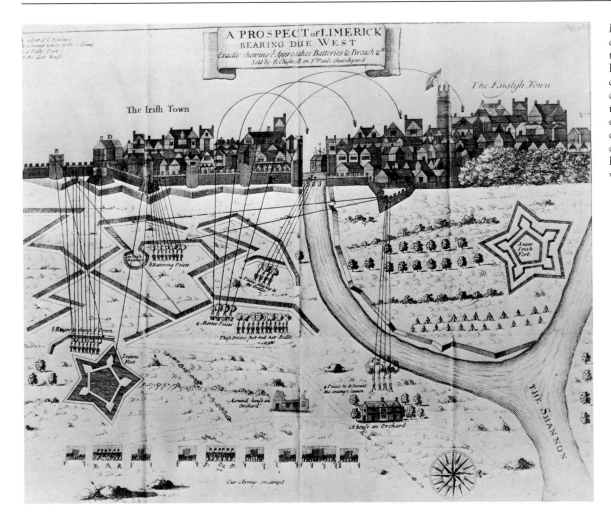

A PROSPECT of LIMERICK
BEARING DUE WEST
Exactly shewing ye Approaches Batteries & Breach &c.
Sold by R. Chifwell in St Pauls churchyard

Left: A contemporary map of Limerick demonstrating the progress of the war for an English audience, as demonstrated by the description at the base of the map of 'Our Army encampt.' Note the division of the town into Irishtown, outside the island, and Englishtown fortified within.

the city, a fatal tactical error. In identifying himself personally with a siege that failed with absolute moral triumph for the victors he massively boosted the confidence of his enemies. The courage and sheer determination of the besieged, who chose starvation rather than surrender, the bravery of the apprentice boys, joined the massacre of 1641 as yet another defining experience

Left: Demonstrating the European interest in the state of the struggle between William of Orange and James II, this contemporary etching of the siege of Londonderry by James Schoonebeck was captioned in both French and German.

for the northern settlers. The city of Derry was re-
lieved at the end of July and on the same day the
Williamite forces at Enniskillen defeated a Jacobite force. The commander of William's army in
Ireland was the duke of Schomberg who had fled
from his commanding position in the French

army after the revocation of the Edict of Nantes.
He was joined by William who took over the role
of commander of his army in Ireland after further
northern victories. The south was in Jacobite
hands, or rather had not seen any Williamite
victories, and James marched from Dublin to

Dundalk to take on William's army, another mis-judged decision. The two armies met at the River Boyne where the superior forces of William triumphed. William marched on Dublin and claimed control of the country. Tales from the battlefield were anxiously awaited in London and throughout the Irish countryside. Most of the reporting broadsides were printed in London, although some were printed in Dublin. It seems clear however that London knew more of the progress of war than the population in many parts of Ireland.

Above: 'The Battle of the Boyne' by Jan Wyck.

CHAPTER 5
THE EIGHTEENTH CENTURY –
A PROTESTANT NATION

THE early eighteenth century in Ireland is a period about which historians have more questions than answers. This is not because of any lack of records from which we can seek to understand it, but merely because it has been viewed since the late nineteenth century, when James Hartpole Lecky wrote his magisterial work on the history of Ireland in the eighteenth century, as a politically uneventful period. Why it has been viewed in this light is easy to see. It was marked by no wars, no plantations and no violent public drama. Catholic Ireland seemed acquiescent and defeated; Protestant Ireland victorious and self-absorbed. There were, however, great changes in the landscape of the country. Dublin was virtually rebuilt, becoming by the close of the century one of the most magnificent cities in Europe. In Cork, Limerick, and in all the other substantial towns of the country, court houses, prisons and churches were built at an unprecedented rate. The major ports were restructured to make them more amenable to commercial demands, the North and South Walls of the bay of Dublin being merely the most dramatic example. Banks and financial houses developed in major urban centers, money and goods were available in remote parts of the country. People still starved in successive mild famines, but agricultural practices changed and in some ways were modernized. In parts of the country life was on the surface little different from one or two hundred years before, but in others the

London and Dublin newspapers kept people in touch with the latest fashions and the international news. Municipal and borough corporations conducted complex negotiations with central authority on the niceties of legal distinctions in a country where many people dressed in tatters, lived in mud cabins and scarcely saw the written word. The machinery of a coherent legal system reached into every area of the country, administered by urbane and educated legal officials in association with landed wealth, while in most of these areas the majority of the population were denied all legal personality by virtue of their religion and spoke a language which the legal system theoretically did not recognize.

On the surface the picture is scarcely unusual for western Europe in these years. One might in fact almost describe it as typical. The life of ordinary people was utterly removed from high political concerns. Matters of principle or of legal complexity were not the primary concerns of those for whom survival was the paramount consideration. How ordinary people saw their lives or made sense of the world that surrounded them is something we can never adequately recapture. By definition those who wrote about or analyzed their state were exceptional, at least in the fact of their literacy. Travellers who commented on what they saw read the lives of these people through the filter of their own culture or prejudices. It is unlikely, however, that the sense of shared oppression that later nationalist commen-

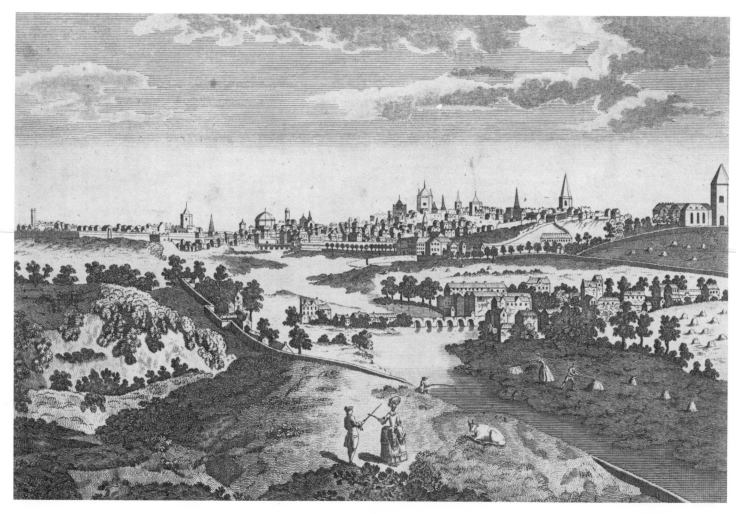

tators have tried to read back into the period was so cohesive as is suggested. It seems likely that if people blamed anybody for their poverty or destitution it was the nearest personalized oppressor or the will of God rather than the existence of an impersonal penal code against the majority of the population on the grounds of their religion. The records of the Irish Folklore Commission seem to indicate that among country people in Ireland over a century later there was a belief in an unadulterated oral tradition of shared oppression passed down from this time, but whether such a tradition owes as much to the romantic strain of publicized nationalism in the nineteenth century is unclear. Thus the public and official history of eighteenth-century Ireland is only a partial history. Economic statistics, demographic returns, details of diet, the accounts of travellers, the intent of laws, the response of the literate – all of these we have the capacity to reconstitute. For how ordinary people thought and felt we have only the conjecture of educated contemporaries.

The Parliament of Ireland in the eighteenth century had little to do with the ordinary people. As elsewhere in Europe the franchise was structured on the ownership of property. Rights were conceived of as the rights of property, which granted admission to the world of power. From this narrow base the legal rights of those not admitted were administered on the basis of what was thought to be just. From this basis, the rights

of the common man were derived. The Irish Parliament was in no way exceptional in its view of these rights. It was not even exceptional in denying the rights that normally accrue to property to those property owners who were Catholic. In other European countries groups of people, like the Huguenots of France, had been denied all rights by reason of their religion. The only way in which the Irish Parliament was exceptional was in denying rights to the property-owning section of a religion that was the *majority* religion of the country, a country moreover where the rights of property had been taken from the pre-existing population of the island in living memory and granted to a newly arrived population. Thus the former property owners had been cast into the undifferentiated mass of their co-religionists and deprived not only of the rights deriving from their property but of the leadership of their people as well. The Gaelic poets of the eighteenth century convey a sense of a leaderless people, cut off from the traditional ties with their own great families. It was not that the new landowners were necessarily harsher than their predecessors, merely that they shared neither language, religion nor culture with their new tenants. Some of the old families became Protestant to survive in the post-Williamite world; these continued to fulfil their old role. Others stayed on and traded or practised the law, keeping a low profile, sending their children to the Continent to be educated, retaining

Above: 'The Custom House, Dublin' by James Malton. The Custom House, along with the Four Courts and the King's Inns, was one of the most notable new buildings erected in Dublin in the late eighteenth century in the Neo-Classical style. All three were the work of James Gandon.

strong links with France and Austria through relations who served in these European armies.

What was the Penal Code? To speak of it as a code is in fact to distort the meaning of a number of laws, passed over a period of more than half a century from the last years of the reign of William, through the reigns of Anne and the first two Georges, that had as their consequence the reduction or erosion of the civil liberties of Catholics on the grounds of religion alone. That is not to suggest that the Parliament of Ireland declared such an end to be their intention. The process began after the Irish House of Commons rejected the Treaty of Limerick. The power of the King was no longer absolute in England. He was forced to rule with the support of Parliament. The option of disregarding that body was no longer possible in the light of the fates of both Charles I and James II, both of whom had lost their thrones for precisely such disregard. William acceded to the wishes of the Irish Parliament. In doing so he in effect recognized the rights of that parliament to deal as it chose with the defeated Catholics of Ireland. In deciding to deny Catholics the right to practise their religion as set out in the treaty, the Parliament of Ireland was not primarily motivated by religious bigotry or the desire for revenge. Its primary aim in denying rights was to ensure that there was no future Catholic capacity to threaten the holding of land and political power. Since Catholics formed so overwhelm-

ingly the majority of the population, since they continued to resent utterly the confiscation of their lands, since it was known that they were merely waiting for an opportunity to reclaim what they believed to be theirs, the clearest course seemed to be to break any remaining power that they had. Certain Catholic landlords like the Kenmares and Fingalls retained their property by complex stratagems. In 1703, 14 percent of land remained in Catholic hands but the possession of land was no guarantee of rights even for that minority. By 1776 five percent was held by Catholics.

In 1691 an act of Parliament made it impossible for Catholics to enter the Parliament without ceasing to be Catholics. To many, indeed most, loyal Protestants this seemed reasonable, given the revocation of the land settlement by an almost exclusively Catholic Parliament in 1689. Laws that prevented Catholics acquiring more land were passed, and incentives were offered to members of Catholic landowning families to change their religion, since if they did all family property would come to them even during their fathers' lifetime. In families that remained Catholic land was to be divided among male heirs, thus ensuring the breakup of formerly substantial estates. Apart from this primary intent to diminish Catholic social and economic powers there were other measures designed to root out the Catholic religion in Ireland. The Banishment

Below: The Great Court Yard, Dublin Castle, which was rebuilt in the 18th century.

Act of 1697 decreed that 'all popish archbishops, bishops, vicars general, Deans, Jesuits, monks, friars and all other regular popish clergy and all papists exercising ecclesiastical jurisdiction shall depart out of this kingdom before the 1st May 1698.' The penalty for failure to comply with these instructions was that of high treason. Any new persons in those categories found entering the country after that date were to be imprisoned for 12 months and then banished. Transportations began in the beginning of 1698 when over 150 priests were shipped from the port of Dublin nearly 200 from Galway and almost 100 between the ports of Cork and Waterford. These priests were provided with subsistence money for their European destinations at the insistence of William who worried about the impact of these banishments on the public opinion of Europe. Some travelled to Lisbon and Corunna but the majority went to French ports. By 1698 there were almost 400 registered Irish religious in the city of Paris and its environs. The exiled former King James commented on their condition, 'I feel the torture of seeing them with my own eyes dying of want, after having shared with them what I needed for my own support.' The treatment of Irish Catholics was, as William had feared, giving rise to unease and alarm in Europe. The Emperor Leopold of Austria, William's Catholic ally conveyed the following through his ambassador:

I have learned with a heavy heart the accounts of the Catholics in Ireland. It is clear from them that the new legislation aims at the entire extirpation of the Catholic religion. This is in direct contradiction of the promises which the king made me at the beginning of his reign. It violates the capitulation of Limerick. It destroys confidence between alies of different religions. Nor will the evil be removed by the plea that the King had to give his sanction, but that he will prevent the laws from being enforced. The King is mortal like all other men and when he is gone these laws may be enforced in their full rigour.

The Catholic Church in Ireland was in a poor and disorganized state. It had scarcely recovered from the Cromwellian period when persecution struck again. The number of vacant sees alone testified to its broken condition: Ardagh, Clonmacnoise, Clogher, Derry, Kilmore, Meath, Raphoe, Kerry Killaloe, Ross, Achonry, Killala and Kilmacduagh. Three archbishops and two bishops had left Ireland immediately after the defeat of James and had not returned. The remaining bishops were further depleted by the Banishment Act, although Bishop Sleyne of Cork was not transported immediately, despite being captured and imprisoned, since William intervened on his behalf. The Austrian emperor's words were, however, proven correct in the case of Bishop Sleyne since after William's death he was transported to Portugal where he died. In 1706 only two Catholic bishops remained at liberty in Ireland and this was reduced to one when Dr Patrick Donnolly, bishop of Dromore and administrator

of Armagh was charged in Dublin in that year. Donnolly was acquitted and remained active in Ireland, protected by different families despite the penalties that they faced if found harboring such a man.

Secular priests fared better than Jesuits, bishops or members of religious orders. In 1697 an enumeration of these clergy placed their number at nearly 900. An Act of the Irish Parliament in 1703 imposed severe penalties on any new priest of this kind found entering the country. Since all bishops were in theory banished the assumption clearly was that in the absence of any capacity for ordination within the country and in view of the denial of entry to priests trained at Continental seminaries, the Catholic clergy would in time simply die out. In June 1704 every Catholic priest in the country was ordered to appear at the sessions held after the 24th of that month and register his name, address, age, parish, the date of his ordination and the name of the ordaining prelate. Each priest was to have two securities of £50, no easy matter in a community so theoretically impoverished, and no priest was to leave the county in which he was registered. Every priest was to exercise his pastoral care alone, and possession of a curate was to be punished with banishment. This Registration Act, as it was called, enabled priests to practise openly in chapels as during the reign of Charles II.

There were 1089 priests in the country at the time of the act and many who were curates registered themselves as parish priests, as did those

Above: Details of Dublin's Georgian architecture can still delight visitors to the city.

Right: Representation of activity outside the Linen Hall in Dublin in September 1785 by William Hincks published with the following dedication 'To the Very Respectable the Linen Merchants and Manufacturers of Ireland, the Conductors of the Great and Beneficial Staple of our Country.'

bishops who had filtered back. In theory this measure was designed to extirpate the Catholic religion over time, without evoking measures that looked bad in the European context. In practice, though most of the Protestants of Ireland would have liked to have seen the end of the Catholic religion, they were not over-optimistic about its chances of being removed. These measures were designed to give an appearance of religious zeal for the purposes of morale, and to remind Catholics that such pleasures of worship as they enjoyed were entirely at the grace of the Protestant establishment and could be limited, altered or simply withdrawn at any time. Quite simply they were designed to maintain that sense of marginality and insecurity that made the Catholics fear the Protestant interest as much as Protestant Ireland feared them. In that respect the clauses can be seen as whistling in the dark by a heavily armed man, but whistling in the dark nonetheless.

Bishops of the Catholic church had been nominated to the Vatican by James II before his fall from power, and this practice did not change when he became the exiled former king. To Catholic Irishmen he was still their king, all the more so since his defeat by William. The pope continued to recognize James as the king of England, and hence continued to appoint James's nominees to bishoprics. In many respects this fact was one of the chief reasons for the suspicion, fear and loathing that Catholics generated in England and among the Protestants of Ireland. Hatred of Catholicism had a long and virulent history since the Reformation, but the potential demonologis-

ing capacity stimulated by the association of the Anti-Christ of Rome, a deposed Stuart king and a horde of dispossessed Irish Roman Catholics in the Protestant consciousness can scarcely be exaggerated. The widespread Irish Catholic refusal to take the Oath of Abjuration (repudiating the claim of James II and all his heirs to the throne of England and Ireland) was a further cause of rage.

The religious issue was never an isolated one, and successive enactments constraining Catholics (retrospectively taken as a coherent whole and designated as the Penal Code) cannot be seen as a coherent body of calculated and premeditated intent. Different enactments took place at different times in response to specific outside political pressures. For instance the news that in March 1708 the Pretender had set sail from France to invade England was greeted by the authorities in Dublin by the summary 'seizing and committing of all popish priests to gaol until further orders.' This is not to suggest that successive penal enactments were devoid of evil intent towards the Catholics of Ireland, or that prejudice, fear and sheer bigotry did not influence the Parliament of Dublin, merely that the laws were contingent, dependent on their immediate context and not on some impersonally preconceived master strategy – that they took place in the political world and not in the rarified chamber of ideology. The priests seized in 1708 were ordered to take the Oath of Abjuration which they summarily refused to do, regardless of the penalty for refusal. Such loyalty to a Jacobite king, who, in his prime had not seemed enthralled by the Catholics of

Left: Another dedicated representation by Hincks, this time showing 'the common method of Beetling, Scutching, and Hackling the Flax.'

Ireland, seems incomprehensible until we recall that James, by taking part in the Irish wars had become the living embodiment of the enduring hopes of the exiled, the dispossessed and the defeated. Only through his reinstatement could hopes of revenge and victory be fulfilled. When the priests did refuse to take the oath there was not, however, very much that the government could do, apart from banishing every one of them from the country, which was impossible. If ordinary people, living in a society where their leaders' economic and social power had been broken, where their language and culture was a matter for amusement if not ridicule, where their religion was excoriated as a cult of idolatrous mumbo-jumbo, had anything from which to take pride or sense leadership in this period it was the behavior of their priests. By the strength of their resistance and the confidence of their faith they seemed unbreakable.

Much romantic pondering and unfocussed speculation has been devoted to the cultural

Left: Limerick Custom House, built by the Sardinian architect Davis Ducart between 1765 and 1769. Ducart also designed some notable country houses including Castletown Cox, County Kilkenny which is held to be his finest.

transformation of the Irish Catholic masses in the eighteenth century. In a panegyric to Irish nationalist triumph in the twentieth century Daniel Corkery wrote of 'The Hidden Ireland', of a culture and a civilization that went underground in the eighteenth century in the face of state oppression. This is a corollary to a view that sees the history of eighteenth century Ireland in classic colonial terms. In parts of England at the same time, however, localized differences and separate 'cultures' were being intruded upon by the forces of trade and the impact of change. Whether one clear 'culture' united the island of Ireland even before settlement is also debatable. Whether one talks in terms of exploitation or modernization is perhaps almost irrelevant. One way of looking gives one perspective, the other another. In a sense the differences are of labels rather than of substance. In the absence of specific research on details of local life, on the manner in which the church addressed the people, on the structures of everyday life, such debates are limited. It is probably, however, true to say that the image of James and the reality of the Catholic Church presence were the only congenial images of authority that the people had.

Maria Edgeworth wrote at the end of the century, but the times that she wrote of were the years before 1750. Her novels are often read as humorous comments on the Irish character, or inaccurately as images of collapsing Protestant power after the Act of Union. Carefully read they are chiefly remarkable for conveying the precise degree of distrust that existed between the landowners and their native tenants. The slithering, jovial, deceptive family retainer is seen as always ready to pounce in the most devious way possible, disturbing and wrongfooting the landlord who hankers after open and honest dealings such as he would find from tenants in England. But in Ireland there is a sense of resentments masked by obsequiousness, of a feigned trust that conceals calculated appraisal, in short of a complete absence of good faith in relations between the rural classes. More particularly there is an acute sense of the treachery of appearances, of living in a country where things can metamorphose without warning. That much of this derives from the seventeenth-century Protestant experience of being slaughtered by neighbors who they had dispossessed is clear, that Protestant distrust, as institutionalized in every arm of the state, fed and nurtured the treachery they so carefully anticipated is even clearer.

The culture of Gaelic Ireland had been preserved during the seventeeth century by descendants of the old learned class and by Old English churchmen like the Jesuits Henry FitzSimons and Stephen White, Luke Wadding and Peter Lombard. In Louvain the College of St Anthony had been founded by Flaithrí O' MailChonaire, Franciscan archbishop of Tuam. Founded in the early 1600s this college became an intellectual center for those Irish educated at Salamanca or Paris. Material of historical significance collected in Ireland was brought to Louvain and worked on by these exiled scholars. These schools did not survive intact into the eighteenth century, though the repositories of materials relevant to Ireland's past stored at Louvain and elsewhere remained protected. There was, however, a popular sense of the country's past, promulgated through the

circulation of works like Geoffrey Keating's *Foras Feasa Ar Eirinn*, an account of the history of Ireland since the conquest of Henry II.

The literary tradition of the bardic schools of poetry and the classical schools of learning did not survive the final defeat of their patrons, the old landowners. In some cases the trained poets transferred their allegiance to those new Cromwellian families who seemed amenable to the glamor of having long bardic incantations to their glory in the Gaelic manner, a tradition that can be seen in the poems to Valentine Brown of Kerry. The strict meters of the old bardic schools, governed by complex restraints of internal assonance and rhyme, became lax and less formalized in the unsupervised conditions of the early 1700s. Purists of the old school heaped derision on the heads of careless rhymers. Poets like Seamus Dall MacCuarta, Aogán O'Rathaille, Eoghan Rua O'Suilleabhain and Brian Merriman retained in their poetry a sense of the meaning and conventions of a culture that had little or no official status in the eighteenth century. The type of verse known as the *aishling* which emerged in this period took the form of a lament for a beautiful but oppressed woman, brutally treated by new arrivals who nonetheless waited patiently for redemption from across the seas. The woman was a personalized Ireland – Roisín Dubh, Caitlín Ni Houlihán or countless other names that were to cloak the idea of Ireland for two centuries. The stranger who oppressed her so cruelly was an embodiment of the new landed class, and the stranger awaited was of course James, and later in the century his son the young Pretender, or *Mac an Cheannai* as O'Rathaille called him in his poems of 1719 and 1720 when hopes of Spanish aid for the Pretender's cause were at a peak. In effect the poem is written when hope has died. The title means literally 'The Merchant's Son', but in this case the term seems to be taken from an old Irish tale where it has the connotation of 'redeemer' or 'savior'. The poetry of O'Rathaille was not in the classical mode but it had not reached that standard of debasement which had prompted Daibhíd O'Bruadair, a poet of the old school, to speak of the new poetry as '*sraid eígse*,' literally 'street' or 'gutter' poetry. One tradition that did survive was the copying and preserving of manuscripts. The printing was informally executed but was adequate and preserved poetry, romances, genealogies, lives of the saints, charms, medical texts, histories, prophecies and songs.

For the first half of the century Catholic Ireland retreated into a culture of the undergrowth, rarely intersecting with the concerns of politics at a high level. It is clear from the Penal Rolls, the listed record of those who altered their religion from Catholic to Protestant, that thousands did adopt this course for a variety of reasons. In terms of the overall population their number was, however, minimal. As the Penal Laws were enforced with differing degrees of assiduity over

the century, many educated Catholics did find the means both to preserve and increase their wealth. The only system of education provided by the state were the charter schools, shunned and rejected by Catholics since they were seen as mere proselytizing agencies. Trinity College in Dublin continued to educate the sons of wealthy Protestants, and through a system of assisted places to educate the intelligent sons of Protestant artisans and tradesmen. Many of the most prominent men in the political and intellectual world of the new élite were such men together with recent converts from Catholicism. Though the Catholic church in Ireland was an underground force, with the image of the Mass rock where outdoor services were held at its core, it retained more coherence of organization and intent than this would suggest, and by the 1760s the orders of friars and monks were beginning to reassert and expand their organization in Ireland. The Penal Laws served to fuse the sense of political and economic displacement on to the religion of the majority, so that for many religion, power and culture became intermingled and interlocked. The Mass rock, the hedge school, the necessity to be educated abroad, if at all, the fighting in European armies as the only means of retaining the status of a gentleman and immersion in trade and the law as an alternative to politics and landed power, all combined to confer on the Catholic middle classes a sense of grievance and a desire for the reassertion of position.

While Catholic Ireland seemed to be a separate and contained world to the class that controlled the country through the ownership of land, the control of all political power and the support of the government in London, of whom it was representative, its existence nonetheless conditioned the terms within which the new politics were generated. As we have seen, the insecurity of this new class was directly related to the meaning of the Penal Laws, and the extent to which they had to push their claims for these laws against the conciliatory tones of English ministers served to distance them from the politics of London. Many of the most powerful men in the Irish Parliament had been born in Ireland. They were the descendants of the settlers of the 1650s. Others were the descendants of Old English or Old Irish families whose families had lived for centuries on the island before converting to Protestantism. But even those first-generation settlers who dominated the upper and lower houses of the Irish Parliament came within a few years of having settled in Ireland to see their interests as separate and distinct from those of the London government. It would be an error to see the divide as a clear one, since in many ways the politics of London and Dublin were utterly entwined. The Irish Parliament was still restrained by Poyning's Law, which in effect meant that the Irish Parliament could pass no law inimical to the wishes of the English Parliament. The government of Ireland was presided over by a lord lieutenant, and the cabinet role was filled by men appointed by the king, men who were not accountable to the Irish Parliament. This left considerable room for tension between parliament and executive. The fact that it did not lead to constant difficulty was due to the energies and strategies of 'parliamentary managers' who worked to maintain parliamentary support for government measures. In the absence of disciplined 'parties' in the modern sense this was the only method of acquiring groups of support, and it was best administered through a well-oiled system of patronage. The lord lieutenant, as head of the Irish administration, did not reside in Dublin. He visited the capital at 18-month intervals and in his absence the executive authority was in the hands of the lords justices who were appointed by commission under the Great Seal of Ireland. At their service in the mechanics of government they had aides-de-camp and secretaries, of whom the under secretaries to the chief secretary and the second secretary customarily served them directly. The power of the lords justices changed over time in response to specific political pressures: for instance, after the political crisis referred to as Wood's ha'pence in 1723-25, during which the lords justices were hostile to the policy of London. The London government saw that this was potentially a dangerous development and ensured its nonrepetition by taking greater care with such appointments. In the future the lords justices were to be assuredly loyal. For this reason the primate of the established church in Ireland was almost always an Englishman, and the Lord Chancellor and the Speaker of the Irish House of Commons were also chosen for their loyalty.

The lords justices were in effect the rulers of

Ireland. They appointed sheriffs and lieutenants of counties. They controlled public order and suppressed riots, administered the Penal Code, supervized corporations and regulated the coinage. A generally English tenor was maintained until 1747 as a result of the clear dominance of the Protestant primate Boulter, who had clear ideas on the necessity of keeping Englishmen in key positions. Since the lords justices 'undertook' the king's business in Ireland in the absence of the lord lieutenant, their control has been described as that of the undertakers. Later in the century their power was a source of alarm to the London government and much of the parliamentary wrangling between Dublin and London in the 1750s was on precisely this issue. The problem, from London's point of view was solved during the viceroyalty of Townshend in the late 1760s and early 1770s. He established a precedent whereby future viceroys remained throughout their period of office in Dublin and ruled directly, with the aid of the chief secretary. The viceroy's prime responsibility continued to be to the English government, to which end he strove to manage the Irish Parliament through his own nominees.

Above: The Irish in the service of France. This print by Ernest Meyer of Paris, dated 1750, is called 'Regiments Irlandais . . . Clare, Dillon, Lally, Roth.'

Above: Edmund Burke (right) and the English radical leader Charles James Fox in a painting by Thomas Hickey. Raised in Ireland and educated at Trinity College Dublin, Burke was one of the leading political thinkers of his time and a strong supporter of Irish political reform.

The legal establishment closely mirrored that of England, with five superior courts: Chancery, the three common-law courts of King's Bench, Common Pleas and Exchequer and the Prerogative Court. The policy of appointing Englishmen to prime positions was as prevalent in judicial circles as in political. All Irish judges held office during the king's pleasure. The headquarters of the courts in Dublin were a warren of cramped chambers near Christ Church Cathedral, until the magnificent Four Courts building was constructed in 1796. The Honourable Society of the King's Inns was a legal body modelled on the English Inns of Court.

The administration of law throughout the country was a complex and burdensome process. Twice a year the common-law judges went on circuit to try major civil and criminal cases. The county grand jury selected the cases to go before them, the jury itself having been selected by the county grand sheriff and consisting of 23 substantial local men. The assizes were major social events. Though these assizes represented the glamour and menace of the law in its most exalted form, the most important of the courts for the lives of the majority of the people were the courts of quarter sessions conducted by the justices of the peace. These JPs were either mayors or primary officers of corporate towns, or country gentlemen appointed by the Lord Chancellor. As such they were political appointments that owed much to the system of patronage. Each county had about 50 justices of the peace who acted collectively four times a year as a court of quarter sessions. For the rest of the year they had a variety of legal duties, including administering penalties that arose out of Penal legislation.

The Irish House of Commons was composed of

300 members. Each of the 32 counties returned two, the 117 boroughs each returned two and Trinity College, Dublin two also. The Irish House of Lords contained 22 spiritual peers of the Established Church and a varying number of temporal peers. It exerted a direct influence on the House of Commons since about half of the borough members of the House of Commons were returned by lay and spiritual peers. There were surviving Catholic peers though these were debarred from taking their seats by the Act of Supremacy. They did receive writs of summons and some took the Oath of Allegiance. Throughout the century their ranks were expanded by the

Above: 'The Irish House of Commons' by Francis Wheatley.

contention. This was contrasted by the libertarian unorthodoxy of Belfast, a city also deeply influenced by intellectual developments in Scottish universities. The Presbyterians had considerable grievances against the Dublin Parliament, though they were not acute as those of the Catholics who surrounded them nor were these grievances ever strong enough to disturb their sense of the community of the Protestant interest in Ireland. The Presbyterian Church was partially recognized by the state as shown by the *regium donum*, or royal bounty, which was first paid to Irish Presbyterians by Charles II in recognition of their loyalty. Though this financial gift con-

tinued as a burden on the Irish exchequer throughout the eighteenth century, it was a sum insufficient to maintain the ministry of the Church, a situation that often resulted in emigration to escape poverty.

The Irish Parliament in the 1760s and 70s took issue with Westminster on a number of points that usually found their focus at the time of the passing of money bills. The 'opposition' or patriot element in Parliament had a loose affinity with the liberal elements in Dublin municipal politics whose views were most clearly articulated by Charles Lucas, the defender of the guild interest against that of the aldermen in city politics. Their

Above: Installation of the Order of St Patrick in St Patrick's Hall, Dublin Castle, 17 March 1783. The figure in the center is the original Grand Master of the Order, the Marquis of Buckingham, Knight of the Order of the Garter.

aims were parliamentary reform and municipal reform and to an extent the demand in Parliament for greater freedom from Westminster restraint came from those who could on certain moderate reforms agree with the trading interest of Dublin. Lucas' demands also overlapped with the interests of certain Catholic tradesmen, who were forced to pay quarterage in order to acquire the rights of freemen in guild membership. Thus on certain ostensibly liberal issues the interests of radical urban politics, Whig patriots in Parliament and conservative Catholic middle-class tradesmen seemed to coincide.

In the optimism for reform generated after George III's accession to the throne in 1760 and the general elections that marked it, the substantial conservative Catholic professional men, some of old families and others of recent wealth, united with elements of the surviving Catholic aristocracy to form a body to press for certain measures of reform within the established order. They were cautious and moderate men, scholars, antiquarians and doctors like John Curry and his friend Charles O'Conor of Belnagare whose letters are the most revealing source that we have for understanding the thinking of such men at this time. O'Conor and Curry were interested in the

history of Ireland for its own sake, but also for the purpose of defending their ancestors from charges of barbarity and cruelty which seemed to justify the English conquest. They were conservative and cautious in their demands, knowing that any dramatic clamor for the reassertion of Catholic power would merely provoke a conservative backlash. They clearly viewed the Protestant community as 'other', and always spoke of 'we' with an unambiguous clarity – meaning the Catholics of Ireland. Measures of Catholic relief were passed in 1774 enabling Catholics who were prepared to take the Oath of Allegiance to play a greater role in public life. From the first tentative meeting of the Catholic Committee in The Elephant tavern in Essex Street in 1760 it was clear that, despite their selfeffacing and chameleonlike demeanor, the Catholics of Ireland had taken a significant step towards re-entry into the political world that had excluded them for over half a century.

During the 1770s the Irish Parliament demonstrated an even greater willingness to flaunt Westminster, generally on financial measures. Ireland, it was declared, was contributing too much to the imperial exchequer. The cry was one of over taxation. There was a popular sense of economic depression, despite the contrary evidence that the building boom and general bustle of Dublin seemed to indicate. It was claimed that Irish trade was unnecessarily restricted by measures designed to protect English industries and the maintenance of Ireland as a primitive economy. There was a corollary to claims of the draining of Irish wealth by imperial contributions in the claim that landlords with principal holdings in Britain were draining Irish wealth in their role as absentees on their Irish estates. This was met by a proposal to introduce an absentee land tax which outraged British politicians who fell into this category – men like Rockingham, Devonshire, Bessborough, Milton and Upper Ossory who protested in the strongest possible terms to the prime minister, Lord North. The argument used to defeat the land tax was the claim that the two countries were as one, and that wealth inevitably gravitated to the metropolis – in this case, London. For the Anglo-Irish, however, Dublin and not London was the metropolis and this served to inflame opinion further.

In the midst of fiscal controversy the American War of Independence began, and Lexington in 1775 was an inspiration to the Irish. Rebellion on the issue of taxation seemed to many patriot and radical Irishmen to be a dramatized enactment of their own complaints against London. The sheriffs and commons of Dublin voted an address of congratulation to the rebels. Liberal clubs and radical Whig societies followed suit. The statements of Belfast radicals like William Drennan were accompanied by banners of 'an infant Hercules strangling the serpents of taxation and despotism.' Clergymen like William Steel Dickson preached sermons against a war with the American rebels, who were seen as brothers. Debating societies and clubs discussed and disseminated the works of philosophers like Locke and Montesquieu. There was a revival of interest in the works of Swift and Molyneux. All of this was radical activity on the fringe of orthodox politics, but it was both widespread and significant. It was not, however, a uniquely Irish development. Radicals all over England mobilized at this time and the unique condition of Ireland merely served to add a more specific political focus to such popular politics. The Parliament of Dublin supported the war, and despite quibbling on the issues of troop supplies and financial support, contrived to appear both loyal and committed to the English war effort. The Parliament refused however to replace the troops withdrawn from Ireland to fight in the war by a 4000 strong band of German-recruited mercenaries. A loose structure of voluntarily recruited men drawn from the leading families in the counties replaced them instead. These were not, however, raised by the Irish Parliament, nor were they under its control, hence their title of Volunteers. A further bone of contention between the two parliaments was the embargo of the export on foodstuffs from Ireland for the duration of the war, except to England and

the colonies. This move was intended to check war profiteering, but in Ireland it was viewed as yet another attempt to maintain the country in a state of depression. In the words of Hussey Burgh, a respectable member of the House of Commons, 'The bounty of the Almighty was perverted into a curse by the poison of prerogative'. In the course of heated debates on this issue and on the related issue of voting monies for the war Barry Yelverton, a lawyer and MP, announced, with more spirit than accuracy, that, 'His Majesty does not rule over this kingdom as king of Great Britain but solely as king of Ireland', thus attempting to recast the constitutional arrangement as that of two equal parliaments under a king who was separately king of both countries. As the nature of the bitter battles between the two Houses of Commons revealed, however, this was simply not the case. The British House of Commons attempted to alleviate the Dublin protest by setting up in 1778, the year that the Volunteers were

Below: The Right Honourable Henry Grattan, 1746-1820, leader of the Patriot Party in the Irish House of Commons.

formed, a committee to enquire into the economic relations between the two islands. The generous and measured recommendations of the committee were, however, dropped, or rather tailored beyond recognition by the political necessity of North's government, who feared offending the commercial interests of their own country more than they desired to propitiate the Parliament of Dublin. The move to reform followed by swift disengagement left public opinion, or rather the opinion of that small public who were politically significant, more dissatisfied than ever. Dublin was aware that the moment of English weakness in foreign affairs was an opportunity to extract domestic concessions.

Buckinghamshire had an extremely unpleasant time as lord lieutenant in 1779. Unpopular in Dublin and ignored by London he spent his time uttering dire prophecies of imminent choas if 'measures' were not taken, but received little satisfaction other than the vicarious pleasure of being subsequently proven correct. Then of course he was blamed for his accuracy. The Parliament of Dublin was supported in its demands for free trade and a weakening of commercial restrictions by the Volunteers operating separately but effectively outside formal politics. 'A short money bill, a free trade, or else,' the banner of the Volunteers proclaimed at a rally in Dublin on 4 November 1779. In Parliament Flood, Grattan,

Hussey Burgh and Bushe sounded equally belligerent. The Volunteers were, however, in the main composed of men of property and wealth, primarily motivated by a desire to protect Ireland from the French, and some felt that the pace of demand was provoking general instability. A more radical minority led by the maverick Dublin businessman Napper Tandy withdrew from the main body of the Volunteers. The use of the Volunteers did not cease to be an effective lever in extracting concessions from England. Nonetheless, the Volunteers were beginning to alarm certain sections of opinion within the Irish Parliament who began to see incipient signs of the tail wagging the dog. Moreover those who opposed the patriot element in Parliament took the line advanced by John FitzGibbon, later earl of Clare, who recognized that the strength of the English connection was vital to the maintenance of Protestant power in Ireland, a country where the majority of the people were Catholic. As he succinctly put it, 'the Act by which most of us hold our estates was an act of violence – an Act subverting the first principles of the Common Law in England and Ireland.' In other words the Protestant settlement was structured and imposed by force and could only be maintained by force. Protestant Ireland did not have the resources to generate sufficient force alone and was therefore dependant on the might and power of the London

Below: A representation of the Irish poor with Henry Grattan at their head, receiving the largesse of the 'Senate and people of Ireland.' It is a rather uncharacteristic representation of Grattan though his characterisation in the words of the leader of the delegation as the 'establisher of our peace' is less atypical.

government. Posturing in the fashion of colonial nationalists, rhetorically articulating a passionate commitment to the community of the English in Ireland, was all very well but Ireland was not America and playing the independence game could prove dangerous. It was a game, however, that the Irish Parliament seemed to win in 1782 when, in the wake of free trade legislation, London conceded autonomy under the Crown to the Dublin Parliament. It was a rushed concession granted in a spirit of exhaustion rather than resignation. The independent parliament was not dramatically different from the preceding assembly – the same men, holding the same views continued to dominate. Certain individuals like Henry Grattan were beginning to come to a view of the political nation of Ireland as being that of all the inhabitants of the island. He and several others were not unwilling to admit Irish Catholics into the political nation that they felt themselves to have fashioned through struggle with Westminster. But the majority of MPs continued to see the Irish Parliament as a Protestant Parliament and intended to grant renewed Catholic demands reluctantly if at all. The repeal of Poyning's Law and the amendment of the 1719 Declaratory Act did not dramatically alter the nature of Irish politics. The lord lieutenant continued to rule with his council as the king's government in Ireland and the issues that dominated the structure of Irish politics outside Parliament remained substantially unaltered. The external focus of London receded, but this merely concentrated

internal issues. The greatest of these was the position of Catholics and the shifting responses within the Protestant community to their demands.

Certain sections of the Volunteers had intended independence to be more than an end in itself. They had fought for the rights of the Irish Parliament over that of London, not for nebulous idealism but for the initiation of specific reforms. These reforms did not relate in any central sense to the rights of the Catholics but rather to a more efficient, just and egalitarian distribution of power within the given political nation. A minority in Parliament supported these reforms, but the majority was violently opposed to them. Electoral reforms and a diminution of patronage were unappealing demands to men who had no objection in principle to the way in which politics was managed. Their only desire had been to ensure that control of that management was rooted in Dublin and not in London. There were 100,000 Volunteers in arms and one of the chief challenges facing the Irish Parliament was to control this formidable force that had proved so useful in the past.

In 1783 it seemed as if there might be an absolute confrontation between the Volunteers and Parliament. Volunteer delegates from all over the country met at the Rotunda in Dublin in successive sessions over months. The elected or nominated delegates seem on the balance to have been representative of the moderate elements within the Volunteers and there was a conspicuous

Above: Lord Aldeborough observes a Volunteer parade, as seen in the painting by Francis Wheatley.

absence of those Volunteers who associated with the fringes of Catholic or extreme radical politics. Lord Charlemont, their nominal leader, and Flood managed to control the energies of the assembly, avert a direct confrontation with Parliament and draft reform demands that reflected their own preoccupations with the old questions of increased political autonomy and further trade reforms with Britain. These politics of the center were further reinforced by the collusion of most conservative elements within the Catholic Committee – led by the lords Kenmare and Fingall who demurely submitted that 'they would receive with pleasure every indulgence granted by Parliament.' This was in marked contrast to the views of the bulk of the Catholic Committee who were thinking along far more serious lines of demand and contemplated appealing directly to London. The Catholic lords had no more desire than the bulk of the Protestant members of Parliament to see the lines of class blurred, and were less than impressed by the control exerted within Catholic politics by crude tradesmen who utterly lacked that tradition of Continental refinement believed to be essential to the composition of an Irish Catholic gentleman.

In 1783 and 84 Flood introduced reform bills based on the demands of the Volunteers. They were defeated on both occasions. The Volunteers had concluded their convention by sending an address to the king emphasising that the reforms that they craved were not due to 'any spirit of innovation in them but to a sober and laudable desire to uphold the constitution'.

In Parliament, presented in the form of Flood's bills, the Volunteer demands were viewed as an outrage. Parliamentary reform was denounced as a 'crude and impracticable scheme of wild and fanciful speculation.' The bill apparently violated the rights of freemen, encroached upon chartered rights and diminished the electorate. Deputies, instead of being representatives of the kingdom were to be the 'fettered deputies of a parcel of petty communities.' Economic development, it was stated, was the area in which gentlemen like the Volunteers should concentrate their energies, not on ludicrous and radical measures to alter the composition of the political world. There was a demand by radicals outside Parliament, particularly in Dublin municipal politics, to which the Irish House of Commons was more sympathetic. This was the agitation for tariff reform for the protection of Irish industries which reached a peak in 1784-85. The demand was precipitated by genuine economic recession and by a clear body of public protest, but the speed with which Grattan leaped on the issue seems to suggest that he welcomed yet another opportunity to test with the English House of Commons the real dimensions of the newly won independence.

Below: An anonymous 18th century view of Dublin Bay.

Already the Irish Parliament had extracted an Act of Renunciation from Westminster, a further underlining of Irish legislative independence that the crudely cobbled agreement of 1782 seemed to leave ambiguous. Moreover radical dissent was more easily continued when it could be absorbed into a shared opposition to English 'control.'

Those in English politics who had a view of a new federated empire which would compensate for the loss of the American colonies felt that the time for a final accommodation with Ireland had come. Shortly after Pitt became prime minister a draft treaty was drawn up to settle relations on trade and defense, for the general good of the empire. This was viewed with satisfaction in Dublin where loyalty to both England and the idea of the Empire retained all of its old potency regardless of recent wranglings. The concessions to Ireland were considerable, representing a departure from the mercantilist principles implicit in all English commercial legislation since the mid-seventeenth century. In effect it meant that Great Britain retained no commercial advantage in trade with Ireland. For commercial purposes the two countries were to be as one. Legislative independence was to be balanced by economic integration. Irish ships could carry colonial products to the ports of Great Britain; there were to be no import or export duties between the two countries. In return for these huge concessions Ireland was to contribute to imperial defence in the form of direct payments to the navy. Grattan negotiated on behalf of the Irish Parliament and ensured that the treaty was carried through the Irish Houses. But the reception of the measure in London was excited and irate. English manufacturers launched a massive press and pamphlet campaign against the measure. The treaty passed through Parliament with amendments so substantial that its original purpose seemed to have been lost. These amendments meant that trade and shipping regulations imposed by the English House of Commons would in the future also apply to Ireland. To Grattan this amounted to a repudiation of the freedoms already conceded. The Irish Parliament rejected the revised treaty terms. The old-style political management of the lord lieutenant in Dublin was reinforced and the movement towards Irish government accountability to the Irish House of Commons halted. The reality, as opposed to the appearance, of legislative independence was seriously diminished. The prospect of a long-term satisfactory arrangement between the London government and an independent Irish House of Commons was clearly lost. It seemed clear that the existing arrangement could not continue indefinitely, a point most forcibly made four years later when the Irish and English Houses of Commons reached quite different conclusions on how the kingdom was to be administered during a period when the king was declared to be insane. This so-called Regency crisis merely underlined what had for some time been apparent, that from the point of view of

The Rt Honble Henry Flood.

imperial unity such a situation required legislative reordering.

These disputes with London were not the primary focus of radical attention in Ireland, which still remained committed to reform of the Irish Parliament. The dissenting Volunteers under Napper Tandy formed a minority within orthodox radical protest, since they demanded, as more fringe and extreme radicals were beginning to demand, a consideration of the Catholic question within the framework of liberal reforms. In 1789 Whig clubs formed throughout the country, frequently overlapping in structure and composition with the Volunteers. Their demands were, however, framed within the tradition of the Glorious Revolution of 1689 and again reflected the community of interests with municipal reformers in Dublin. They demanded a Place Bill and a Pension Bill – both to root out patronage abuses – the disenfranchisement of revenue officers and the exemption of barren land from tithe. This latter demand was in response to northern Presbyterian and southern Catholic violence and protest at the payment of monies to the Established Church. While the Volunteers were unwilling in principle to concede to peasant demands, the demand for concessions on barren land was designed to limit discontent and ensure that landlords did not suffer.

Above: The Right Honourable Henry Flood, with Grattan the leader of the Patriots.

CHAPTER 6

THE UNITED IRISHMEN

THE French Revolution of 1789 had an initial effect similar to that produced by the American Revolution over a decade earlier. Throughout the British Isles radical clubs and debating societies flourished. Thomas Paine's *Rights of Man* was disseminated by the Whigs who formed a committee for precisely that purpose. In the north of Ireland in particular the language of liberty, equality and fraternity struck a cord in Presbyterian intellectuals who felt willing to see such principles as relevant to the four million Roman Catholics of the island. In July 1791 the Volunteers under Napper Tandy celebrated the fall of the Bastille. Men like William Drennan, his friend, the Cork man Thomas Russell and Drennan's sister Martha McTier were at the center of the northern Whig radicals. They asked the radical pamphleteer Theobald Wolfe Tone, a Protestant, to come to Belfast and prepare an address. Tone was the son of a Dublin coach builder, had been educated at Trinity College and had spent time ostensibly studying for the Bar in London. He was intelligent, energetic and efficient. As his diaries reveal he was also complex, sociable, witty and urbane. He was not unique among those of his background in ultimately deciding to throw in his lot with his Catholic fellow countrymen. He shared with those establishment rebels like Lord Edward FitzGerald a romantic streak, though he was certainly no dreaming aristocrat. To see him merely as a man alienated by his own community and therefore turning for position or place, albeit of an unorthodox kind, to alternative politics is to deny the complexity of his position and the ambiguity of his perspective. Clearly he put himself outside his own community by his radical politics, but then so did many of his contemporaries. But they fought not for romantic or idealistic ends but for the concrete achievement of those ideals.

Tone published the address that Drennan had asked him to prepare but did not use, since it was too radical even for him. Moreover he suspected that it was seditious. Signed, 'A Northern Whig,' the pamphlet, published in 1790, voiced such heresies as the view that rhetorical phrases like 'the good of empire' were mere euphemisms for the good of England. Tone proclaimed himself to be a radical, a republican and a supporter of the rights of Catholics. Even by the standards of the most extreme Whig radicals this was excessive and dangerous talk, talk that only a very small minority of radicals in the previously understood sense of the term would agree with. In 1791 he published a further pamphlet, *An argument on behalf of the Catholics of Ireland*, which clearly brought the Catholic issue to the center of radical politics.

In October 1791 the Belfast Society of United Irishmen was formed. Its declared goal was the radical reform of the representation of the people with the aim of effecting the limitation of English influence. This demand was in the orthodox tradition of Whig, radical or patriot demands in or out of parliament for over 30 years. The society's further aim of the reinstatement of Irish Catholics into the political nation was one shared only by a small minority of those who would support parliamentary reform and further separation from England. Napper Tandy and Drennan rapidly formed a Dublin branch. While the United Irishmen were from the beginning an open propagandist public political pressure group they had from the start a less public if unconcealed dimension of independence, republicanism and brotherhood. Groups were formed in the north, and were strongest in Leinster but had some hold in east Munster. The newspaper the *Northern Star* was their mouthpiece, or more officially the mouthpiece of the northern Whigs. They produced pamphlets, manifestoes and speeches. The number of profiled urban activists never exceeded more than about 300, but throughout the country membership numbers were in some areas considerable. Moreover in the country there was a degree of informal contact between these gentlemen's or intellectuals' debating clubs and secret organizations know as Defenders which Catholic tenants ran as their own defensive or offensive agencies. Catholics and Presbyterians were free to join the United Irishmen. While educated

Left: How the establishment saw the rural protesters *before* the outbreak of the 1798 rebellion. Many of these men were to swell the ranks of the Defenders. This is sarcastically entitled 'The Right Boys Paying their Tythes.' It dates from *circa* 1785-6. To the tree is tied a naked tithe collector, a threatening notice pinned over his head marking him out as an example to all others. Chaos, evil and danger from a sinister native population. This was the perspective of establishment Ireland in the late 1780s.

Below: A highly stylized subsequent depiction of the 'United Irish Patriots of 1798.' From left to right they are: Samuel Neilson, Michael Dwyer, John Sheares, William Corbett, Arthur O'Connor, A.H. Rowan, William Jackson, W.J. MacNevin, Matthew Teeling, Robert Emmet, Henry Sheares, T. Wolfe Tone, J. Napper Tandy, T.A. Emmet, James Hope, Thomas Russell, Henry Joy MacCracken, Lord Edward FitzGerald.

Catholics shared the ideological framework of Protestant fellow-members those on the United Defender margins tended to see the organization as a potential source for the vindication of their local and specific aims.

Early in 1790 the Catholic Committee pondered 'the best and most concrete means to apply for further advantages'. Their specific and short-term aims were the admission of Catholics to both branches of the legal profession, Catholic

Above: Contemporary English propaganda, 'United Irishmen in Training.'

eligibility to hold commissions of the peace and to sit on grand and petty juries, and to vote in parliamentary elections in the counties for Protestant candidates provided they possessed a freehold worth £20. Just half of the members of the Catholic Committee were to become United Irishmen, although the other half were wary, suspicious and anxious to keep the secular egalitarian United Irishmen at a distance. As Drennan said of such members, 'They dread us as republicans and sinners and don't like to have much communication with us.' Drennan, however, had his own doubts about his Catholic allies. Speaking about the Defenders, the men who committed dark deeds at the dead of night, he confessed the ignorance and fear of even the most valiant proposers of the Catholic cause: 'Why should we tolerate, why should we commit arms and rights to such savages as these Catholics?' On reflection he said that the only answer was: 'Why did you make them and keep them savages, for that they are is without question.' He claimed to see 'as far into the Catholic mind as others. I do not like it. It is churlish soil, but it is the soil of Ireland, and must be cultivated, or we must emigrate.' His sister Martha McTier put it even more succinctly. She said that on seeing a singing procession of Catholics, 'I began to fear these people and to think, like the Jews they will regain their

native land.' Edmund Burke's son was secretary to the Catholic Committee for a couple of years. He was a somewhat useless appointment, although he did show the committee the mechanisms whereby they could bypass the Irish Parliament and deal directly with London in seeking to redress their grievances. As a member of the committee said when they had decided to petition the King directly at the end of 1792, 'African slaves would not petition their masters.' Edmund Burke closely monitored the development of the Catholic Committee and warned Pitt that the only way to counteract the widespread dissemination of 'French ideas' was to make rapid and far-reaching concessions to the Catholics, regardless of the views of the Irish Parliament. The old Catholics like Gormanstown, Fingall, Kenmare and the Catholic archbishop of Dublin, Troy, viewed such behavior as reckless and did temporarily succeed in splitting the organisation of the Catholic Committee throughout the country.

There were measures of Catholic relief in 1793 during the period when Tone was secretary of the Catholic Committee. In the previous year the United Irishmen of Dublin had published a 70-page report entitled *Report on the Penal Laws.* Though the personality of Tone and a certain overlap of membership gave an appearance of strong links between the committee and the

United Irishmen, in reality their respective philosophies were wide apart. The United Irishmen wanted a new egalitarian democratic republic in which Protestant, Catholic and Dissenter would bear the common name of Irishmen. The members of the Catholic Committee were hardheaded businessmen inured to political disappointment, supreme realists as a result of their deprivation for over a century and well aware that the backlash of state power could strike at any moment. To them the United Irishmen may have seemed like hotheaded idealists, or faintly condescending dreamers who imagined that the past could be written away. Defenders, the nameless men who ran secret societies, had links with both organizations, but a clear identity of interests with neither.

In their hardheadedness the Catholic Committee had more in common with FitzGibbon and the Parliamentary reactionaries than with any other group. Both saw that matters could not be indefinitely allowed to drift without restraint toward revolution. Ireland was a complex of militias, Volunteers, protest organizations, committees, debating clubs and secret organizations. The old Volunteers were disbanded by parliament in 1793. In their place a government-controlled militia was formed which permitted Catholics to enlist at the lowest level. This meant putting arms in Catholic hands, which was viewed by the Protestant workers and labourers of the northern counties as anathema. While intellectual northern Presbyterians spoke of a unity of all religions, the incipient sectarianism of the politics of the poor was reactivated. While the new bourgeoisie might see the prospect of a new beginning, neither the traditional holders of power nor the congenitally denied could so swiftly adapt to new political ideas. Presbyterian Ulstermen may in the past have been as poor as their neighbors who were Catholic but they had at least felt themselves to be superior through the law, through their intimate relations with their own landlords, through a sense of order and power being on their side. Arming Catholics, together with the fact that many of them were their competitors in pursuit of work in the linen trade combined to make the Protestant lower orders feel betrayed, insecure and in pursuit of a reassertion of their power. Moreover, Catholics were now entitled to the vote if they were 40-shilling freeholders. Though Catholics were members of the militia they were still in law not entitled to carry arms. In areas like South Armagh bands of Protestant working men took it upon themselves to launch raids into Catholic houses for the purpose, it was alleged, of finding arms. The Protestant gangs were called the 'Peep o' Day Boys' and their Catholic opponents 'Defenders.' As a generic term, however, Defenders was used to cover all Catholic secret societies – Terry Alts, Whiteboys, Rightboys. In reality these societies had more to do with economic competition than political or sectarian ends, but

badges of religion were useful differentials in the struggle for more than subsistence. Ironically the United Irishmen moving out from the cities and attempting to preach an anti-sectarian gospel found themselves confronting a society where economic change was fanning sectarian enmities. Defenders were also organized by travelling educated Catholics who attempted to control this movement that had grown up from below. Prophecies of imminent attack or doom circulated wildy through both communities throughout the 1790s, spreading fear and brutality. In 1795 Defender gangs were active in Armagh where they spent weeks looting Protestant farms. This led to a pitched battle at the Diamond, near Loughill, which the Peep o' Day Boys won. One of the Protestant leaders refused to join an organization proposed by the victors since he had no desire to lead a sectarian organization. Another took his place and the Loyal Orange Order was founded. Excited by victory its first aim was to drive neighboring Catholics from their homes. Orangeism was an exclusively lower class and Anglican movement initially, though as the extent of its power and influence emerged Protestant landowners and men of substance joined to control and direct it. On 12 July 1796 over 5000 Orangemen marched at the Diamond to com-

Below: The parliamentarian and barrister John Philpot Curran, 1750-1817. Curran was a supporter of the Patriots in the Irish House of Commons but became best known for his legal oratory in defense of the rebels of 1798.

Right: Another drawing by George Cruikshank. This one is part of a series in the *St Stephen's Review* and is called simply 'Scenes from the Irish Rebellion of 1798.'

proclaim a county or part of a county to be 'in a state of disturbance.' This proclamation enabled magistrates to search for arms and to introduce a curfew. It further empowered two justices of the peace to sentence 'idle and disorderly persons to serve in the fleet.' Local district yeomanry corps enforced law under the command of officers commissioned by the lord lieutenant. In effect this meant a marginalization of the militia, composed as it was of many Catholics, and a rearming of loyal Protestants.

Most of Ulster under the command of General Lake was proclaimed 'in a state of disturbance' in 1797, all of Sligo and parts of Leinster in the same year. From 1798 the practice of soldiers living 'at free quarters' – literally in the homes of suspects – was employed in the south and midlands. The pace of government oppression presented the United Irishmen with the choice of acting soon or not at all. In March 1798 the government delivered the supreme command an almost crushing blow at a time when the military committee seem to have had no very clear plan of insurrection. Thomas Reynolds, a protégé of Lord Edward Fitz-Gerald, decided on balance that aiding the government was perhaps wiser than maintaining loyalty to a patron who seemed condemned to exile. Consequently he revealed all that he knew about the Leinster command. What he knew was considerable and the Leinster executive was decimated by arrests. All that remained of the Leinster leadership were Lord Edward and the Sheares brothers whose attempts to reconstitute the leadership were terminated by their own arrests a few days later. Rebellion broke out nonetheless. Ulster had already been almost successfully suppressed by General Lake. The Presbyterians of

east Ulster, particularly Antrim, had been considerably reduced, often due to the exertions of Catholic militiamen under Lake's command. The most formidable insurrections were in areas around Dublin – Kildare town, Prosperous, Rathangan, Rathfarnham, Ballymore Eustace, Kilcullen, Clane. The main thrust was, however, in south Wicklow, the towns of Wexford and Wexford/Carlow borders. It seems that in areas near an urban center or in small towns the organization of the United Irishmen, despite the removal of central leadership, could improvise effectively. In scattered baronies where settlement was in the form of isolated houses or scattered hamlets it seems to have been easier for the authorities to enforce the law. Despite the leadership of United artisans and tradesmen, the rebellion rapidly took the form of a *jacquerie*, or peasant rising. Many had as their principal aim the avenging of years of interference and irritation by protestant yeoman who served as government troops. Catholics slaughtered both innocent Protestants and yeomen troops, thus fighting their own most immediate oppressors. Nonetheless, the echoes of liberty, equality and fraternity may be heard in their songs. Their urban leaders reminded them of the United ideals, they welcomed the leadership of the Protestant landowner Bagenal Harvey, but their higher ends were subsumed under a desire to avenge themselves upon a local yeomanry, many of whom were their neighbors. The mainly Protestant uprising in Antrim and Down was also rapidly put down. The French did come from across the sea, but too late. The invaders consisted of a force led by Napper Tandy which occupied Rutland Island off the coast of Donegal, a more significant force of about 1000 men that landed in Killala under General Humbert, and a final force lead by General Hardy which was captured off the Donegal coast. In one of Hardy's ships, the *Hoche*, was Wolfe Tone. He was seized in his role as an invading French officer, brought to Dublin and sentenced to be hanged. He cut his throat before the sentence could be carried out, and became the legendary hero of the insurrection in that act. There was a rising of the peasantry in the west in support of Humbert, but despite impressive temporary achievements they were defeated and their glory was ended at Ballinamuck in County Longford in early September 1798. Effectively the rebellion was over.

Perhaps 50,000 people died in 1798. After the official rebellion ended the country remained in chaos and violence of a sporadic kind. The troops of the Irish Parliament viciously rampaged through the country, angry and vengeful at a rebellion that they viewed as yet another act in the old play, altered merely by the gloss of French ideas. While on one level their analysis was correct, it was also limited. The death of Tone, the political philosophy of United Irishmen and the non-sectarian ideals of Irish republicanism articulated in these years were to be passed down in all subsequent chronicles of the past and to remain as an idealized manifestation of the idea of an Irish nation composed of Protestant, Catholic and Dissenter. More strangely, the independent Irish Parliament, which so ruthlessly repressed the rebellion, was to become for constitutional nationalism in the late nineteenth century a lost idyll of native control. In terms of English politics, the result that the rebellion precipitated

was one toward which Pitt had for some years been moving – the absorbtion of Ireland into Great Britain, the Union.

Above: The trial of Robert Emmett. Emmett tried to organize a rebellion in Dublin in 1803. It was a complete failure and Emmett was captured and executed. His speech from the dock contained the instruction that no one should write his epitaph until Ireland became a free nation.

Left: 'Whipping a victim at Marlborough Green,' 1798, from the *Irish Magazine*. The rebellion of 1798 was marked, as so often in the past, by atrocities on both sides.

CHAPTER 7

EMANCIPATION, REFORM
AND REPEAL

After the rebellion of 1798 the independent philosophy of the 'patriot' Parliament was replaced by an élite fear of Catholic Ireland that outweighed the former focus upon the English House of Commons as the prime enemy. Though creating a non-sectarian ideal of Irish nationalism that was to be appropriated by successive nationalists in the future, 1798 also hardened sectarian configurations. The Parliament of Dublin struggled against Pitt's scheme for its abolition, but the effectively deployed skills of parliamentary managers who oiled the Act of Union's passage through the Irish Houses of Commons and Lords proved effective. The managers bought acquiescence, abetted by committed unionists like Lord Clare who had believed for many years that the only means of defeating the potential contained in the numerical superiority of the Catholics was to subsume the island of Ireland into the larger unit of the two islands. Acquiescence to the Union was purchased with some difficulty. Lord Cornwallis, lord lieutenant of Ireland at the time of Pitt's government, warned him that the attempt to include further measures of Catholic civil relief in the settlement would jeopardise the union itself. If anything, the conservative members of the Irish House of Commons were more unwilling now than they had previously been to concede such rights. Politically active Catholics in general initially supported the Union, thinking that within it they might stand a better chance of having their religious grievances assuaged. The commercial interest of Dublin opposed it with a vengeance, realising the damage that the removal of Parliament would do to their trade. But though the members of the Irish Parliament eventually voted for the act's passage, they did so in the face of impassioned speeches from Grattan and the old patriots, who claimed that the Irish nation was being betrayed and the achievement of the English in Ireland during the eighteenth century abandoned. The English in Ireland were described by contemporaries in a variety of ways. By 1800 most of them would have called themselves Irishmen. It is claimed that the term 'ascendancy' in association with the Protestant or English interest in Ireland first entered the political vocabulary when the Corporation of Dublin in the 1790s proclaimed themselves to be committed to the maintenance of 'Protestant Ascendancy.' To move however from this to the term 'Protestant Ascendancy' employed as a descriptive noun to cover a whole class is somewhat difficult. It seems unlikely that we can precisely date the common usage of the term, if indeed it was even widespread.

Under the terms of the Act of Union Ireland returned 100 members to the Westminster House of Commons. The redrafting of constituency boundaries essential for this new arrangement resulted in an accidental reform – the removal of

Previous pages: 'Emigrant ship leaving Belfast, 1852' by James Glen Wilson.

Below: A map of Dublin, engraved by J. Needle, 1797.

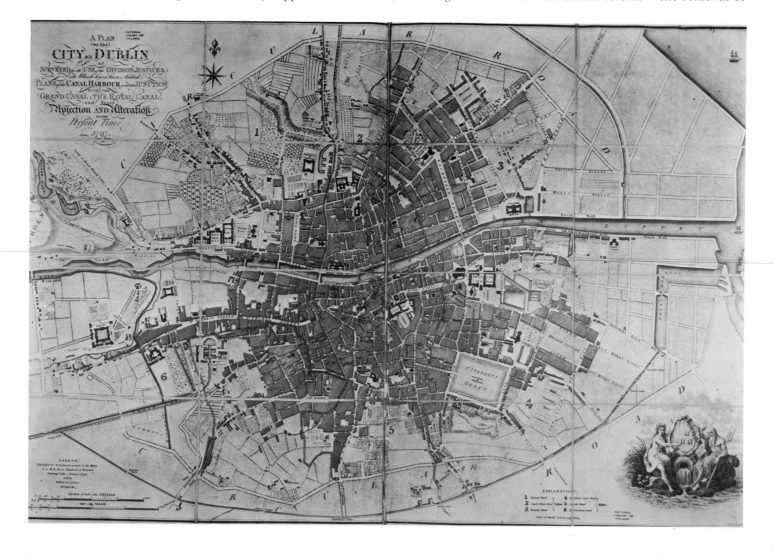

the bulk of borough representation. Each of the 32 counties returned two members and Cork and Dublin also returned two each. One member was returned by Trinity College in Dublin and 31 by the 'considerable boroughs'. The United Kingdom of Great Britain and Ireland was a free trade area and the Irish area of the new United Kingdom was to contribute to the expenses of that kingdom in the proportion of two to fifteen. The country, in an anomaly in the context of proclaimed total integration, was to continue to be administered from Dublin in a fashion substantially unchanged, without of course the necessity of 'managing' an Irish Parliament. The lord lieutenant was usually a member of the British Cabinet and the lines of policy were henceforth to be decided in London and effected in Dublin. This arrangement appeared to contradict the essence of the Union which was that the United Kingdom was in effect one country. The very existence of an administration in Dublin Castle was an invitation to a continued sense of separateness. Ironically, though the events of 1798 were seen in retrospect to be the catalyzing force in bringing about the Union, plans for its introduction were already in progress before the rising even began. From the perspective of London the reasons for the Union were simple and straightforward. Ireland presented a serious security threat to Great Britain in times of war. The Dublin Parliament did not seem capable of containing the revolutionary forces within the island, therefore London was forced to do so. The decision to impose a Union had therefore almost nothing to do with the need of the population of the island of Ireland and everything to do with the imperatives of Great Britain. Great Britain found, however, the politics of a highly complex contemporary situation introduced onto the floor

Arrah now, be asy, ye devils, be asy! I'm thinking how I shall pay Dan two thirteens out o' one. Och now! and Dan's a dear crater! —

The Gemman as pays the Reglar Out-an'-Outer vot drives the HERO!!

Above: A Cruikshank cartoon of 1829, the year in which Emancipation was achieved. Representation of the Irishman in English or Anglo-Irish cartoons reached a high pitch of excoriation as a result of the successes of Daniel O'Connell. Paddy is ragged, revolting, decrepit and above all slow witted.

Left: 'Scene in an Irish cabin, 1851' by Nicholas Erskine.

CAP.ᵀᴺ SWAYNE
Pitch Capping the People of Prosperous

Above: A later representation of punishment after 1798, from the *Irish Magazine*, 1810.

the Irish population by famine, disease, emigration and changed marriage patterns. Indeed by the end of the century the new industrial towns of the north of England had outstripped Dublin and the relative balance of population of the two countries was startlingly different.

Administratively little changed as a result of the Union, though as the century progressed administrative developments took place as elsewhere in the United Kingdom. In many areas of administrative reform Ireland was first, sometimes for reasons of perceived need, sometimes for the simple reason that the centralized nature of Irish administration facilitated easy reform. The Union is a landmark only in retrospect, or only in terms of the question of what an independent Irish Parliament might have become in a democratic age. Popular representation was not a reality in 1800 and therefore the Union touched immediately only on the lives of former members of the Irish Lords and Commons, their social circle and the trade and municipal bodies of the city of Dublin. English troops had always been garrisoned in the country and continued in the same fashion. The legal system continued to be administered as before. Local government, insofar as it existed, continued under the justices of the peace and local notables. Only the degree of attention which a specifically Irish Parliament could give to the island was removed. A more significant change was perhaps the transformation of Dublin, the political focus of the island, into an empty stage, its massive and impressive Parliament houses on College Green reduced in time to providing premises for the possibly more potent political seat of mammon – the Bank of Ireland. The alteration from parliament to bank was strangely apt for the political history of nineteenth-century Ireland was no more than surface squabbling on an economic quagmire.

Why was Ireland so poor? It is an economic question for which there is no clear answer, but also the key to understanding politics. The proposition that Ireland was poor is a relative one. It was an island of sharp contrasts and extremes of wealth and poverty. So was all of western Europe at this time. It appeared poor because it was ostensibly a background fringe area in the most rapidly developing country in the world. The arguments advanced for Irish 'poverty' run the spectrum from the denials of God (lack of mineral resources) to the evils of man (grasping landlords and a machiavellian London government determined to keep Ireland poor and therefore impotent). The other arguments advanced were the popular wisdom of Malthus (the island was inherently economically incapable of sustaining a population as large as had been spawned there); and a theory of 'Irish character' which emphasized an innate fecklessness, lack of initiative and sluggishness, with a religious variant which saw this as in some way emanating from a religion that encouraged passivity and the refusal of responsibility for self.

of the House of Commons. While the absorbtion of Ireland was seen to be a strategic necessity, the occupation of hours of parliamentary time by the problems of an island most members knew little and cared less about was less appealing. The population of Ireland in 1800, at almost five million, amounted to just one-third of the population of the British Isles. Dublin was the second city after London. The relative weight of Ireland in the internal politics of the kingdom was therefore considerable. As the century progressed this balance was utterly altered by the decimation of

The relative merits and demerits of these arguments can be argued ad nauseam but what seems clear is that a disproportionate number of the rural inhabitants of Ireland lived barely at the subsistence level. To an extent this is evidence of a form of relative rather than absolute poverty. Many more lived just above the margins of subsistence and it seemed in the period of boom that ended with the close of the Napoleonic Wars in 1815 that this subsistence level could be maintained for indefinitely spiralling numbers, in other words a few acres and a potato crop was sufficient on which to survive and the plots of land on which this version of living took place could be indefinitely subdivided. The average marriage age was low, the number of children born per family high and the mortality rate by the standards of the newly industrializing towns of northwest England was low. In good times, then, living at the very margins of subsistence was relatively easy. Inherently, however, such an economy was unstable because any swing of the pendulum, in terms of falling agricultural profits which lessened the demand for labor and increased the demand for rent, or a collapse or even partial failure of the potato crop, went to the very roots of the balance. The Irish rural economy can then be seen as a rickety house, teetering always on the brink of danger. The complete failure of the potato crop in 1845, 46 and 47 in so precarious and vulnerable an economy knocked the whole structure to its foundations and occasioned the greatest and most devastating famine in the advanced world for centuries. To see all before the famine in terms of the nightmare ahead is of course to distort the reality which seemed secure and safe enough in its accustomed misery.

Increased competition for land in the early years of the nineteenth century ensured the continuance of an established tradition of agrarian

Above; An article from the *Cork Constitution* in 1858 describing the activities and procedures of the agrarian secret society, the Ribbonmen.

EMBER 4, 1858.

RIBBONISM IN THIS COUNTY.

For some time past delegates from the Ribbon Society have been actively engaged in the west of this county holding nightly meetings, at which they are swearing in members, in the neighbourhood of Bantry, Skibbereen, and Clonakilty, and extending into Kerry. The proceedings appear to be entirely confined to the class of labourers and farm servants, the farmers holding aloof, and appearing not to be altogether at ease with regard to them. Strenuous efforts, however, are being made to entrap farmers' sons into the conspiracy. Some of the delegates are known to the police, and the Government is fully aware of their movements. The principal delegate arrived in this city yesterday, but his object here is at present unknown.

On next Tuesday one of the best meetings of the Southern Coursing Club for this season will take place at Killady Hill. The entrance for each dog is £3, and the challenge cup is £50 in money, so that the lucky winner will be able to gratify his own taste in the selection of plate. Mr. HAWKES will act as judge. On the 20th of September thirty-two puppies from various parts of Ireland were nominated to run, the greater part of which will come to the post, and perhaps four or five will pay forfeit. Complaints have been made of the great danger arising from gentlemen mounted galloping over the fields, but at a late general meeting of the Club it was unanimously determined to put a stop to so dangerous a practice, and also not to allow horse-trainers or gentlemen's servants mounted to accompany the meeting. On the previous evening the members and friends will dine together at the Imperial Hotel. The following gentlemen have nominated dogs to run :—

1—Mr. Robert's bk. w. d. Mark, whelped April, 1857 ; pedigree Ranter, out of Alice.
2—Mr. Robert's bk. w. d. Colleen, whelped April, 1857 ; pedigree, Ranter, out of Alice.
3—Mr. Robert's bk. w. b. Bella, whelped April, 1857 ; pedigree, Ranter, out of Alice.

Left: An Irish hedge school. Such informal schools had helped preserve Gaelic traditions.

Above: Another Catholic Emancipation cartoon of 1829, this time by Tregear. Here again O'Connell is depicted as the leader of an ignorant, unlovely, grasping collection of time servers and near half-wits.

protest and of in-fighting. While Defenderism with its overt political associations remained active in the north, the three southern provinces were more clearly characterised by combinations and groupings opposed to specific local grievances. In 1813 Lord Lieutenant Whitworth wrote about the state of agrarian disturbance:

In the early part of 1813 and during the whole of that year, many daring offences against the public peace were committed in these [Tipperary, Limerick, Kilkenny] and other counties, particularly Waterford, Westmeath, Roscommon and King's county, the nature of which sufficiently proved that illegal combinations and the systematic violence and disorder, against which the special commission of 1811 had been directed, still existed. . . . The principal objects of hostility, or rather the principal sufferers on account of their inadequate means of defence were those persons who; on the extirpation of leases, had taken small farms at a higher rent than the late occupier had offered.

Land was held by an élite numbering no more than about 10,000, the majority of whom were Protestant. They tended to let their land on long leases to substantial tenant farmers. They in turn sublet, sometimes on leases but more usually by informal arrangement to tenants at will. The long fixed leases of the more substantial tenants

usually provided for fixed rents for the duration of the lease, but the sublettings tended to allow for changes in rent at the whim of the landlord or of the exigencies of the market. At the very bottom of the scale were cottiers holding merely a few potato-growing acres or laborers who possessed no security of residence, tenure or work. Within this rural society there was a medley of class interests all having their own self-protective mechanisms for resisting intrusions on their own present and future survival. A series of commissions of enquiry into the reasons for specific outbreaks of violence tended to obscure rather than clarify what exactly was going on. This was further complicated after 1798 by the willingness of the authorities to ascribe political motives to all agrarian trouble. There was an underlying political bias in rural society that was anti-authoritarian, anti-landlord often anti-Protestant and in a more unfocussed way anti-government and anti-English, but to see political purpose in all rural violence is simply wrong. People protested, as they had protested throughout the eighteenth century against the payment of tithe to the Established Church. They protested as in the earlier period against taxes imposed during the French wars. They protested against sudden or sharp rises in rent. They punished those who sought to minimize another man's bargaining power with his landlord by offering to pay a higher rent. They resisted the kind of clearances that were taking place in Scotland by a stubborn campaign of attrition. Catholic laborers and cottiers struggled with more substantial Catholic tenant farmers who sought to oppress them. All classes displayed a remarkable commitment to land in terms of place – they were unwilling to look on land as a commodity, one portion of which could be traded for another. The historical reasons for this are not hard to see. Moreover that sense of alienation to which the Penal Laws of the eighteenth century had contributed proved a useful weapon in a defiance of the economic logic of the market. There were few industrial towns to move to. Land was the focus of all aspirations because in the eyes of most people it was the only means of survival. The politics of Westminster intruded on this world in the form of the attention which its committees or members gave to these problems. Committees of inquiry resulted in various improvement schemes involving the construction of roads or model towns like that at King William's Town (now Ballydesmond) on the Cork/Kerry border.

Local magistrates were often taken to task for their supine reaction to the disorder around them. Lord Norbury took magistrate reaction to the Shanavest and Caravat violence in Tipperary to pieces in the following manner:

By the unfortunate want of confidence or co-operation amongst the magistrates of Tipperary (many of whom are my closest friends) this spirit of avowed outrage has raised its crest so high, that gentlemen of old authority and respect have lately been driven from their public affairs in terror and dismay, with a volley of shots fired at them in the noonday, when attempting to keep the peace. Some of these gentlemen have quitted their family residence and the county has become a theatre for the bloody conflicts of the Caravats and Shanavests.'

There were organizations primarily political in motivation like the Ribbonmen who were largely based in Dublin, and who saw themselves in the tradition of United Irishmen, or more particularly in the mould of Robert Addis Emmet who had desperately led a rebellion in Dublin two years after the passage of the Union. Sentenced to a brutal death he ordered that his epitaph was not to be written until his country had 'taken her place among the nations of the earth,' thus firing romantic nationalist imaginings for the following century and beyond. But though the Ribbonmen attempted to recruit the complex of rural secret societies to their specifically political goals they encountered little success. Caravats, Shanavests, Rock Boys, or Rockites, Terry Alts, Threshers, Carders, Whitefeet, Blackfeet – all generically styled as Whiteboys by the authorities – continued in pursuit of their localized specific ends.

The Ribbonmen were particularly active among artisans, laborers and shop-keepers in Dublin in the years between 1818 and 1822. Their members travelled the country and their influence can occasionally be seen in the wording of local threatening notices or pasted insults

Below: The O'Connell family home at Derrynane on the Iveragh Peninsula in Kerry.

Above: Daniel O'Connell, in a typical 19th century romantic pose.

which played a major role in rural intimidation. As Michael Beames has observed in a study of the Whiteboy movement, a notice of Whiteboys pasted in Tipperary in 1821 states among the usual specific Whiteboy grievances, 'English laws must be curbed in; for we will never be satisfied until we have the Irish parliament and King crowned in Ireland as was formerly the case.' It is equally clear from this demand that anti-English feeling was by no means necessarily republican. The Ribbonmen had some success in centralizing the Cork Rockites, as an interview with William Hickey the Cork Rockite just before his execution demonstrates. Hickey said that all printed catechisms and orders came to them from Dublin and that the head committee was in Dublin.

He said the committee men are appointed; a head committee man is ordered to move to the next parish or district, and the men composing the committee in the said parish are ordered by summons . . . to attend on a certain day . . . under forfeiture of life; and the next head committee man knows the other; they have also signs. You will be quiet by and by in this country; but the business will proceed eastwards; it will be slow. When destruction of property, and the system is established in each country, there will be a general rising.

The Ribbonmen thought in terms of overall uprising, something distinct from the economic realities that fuelled local movements. In their limited view 'the reason for the premature commotions in the south is that human nature could no longer bear the slavery they are in and it is better to be shot than to die of hunger'. Under the terms of the Insurrection Act of 1814 much of the southwest was proclaimed. It was seen to be a useful and effective deterrent: 'I have gone on the home circuit and I have been present at many trials, where persons have been capitally convicted, and I never saw a stronger impression of feeling upon the public mind upon any conviction . . . I mean the expression of agonised feeling, lamentation of women, cries and exclamations, continued for a long time after sentence is passed.'

Another approach to the problem of endemic violence was to make an attempt to alleviate the condition of the poor and to take the responsibility for education out of the hands of unsupervized hedge-school masters. Ireland had no system of poor relief. The Poor Enquiry of 1833-36 resulted in a system of poor relief that was largely the work of two men – George Cornewall Lewis and George Nicholls. Lewis was assistant commissioner to the enquiry and as a result of his researches produced a book called *On the Local Disturbances in Ireland.* His personal recommendations were preferred over those of the formal commission report and the responsibility for the final form of the system was given to Nicholls. Both, curiously saw the new Poor Law as a system to aid the country through a 'transition period'. In the words of Nicholls,. 'By the term "transition period" I mean to indicate that season of change from the system of small holdings, allotments and sub-divisions of land which now prevails in Ireland, to the better practice of day labour for wages, and to that dependence on daily labour for support which is the present condition of the English peasantry.'

The majority of the rural Irish population was English speaking by the early 1800s. In the province of Connacht, the west of counties Kerry and Donegal and an area north of Louth, Irish continued as the first language. In many areas of the west it was the only language of the people. Leinster and the cities were almost exclusively English speaking and in the remaining counties bilingualism was the norm. Irish was increasingly the language of private domestic conversation as English increased its hold due to the increased bureaucratization of the public domain. Literacy levels were low. (The first reliable figures that we have are for 1841 when average illiteracy figures stood at 72 per cent).

The introduction of a state system of national education in the 1830s improved the level of literacy over time, but as a corollary diminished the standing of the Irish language which was not taught in the schools and which did not have a printed literature to compete with the English-language publications that circulated with great rapidity from the mid-century. Public figures like

Archbishop Mac Hale of Tuam claimed that the national school system was inherently anti-national. The most often quoted defense of this view is the rhyme which appeared in a set text book for Irish schools:

I thank the goodness and the grace,
Which on my birth has smiled,
And made me in these Christian days
A happy English child.

Cultural nationalists of the early twentieth century were to indict the state system of education as the 'murder machine,' and to represent it as a deliberate agent of imposed cultural change. This analysis is not incorrect, but it would be an error to see the system as uniquely devoted to the undermining of Irish language and culture. All of the agencies of the state, the Poor Law, education, the penal system, displayed from the early 1830s an implicit charge of 'improvement.' The primary aim of these agencies was to alleviate perceived need among the poor and to 'improve' their moral and social values. The Irish language was merely one of many recessive attributes with which the system was committed to contend. It was not merely that speaking the Irish language was punishable by the tally stick. The general aims of the curriculum were to incorporate a disrespect for any knowledge that was not standardized and 'useful.' Thus the limited classical education provided by the hedge-school masters was abandoned in favor of a rigid commitment to the three Rs and such ancillary virtues as thrift, deference, punctuality, abstinence and self-improvement. These were the virtues that were to prove so useful in creating a decorous industrialized proletariat in England. In Ireland the absence of a general industrialized forum for the display of these virtues was to ensure that the literacy which education certainly created often contributed to the public articulation of values at sharp variance with the system. In 1800 Irish was the language of about half of the population. By 1851 less than a quarter of the population spoke the language and only a tiny percentage were monolingual Irish speakers. Clearly the educational system alone did not bring about this massive transformation, though its contribution should not be underestimated. Certainly a general system of education was firmly established in Ireland before anything comparably comprehensive had emerged in Great Britain.

Improved communications, more centralized markets, in short a more capitalized economy diminished the sense of regional separateness after 1800. The most significant unifier was, however, the standardized bureaucracy that touched on every area of life. People from north Donegal and west Kerry shared, despite their differences, the same legal system, the same school curriculum, the same economic exigencies of a market that was increasingly standardized within the island. But the greatest conscious movement towards homogeneity was provided by the campaign for Catholic Emancipation in the 1820s.

The level of rural discontent, the multiplicity of social grievances and the insecurity and instability engendered by zealously proselytizing evangelical preachers made rural Ireland in the first two decades of the nineteenth century a network of conflicting energies. The Protestant churches, buoyed up by a new resurgence of evangelical fervor, sent out a range of missionary biblical societies to reveal to the Irish rural classes

Left: One of O'Connell's famous mass meetings for the repeal of the Act of Union at Tara, 1843.

Right: Fr Mathew, the Capuchin temperance reformer was outstandingly successful in his crusade for teetotalism. However, he realised that in order to succeed he was obliged to conform to the politics of Repeal. This particular reconciliation unites nationalism and temperance in a way that was to remain fundamental to certain nationalist movements in the future 'Ireland sober, Ireland Free.'

the error of their ways. Itinerant preachers and scripture readers ventured even into the exclusively Irish-speaking areas of Achill and Corca Dhuibhne Peninsula in Kerry to show deluded papists the path to light. In a ten-year period two of these organizations, the Hibernian Bible Society and the Religious Tract and Book Society distributed over four and a half million tracts texts, pamphlets or bibles. If the level of literacy was as low as we are led to believe this figure seems extraordinary, but whatever one thinks about the success of proselytism in effecting conversions, it certainly succeeded in disseminating throughout rural Ireland the biblical language of damnation, apocalypse and spiritual immediacy. The most dramatic demonstration of the popular consequences of such dissemination is to be seen in the widespread credence given to the millenial prophecies of Pastorini which reached a high point during the typhus epidemic of 1817. A potent misreading of the work of Charles Walmsley led to a popular belief in the imminent destruction of the landowning classes. Writing in 1824 the Rev. Mortimer Wheeler, Protestant curate and schoolmaster in Tipperary, wrote:

Anyone who have been a resident in the country parts of Ireland may have observed that about seven years since a considerable change began to take place in the little penny tracts and ballads with which the itinerant pedlars were supplied. . . The fact is certain that love songs and stories were no longer the principal wares of the book vendors; and that stories of martyrs, deaths, and judgement and executions of obstinate heretics,

and miracles performed in the true church were now in very general circulation. By one class of these productions the animosity of the faithful was whetted against b----y Protestants; in another they learned how the heretics ought to be treated; and the miracles . . . sustained them by a hope that at last God would fight for them and exterminate their oppressors. At the same time prophecy, the constant resource of a depressed people, afforded them its consolations. Pastorini, circulated in various forms became a favourite study.'

A supporter of an imminent uprising to defeat the landlord interest, when taxed with the failure of the rebels of 1798 replied, 'The devil mend the scoundrels; they began twenty five years before it was the will of God they should.'

In the climate of this sense of imminent salvation in rural society the political directors of the campaign for the Catholic Emancipation tired of the old, repeatedly refused, parliamentary supplications. The Catholic Committee had fallen into a fossilized stagnation by the early 1820s. The more manifest grievances of the Catholic middle classes had been removed in the last decade of the independent Irish Parliament but the essential question of equal rights before the law, epitomized by the capacity to be elected to Parliament remained unresolved. Pitt, on setting up a college for the education of Catholic priests at Maynooth in 1795, had introduced the principle of state control of a limited variety for church support. Such plans as Grattan and the Catholic gentry had for the 'Emancipation' of Catholics incorporated the notion of a clergy paid by the state in return for Church support for the status quo. This provision was quite acceptable to the Catholic conservatives and to the bishops themselves, most of whom had been educated on the Continent and who were grateful for any state concessions. To a certain extent such agreement was academic because even under the sympathetic rule of Canning, prime minister in 1827, or his successor Goderich, the agreement of the Commons to such a proposal was ultimately futile since the Lords were committed to blocking such a concession and the king was even more violently opposed.

Despite the academic nature of the problem a section of young radical lawyers whose leading spokesman was Daniel O'Connell insisted that such an intimate arrangement between Church and state was unacceptable to them. They broke with the Catholic committee in 1823 and constituted themselves as the rival Catholic Association. This was a predominantly middle class association, based in buildings in the Corn Exchange in Dublin and its membership fees were considerable. At the end of its first year it had at most a few hundred substantial members. O'Connell then decided to initiate a class of associate members who would pay a subscription of a penny a month. This was to be the secret of the power of the movement.

O'Connell was himself a member of that strange class of Catholic gentry who had survived the trials of the eighteenth century. The family had held on to their lands on the Iveragh Peninsula in Kerry and retained a considerable family residence at Derrynane. The family's fortunes had been revived by O'Connell's uncle, Maurice 'Hunting Cap.' A judicious blend of smuggling, trading and farming had made Maurice a very wealthy man. The family had been educated in France for many years – O'Connell himself was at Douai at the time of the French Revolution. They had served as officers of the French army and O'Connell was an example of the post-1790s generation of Catholic gentry, free to earn his living as a Catholic at the Irish Bar. He had read for the Bar in London where he seems for a time to have become a Deist. In sensibility he was very much of the eighteenth century, tolerant in matters of religion and contented by a secular public sphere. His earnings as a barrister were prodigious. Even by the standards of the London Bar he earned a fortune, an even more exceptional achievement when one appreciates the relative poverty of the population among whom he worked. His family advised him to skip politics and to devote his energies to his own profession, that is, to making money. As Catholic survivors of the eighteenth century they took a cautious view of meddling in the public domain. 'Hunting Cap' believed that it was only by demonstrated loyalty and a grateful demeanor that Catholics would ever gain. Any other course would provoke reaction. The ethos of the O'Connell family was forward looking. They spoke English in all official transactions, and corresponded in English on important matters. O'Connell was a fluent Gaelic speaker and used the language among the women, tenants and staff in Derrynane. He was not a sentimentalist and though his aunt had written one of the greatest poetic laments in the Irish language on the occasion of the death of her husband, '*Caoineadh Airt Ui Laoghaire*,' or the 'Lament for Art O'Laoghaire', he viewed the language as an encumbrance to the Irish people in the modern world and would have viewed schemes for its preservation as the typical undertakings of a condescending Protestant superiority. Balzac said that O'Connell 'incarnated a whole people,' and though the sentiment is romantic it is difficult to refute.

O'Connell organized the Catholic Association in a dramatic manner. The collection of the 'Catholic rent' of one penny a month became a focus for energy and a reason for determination. In each county a treasurer, secretary and committee were appointed to administer the collection. By 1824 200,000 copies of the rent plan and 4000 collectors' books were in circulation. Subscriptions were forwarded to Dublin and published in the Dublin newspapers which were in turn posted locally. One area vied with another for the honor

Below: Cancellation notice for Clontarf Repeal Meeting, October 1843.

NOTICE.

WHEREAS, there has appeared, under the Signatures of " E. B. Sugden, C., Donoughmore, Eliot, F. Blackburne, E. Blakeney, Fred. Shaw, T. B. C. Smith," a paper being, or purporting to be, a **PROCLAMATION**, drawn up in very loose and inaccurate terms, and manifestly misrepresenting known facts; the objects of which appear to be, to prevent the **PUBLIC MEETING**, intended to be held **TO-MORROW**, the 8th instant, at **CLONTARF**, *to petition Parliament* for the **REPEAL** of the baleful and destructive measure of the **LEGISLATIVE UNION**.

AND WHEREAS, such Proclamation has not appeared until *late in the Afternoon of this Saturday, the 7th*, so that it is utterly impossible that the knowledge of its existence could be communicated in the usual Official Channels, or by the Post, in time to have its contents known to the Persons intending to meet at **CLONTARF**, for the purpose of Petitioning, as aforesaid, whereby ill-disposed Persons may have an opportunity, under cover of said Proclamation, to provoke Breaches of the Peace, or to commit Violence on Persons intending to proceed peaceably and legally to the said Meeting.

WE, therefore, the **COMMITTEE** of the **LOYAL NATIONAL REPEAL ASSOCIATION**, do most earnestly request and entreat, that all well-disposed persons will, **IMMEDIATELY** on receiving this intimation, repair to their own dwellings, and not place themselves in peril of any collision, or of receiving any ill-treatment whatsoever.

And **We** do further inform all such persons, that without yielding in any thing to the unfounded allegations in said alleged Proclamation, we deem it prudent and wise, and above all things humane, to **DECLARE** that said

Meeting is abandoned, and is not to be held.

Signed by Order,

DANIEL O'CONNELL,

Chairman of the Committee.

T. M. RAY, Secretary.

Saturday, 7th October, 1843.
3 *o'Clock* P. M.

RESOLVED—That the above Cautionary Notice be immediately transmitted by Express to the Very Reverend and Reverend Gentlemen who signed the Requisition for the **CLONTARF MEETING**, and to all adjacent Districts, **SO AS TO PREVENT** the influx of Persons coming to the intended Meeting.

GOD SAVE THE QUEEN.

Browne, Printer, 36, Nassau-street.

Above: 'John Blake Dillon, Young Irelander', by Henry MacManus. John Blake Dillon, 1816-66, spent 1845-55 in exile because of his 'Young Ireland' views but returned and was an MP in the last years of his life. His son, John Dillon, 1851-1927, was also prominent in nationalist politics as a Parnellite in the 1880s.

of making a 'decent' contribution, so both local pride and a shared national goal complemented one another. In late 1824 the average rent was £300 each week. In March 1825 almost £2000 was obtained in one week and by that time over £19,000 had been collected in all by the Association. O'Connell was to be described as 'king of the beggars'. The remark was not unkind, merely accurate. For these monies were contributed not by the substantial farmers or the comfortable middle classes but by the abjectly poor and miserable in many cases. True, laborers have been quoted as asking rhetorically what difference Catholic Emancipation would make to their lives. The answer in direct terms was, of course, none. But the crowds that flocked to the mass meetings that O'Connell held on historic sites throughout the country were stirred and enthused, not by the concrete meaning of Catholic Emancipation, but by the fact that they had a leader who was 'one of their own,' who was not afraid and who cajoled, rebuked, mocked and demanded from the British government in a fearless and confident fashion. The culture from which they came had fed on images of failure and of degradation for generations; these images included memories of their dispossessed landed class, the taunts of Cromwell, the memory of the

Mass rock in Cromwellian times and a public awareness of the Penal Code throughout the eighteenth century. Devoid of leadership, accustomed to failure and sustaining hope through the now meaningless songs of Jacobite deliverance it was a culture with a profoundly depressed and hopeless sense of its own past and future prospects. Such a view of this culture is not idle projection. We have ample records of the stories, songs and lore that people passed down through oral tradition. The reports of witnesses before parliamentary commissions reveal a similar depressed sense of life's possibilities. O'Connell's real achievement was to give a sense of pride and potency back to these people, to remind them that in the political process it was possible for them to win. The moral force of his massive peaceful mass meetings was to mark him as the first great leader of a peaceful popular pressure movement in Europe. His methods and tactics were to be adopted by the great mass movements of early nineteeth century Britain such as the Anti-Corn Law League and the Chartists. But naked moral force alone did not bring about any government concessions.

Thomas Wyse, a Waterford man of substance, decided through his local Catholic Association to try a new tactic. In 1826 he placed a candidate who supported the Emancipation interest against the local Beresford candidate. For a variety of technical reasons the bulk of the Irish electorate was composed of 40-shilling freeholders. This was a relatively low property threshold, and many of these men were in fact small Catholics holding from more substantial Protestant landowners. In general they were merely electoral fodder, voting precisely as their landlords directed. Indeed in many cases the only reason that they were allowed to retain their holdings was for precisely this purpose. On this occasion many rebelled and voted for the Emancipation candidate who won.

Initially this victory was treated with a degree of scepticism. Brunswick Clubs were organized to oppose Emancipation, proclaiming the imminent collapse of Protestant power if the issue were conceded. Government measures to quash the movement through the law seemed temporarily successful but in 1828 the Association was revitalized and reorganized. The election of O'Connell by the 40-shilling freeholders of Clare indicated to the government that however distasteful concession was it was preferable to perpetual turmoil. Wellington and Peel advised the king to grant Emancipation and despite initial refusal and constitutional complications he reluctantly conceded.

In real terms the victory meant that Catholics were now eligible to sit in Parliament and to hold the highest offices in the land. In practical terms it meant the disenfranchisement of the 40-shilling freeholders as the price of its passage. This reduced the Irish electorate from about 100,000 to 16,000. This was presumably to ensure that concessions would not again be obtained by such leverage. Certainly the accusation that O'Connell threw the 40-shilling freeholders to the wolves after they had played their part is simplistic, but it was an electoral loss which he was later to feel acutely. The changes which it most clearly brought about were in demonstrating that a national movement could be successfully organized, that victory could be achieved. It has been criticised, by those who find the 'might-have-beens' of the past more entrancing than the reality, for identifying Catholicism and national identity so clearly, for drawing the priests so firmly into its organizational structure, for heightening sectarian divides. The issue of Emancipation was a sectional grievance and to that extent such accusations are undeniable. It is difficult however to see how any political goals could have been pursued by the mass of the population without its concession. As Gearoid O'Tuathaigh has remarked in his study of Ireland before the famine, to blame O'Connell in this fashion is tantamount to blaming him for the denominational composition of Irish society.

O'Connell's declared ambition after the achievement of Emancipation was the Repeal of the Act of Union, a more difficult, less likely and effectively more millenial goal. While the issue of Catholic Emancipation was one which had been considered in government circles for a number of decades, Repeal was an unthinkable end to all English parties. The tactics that had proved so successful in the Emancipation campaign were employed with equal organizational vigor. Repeal Clubs, membership lists, subscriptions and meetings mounted in a crescendo, but the authorites had at no stage any intention of even countenancing such a measure. The unity and integrity of the Empire itself were at stake and the government was prepared to meet passive resistance with weapons if necessary. O'Connell again brought his people to the plateau of the approach to the promised land, on this occasion without the slightest leverage with which to force an entry. When the government called his bluff and threatened to fire on monster meetings of unarmed civilians he, a pacifist, had no choice but to desist as commanded. Although the drama of the meetings had obscured the fact by their achievement of a new sense of community, it was not the meetings that had brought about the success of Emancipation but the concrete political leverage of the votes of the 40-shilling freeholders, votes that O'Connell had signed away. His achievement in the failed Repeal agitation was no less potent than his achievement in the successful campaign for emancipation. In both cases he conceived a vision and created a rhetoric. In the former he had created a sense of political possibilities and an organization that was to effect them, in the latter he created a goal that was to endure as the overriding aspiration of Irish constitutional nationalism until 1914.

During the 1830s O'Connell, under the so called Linchfield House compact, suspended his Repeal agitation, with its shamrocks and harps and iconographic jumble of nationalist representations, and co-operated with the Whig government of Melbourne with the aim of securing specific administrative reforms. The under-secretary for Ireland in this administration was Thomas Drummond who had worked on the Ordnance Survey of Ireland and was sympathetic to O'Connell's demands. A great deal was accomplished administratively by Drummond, but it was not enough to satisfy O'Connellite demands or to go to the root of the tithe protests that disturbed every area of the country and had led to a new Coercion Bill in 1833. In hindsight,

Left: 'Destitution in Ireland . . . Failure of the Potato Crop.' *Pictorial Times,* 1846.

however, Drummond's time in office stands out starkly as a period during which almost every area of Irish bureaucracy was structured or reformed . . . the police, the schools, the Poor Law, which O'Connell opposed, the Board of Works, which changed the whole system of public communication and transport on the island. O'Connell was forced to repudiate the Whig achievement during his period as Lord Mayor of Dublin in 1841 as his less than unsullied nationalist credentials were attacked by the young purists and revolutionaries who found their voice in the journal *The Nation*. These impeccably educated bourgeois or déclassé upper class young men never stooped so low as to consider sordid questions of administrative reform or trivial issues of economics. They despised O'Connell as a compromiser and procrastinator. Their organization 'Young Ireland' was modelled on organizations of other similarly glamorous young men yearning for sacrifice of self and usually others all over Europe in the years before 1848.

The Nation was edited by Charles Gavan Duffy from Ulster, but the style of writing and political philosophy that was to be specifically identifiable

as that of 'Young Ireland' came from the pen of Thomas Davis, a Protestant from County Cork. He wrote of the spirit of Irish nationality living underground in times of oppression, of a mystical sense of Irish nationhood going back to Celtic times and sanctified by the rebellion of 1798. Lord Edward FitzGerald, Wolfe Tone and Robert Emmet were the heroes in this canon of unbroken tradition, carrying and passing on the flame of liberty to a new generation. The leaders of 'Young Ireland' were upper middle class, well educated and excited by the work of antiquarians and historians on the early history of Ireland. They were enthralled by the work of scholars like John O'Donovan who had worked with Larcom on the Ordnance Survey of the 1830s and were attracted by the scholarly preoccupation of the Royal Irish Academy with the linguistic heritage of the Irish language. 'A people without a language is only half a nation,' Davis proclaimed, and he popularized the romantic view that some irreducible essence of nationality was implicit in language. *The Nation* became the most widely circulated newspaper in Ireland, circulated through the Repeal rooms in provincial towns. The 'Young Ire-

Below: The Cork Society of Friends' Soup House, 1848. The Society of Friends was one of the first groups to recognise the disaster of the famine and to provide charitable relief.

IRELAND.

land' and Repeal movements seemed publicly to coexist until the disaster of the Clontarf meeting in 1843 when O'Connell was forced to bow before government threats. O'Connell was now an old man and *The Nation* increasingly advanced its own philosophy of violent revolution. The ballads and songs written by Davis were martial and stirring. There was little 'distinctively Irish' in their language and expression, though their words preached defiance and resistance in a language that looked back to a tradition of European freedom that emanated from 'Greece and Rome.' *The Nation* created a popular optimism and built upon O'Connell's achievements in representing grievances as caused by the rule of an alien and unsympathetic government rather than from a medley of individual culprits. 'Young Ireland' was a modern, cosmopolitan movement, European and secular in style if not commitment but while it was at its prime Ireland was engulfed by a tragedy that made the neat modern order of Repeal houses and debating clubs seem more like a grim mockery.

The famine made all political considerations seem at least temporarily irrelevant, and when it finally ended in 1847 the structure of Irish society had been changed beyond recognition. The bad season of 1845 caused failures of crops all over

Europe. In Ireland the potatoes were afflicted by a blight which caused them to rot in the ground. Again in the following year, despite initial hopes of a good crop, the potato failed again. This time, more distressingly it putrefied after harvesting. Ireland was not a homogenous society of subsistence potato eaters, contrary to the common representation. The southern cities of Dublin, Cork, Limerick and Waterford to name only the main ones were sophisticated urban economies. Considerable tenant farmers tilled the land of Leinster and produced a variety of crops for export. Huge markets at centers like Ballinasloe traded in thousands of pounds worth of livestock at regular intervals. The banks and joint stock companies held considerable deposits of cash. The new railway and canal systems had been invested in to the tune of many thousands of pounds. The revival of Catholic organization in the late eighteenth and early nineteenth centuries resulted in massive financial investment in church buildings. The cities were populated by the usual social classes found throughout the British Isles in these years. In terms of aberration from class norms elsewhere the only significant difference was in the relatively small size of the urban proletariat and the comparatively few industrial entrepreneurs. The only area in which

Above: Famine in Ireland from a contemporary cartoon. Here politics and starvation meet. The popular view of the continued export of food while people starved was that it was a deliberate policy of starvation. Note the ship bearing foodstuffs away to foreign markets is represented as being *The Orangeman of Galway.*

NOTICE

TO

THE EARL OF CHARLEMONT'S TENANTRY.

IN consideration of the extensive failure in the POTATO CROP this Season, willing to bear his share in the general calamity, and anxious to relieve, as far as in him lies, his Poorer Tenants from an undue share of suffering under the Divine Will, LORD CHARLEMONT has directed that the following Scale of Reduction, in Payment of Rent, shall be adopted for this Year, upon his Estates in the COUNTIES of ARMAGH and TYRONE, viz. :—

25 per Cent. on Rents under £5	10 per Cent. on Rents under £20.
20 per Cent. on Rents under £10	5 per Cent. on Rents under £30.
15 per Cent. on Rents under £15	No Discount on Rents exceeding £30.

Abatements, according to the above Scale, shall be made only to Tenants holding under Lease paying the present Annual value; and Tenants-at-will, not being occupiers of Town Parks, upon their paying the Year's Rent now in course of Collection, on or before the days appointed underneath :—

ALTATULE, AUGHNACLOY, ANAGHA, & ANAGHNACMANUS,	On Tuesday, 3d Nov., 1846.	GRANGEBLUNDELS, GRANEMORE, GRANGEMORE,	On Wednesday, 25th November, 1846.
AUGHNAGURGAN, BALLYLEAN,	On Wednesday, 4th November, 1846.	KILLMAKEW, KILLMAKEW, DRUMMONBEG, LURGABOY,	On Tuesday, 1st December, 1846.
BALLYMACNABB, BALLYBRANNAN, BALLYMACAULLY,	On Tuesday, 10th November, 1846.		
CARRICKATOAL, CARNAVANAGHAN, CAVANAGROUGH,	On Wednesday, 11th November, 1846.	LARAGHASHANKILL, MAGHERY, RATHDRUMGRANA, TASSAGH,	On Wednesday, 2d December, 1846.
CASHILL, CLADYMORE,	On Saturday, 14th November, 1846.		
CLADYBEG, CLOGHFIN, CREEVEROE,	On Tuesday, 17th November, 1846.	TERNASCOBE, TYREARLY, TULLYSARRIN,	On Tuesday, 8th December, 1846.
CORR and DONAVALLEY, CORCLEA,	On Wednesday, 18th November, 1846.	DRUMCART, DRUMGRANNON, LISROAN,	On Wednesday, 9th December, 1846.
DAMFLLY, DRUMATEE, DRUMACHEE,	On Saturday, 21st November, 1846.		
DERRYLARD, FOLEY, ENAGH,	On Tuesday, 24th November, 1846.	LISTAMNET, MOY, TYRLEENAN,	On Saturday, 12th December, 1846.

** Where a Tenant is subject to the payment of more than One Rent, the abatement shall be made according to the Gross Annual Amount to which he is liable.

☞ Where Two or more Occupiers hold under one Lease, the Total Rent reserved by the Lease shall be taken as the sum to regulate the per Centage to be allowed.

W. W. ALGEO.

ARMAGH, 13th October, 1846.

ARMAGH—PRINTED BY J. M'W.

Above: Notice of voluntary rent abatements by a sympathetic landlord in response to the 'general calamity' in 1846.

these classes predominated was in the industrialized northeast and certain areas of southern cities.

The initial scare produced by the first crop failures raised demands to 'keep corn at home and keep it at its present price.' The class that most clearly suffered initially were the laborers who worked for tenant farmers for a low wage and a plot of land on which they grew their staple diet – the potato. Frequently cash was a negligible element in these arrangements with cottiers, but when the crop failed they demanded payment in cash rather than in land which could demonstrably not feed them. Any good potatoes dug in 1846 were eaten rather than replanted as seed potato in view of the need to survive. The potato crop declined from an area of over 321,000 acres in 1846 to less than 40,000 in the following year. Clearly this did not merely have implications for laborers living on a conacre or small leased plot who required the crop for their staple diet. It had severe implications for the entire rural economy. Laborers sold what little livestock they possessed to get cash with which to purchase food. Their greatest drawback was that they were scarcely assimilated into a cash economy in the normal course of events, and in the panic of near starvation sold anything that they had, which was

usually very little. Having done that they were at the mercy of private charity or the workhouses which very quickly demonstrated that they were in no way sufficient to the task. By 1848 most of the workhouses were merely centers of disease and despair in which mothers and fathers of children could die apart rather than together. The greatest numbers of deaths from starvation took place in the west, northwest and southwest, in places furthest removed from urban centers and remotest from public communication. The most horrifying accounts of deaths, starvation and indescribable poverty come from the Quaker reporters who delivered aid and posted back accounts to London from the western counties.

Peel was prime minister when the famine began and he arranged for maize purchased in America to be shipped back and sold at moderate prices. A relief commission was organized to coordinate the distribution of food by landlords and the middle classes. Public works were provided to give employment to the penniless laborers to enable them to purchase the imported foodstuffs. But Peel was defeated in his attempt to pass an Irish Coercion Bill through the House of Commons in 1846. The Whigs opposed him on grounds of liberal principle and Lord John Russell took over as prime minister. The Whig government was more doctrinaire than that of Peel which had acted with pragmatic conservative charity in response to massive perceived need. The overriding concern of Russell's government and Charles Trevelyan, the chief civil servant who administered the policy, was to avoid the demoralization of the indigent poor and to avoid competition with private enterprise in the provision of public works. Similarly such concern for 'normality' involved using troops to prevent starving people attempting to seize food destined for export. The administration of famine relief in Ireland under the supervision of Trevelyan was a source of bitterness and grievance at the time as it still is. He was a product of a particular school of *laissez faire* political economy determined to protect the free market at all costs. He shared the prejudices of his class and generation about the potentially morally corrosive effects of relieving the indigent lest this corrupt the deserving poor who sustained themselves. Moreover he had the usual English bureaucratic qualification for managing Irish affairs, an utter unwillingness to see the situation for himself. Whether a famine occurring in the northern borderlands of England would have been treated in so cavalier or doctrinaire a fashion is debatable. It is certainly possible that a similar event in the Scottish Highlands might have been as meagerly responded to. The government fulfilled scrupulously the limited commitments which it recognized. Meal replaced maize and was sold at a controlled price. Relief works still scatter the Irish landscape . . . piers leading nowhere, roads with no end in view, walls with no purpose. None could be described as competing with private enterprise since no private entrepreneur could have conceived such useless projects. In areas where the wages paid by private employers might be inflated by relief competition no relief works were erected. Thus starving men travelled great distances to perform work for no purpose to earn money to purchase imported foodstuffs which were frequently unobtainable due to the absence of retailers or transport, all in defense of an idea of political economy. It is no more absurd perhaps than the destruction of foodstuffs in one part of the world when people starve elsewhere as happens in the late twentieth century if one considers the relative change in the concept of distance over one century. The only difference perhaps being that late twentieth century notions of political economy are international. Those who had lived on the margins died in their thousands. Writers' reports of starved bodies dead on the sides of the roads abounded. The greatest relief work was done by the Society of Friends who saved thousands from death in the west. Many landlords bankrupted themselves to feed the starving. Many more went to the wall, as the consequences of unpaid rents climbed up the social scale. Many landlords and middlemen saw the famine as a divinely inspired Malthusian solution and if workers were absent on relief works, in pursuit of food or in workhouses, the owners cleared their land of the tiny huddled cabins and plots of the agricultural laborers. In the southwest many solid dry-stone cottages from this period still stand deserted. Some along the seashore are evidence of later emigration since those who lived by the coast tended to survive.

At least 888,000 people or ten percent of the population died from starvation or disease between 1845 and 1851. Despite this massive loss the population in 1851 still stood at 6.6 million. By 1911 it had fallen to 4.4 million. There had been earlier famines in Ireland. Those of the early nineteenth century had been localized and negligible in longterm effects. Famines of the eighteenth century had approached the Great Famine in scale but not in the longterm consequences. For the famine of the late 1840s was to alter utterly the structure of rural society, to make Ireland in European terms a demographic freak

Above: An illustration entitled 'The Causes of Emigration in Ireland' from *The Lady's Newspaper*, Saturday, 13 January 1849. Rent collectors and bailiffs are active while America beckons on the horizon.

Left: The village of Moveen, 1849, typical of ruined settlements around Ireland.

and to lay the foundations for an Irish community in the United States who were financially to control the direction of Irish politics at least until 1922, and arguably to the present day. The precise figure for emigrants during the famine years is not known, but it approaches a quarter of a million. Even more significant than the number who left in these years was the pattern that this initial emigration established.

The Irish who went to North America displayed a steadfast fidelity to their families and friends at home. They saved the passage money to enable families and friends to follow them and very often whole families emigrated one by one in this fashion. Attitudes toward emigration were complex. A wake, as if for the dead, was held on the occasion of every departure, for return was never contemplated, so enormous was the step. There was despair at leaving but also hope since many wished to put the memories of misery and failure behind them. Those who were left behind seemed abandoned, and to many it seemed as if the dynamic elements in Irish society were being slowly sucked out. In the cities of New York and Boston the Irish found a welcome that was less than favorable. Excluded by polite WASP society, looked down upon for their lack of educa-

tion, finesse, Protestantism and virtues of thrift and forward planning, their fate was similar to that of the most recently arrived emigrants at successive stages in the development of the United States. Though poor by American standards this new community was rich by the standards of what they had left behind, and in the decades after the famine many communities, particularly in the west of Ireland were merely remittance communities, that is, they lived exclusively on the monies sent by American friends and relatives. Those who emigrated were of course not exclusively of one social class. Many considerable tenant farmers simply decided for reasons of ambition to sell up and these classes travelled in style. The image of the famine ship with the abjectly poor dying on board of disease and starvation in their hundreds is real, but only part of the story. In many cases these were poor laborers paid a sum by the landlord or middleman to quit their meager patches of conacre to clear the land for livestock. But from whatever social class they came many went to the United States with a deep and abiding hatred of English government in Ireland. Whether justly or unjustly, they blamed the suffering of the famine years on the English government or the landlord class. Countless ballads

Right: Emigrants coming to America aboard the SS *Westernland, circa* 1890.

Left: Contemporary mid nineteenth century engraving of Irishwomen at work in the fields of Roscommon.

composed in these years kept that feeling alive, and the remarkable degree of political organization displayed by the Irish in America owed much to this shared sense of terrible grievance. Communication between the emigrants and their relatives was good. The number of letters exchanged across the Atlantic is prodigious, and news of the New World acted as force for modernization in even the remotest regions of the country. The pull of emigration made people more anxious than ever to discard the Irish language which was now seen as a badge of failure and limitation. It also increased the already high peasant respect for education which was seen as vital. The population who remained behind were less clear in apportioning blame for the famine. Discussing the notion of trauma in a community is by definition dangerous, but the remarkable change in the pattern of life after the famine seems to suggest that all change cannot be accounted for in terms of revised economic choices. The chief casualties of the famine were the laborers. These were the first to go to the wall. In the famine years their numbers fell by 40 percent, and fell by the same amount again in the following half century. This decline was not exceptional in United Kingdom terms, but elsewhere such men tended to migrate internally to industrial centers. From Ireland they went to the north of England, to London or to the United States. In general those who went to Great Britain were the poorest class, who could not afford the passage money to America. Before the famine Ireland had a low average marriage age, after it the age was exceptionally high, the age for men increasing from 25 to 33 and for women from

21 to 28. The proportion of women who never married rose from 12 percent in 1851 to 26 percent in 1911, an extraordinary proportion in any society. The studies of the anthropologists Arensberg and Kimball on the structure of Irish rural family life in the early twentieth century are open to many criticisms, but in their delineation of power within rural families they echo observations of all observers since the mid-nineteenth century. The famine was believed by many, it would seem, to have been the product of their own reckless subdivision of land. After the famine the cardinal sin in Irish rural life was division of the family farm. The eldest son inherited, but not until the death of the father. Much Irish literature reveals the tensions produced in this society where men were always 'boys' until the death of the father. Then they were often at the command of the widowed mother. Marriage was no longer a private decision but a weighted choice determined by the exigencies of land and livestock. Lady Waterford commented on this in less than sympathetic terms when describing the character of 'the Irish' to the Liberal chief secretary John Morley in the 1890s: 'She had come over full of illusions. They had slowly been dispelled. Call the Irish imaginative. So they are on one side or on the surface, in substance they are not imaginative at all. They are sordid and prosaic, love no part of it, an affair of so many cows; sentiment, not a spark of it . . .' The further side of this was the sharpening of the social divide between farmers and laborers. The greatest sin in this rural society was to marry the landless, thus failing to add to the family's security. Younger sons and daughters frequently emigrated. Sons

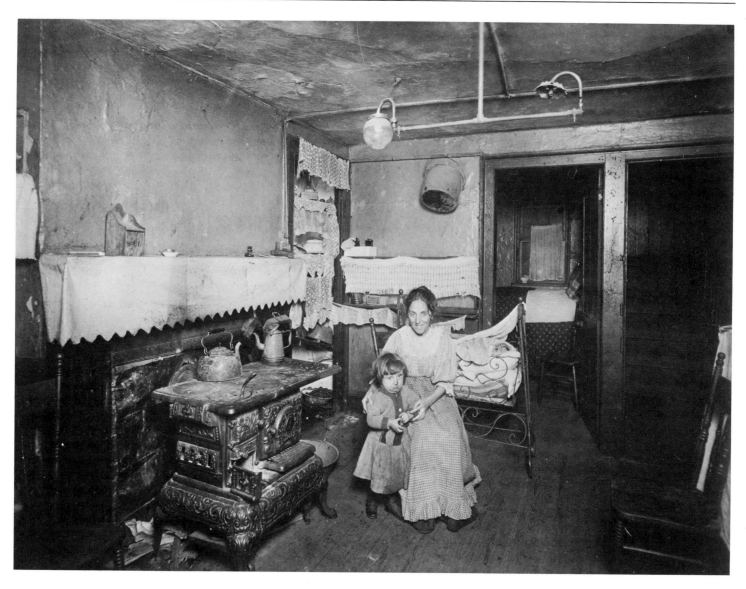

Above: New York City tenement room, 1911. Most Irish immigrants to the USA settled in the major cities of the north east.

who stayed at home on the family farm were themselves by definition landless and as such rarely fit candidates for marriage. Daughters preferred to remain as spinsters on the family farm rather than marry a man socially 'beneath' them. So Irish rural mating was conducted with the nicety of dynastic liasons, the only difference being that at stake was usually a plot of under 50 acres. Like disdainful aristocrats, unmarried sisters and brothers lived in arid caution on their shared farm. Pride and reputation were all in such a society and a woman's virtue her greatest commodity in her family's expansionist interests.

The Catholic Church had from the late eighteenth century educated priests at Maynooth and diocesan seminaries. Their social background was usually that of tenant farmer. The orders of nuns from the Continent brought in to nurse and teach were joined in the nineteenth century by orders like the Irish Sisters of Charity, who tended to come from the same background. The Irish Christian Brothers educated the sons of tenant farmers, the urban petit-bourgeoisie and the deserving poor when they could be located. For the sons of substantial Catholic professional men, merchants and large farmers the Jesuits and Holy Ghost fathers were the usual teachers. Girls from this social background tended to attend the

schools of the Loreto or Ursuline nuns. The massive campaign of church building begun in the early years of the century continued, and reflected, under the disciplined leadership of Archbishop Paul Cullen of Dublin, the increased standardization and order of the Irish Catholic Church. The 'patterns' or festivals of the people, local shrines and distinctively Irish flavor of Church folk culture were checked under Cullen, and more orthodox observances like the Mass and confession were placed at the center of liturgical obligation. Certain particularly native preferences endured, such as pilgrimages to Lough Derg, the centrality of Mary to Irish Catholic belief and the saying of Mass in local houses. After the papal declaration of the Doctrine of the Immaculate Conception in the 1880s the church organized a regular litany of Marian devotions, sodalities, retreats, with their attendant scapulars, sacred hearts and lurid statuary. This tradition was largely imported from Italian and Spanish Catholicism, though by the mid-1920s was seen as pre-eminently and distinctively Irish by most Catholics.

The changes in the structure of rural society cannot of course all be seen as having been directly 'caused' by the famine. It is, however, clear that the famine was a watershed, accelerat-

living at subsistence level in a world scarcely changed since the seventeenth century. The famine smashed the divide between them and brought starvation before the eyes of the 'modern.'

The northern counties of Ireland, in common with the east, east midlands and southeast, had avoided much of the famine, with the exception of Donegal and parts of Leitrim and Cavan. More, however, than the other 'modernized' areas of Ireland, the northeastern counties seemed to have much in common with the industrializing areas of the north of England. Traditional ties with Scotland had been maintained throughout the century. Wealthy Presbyterians continued to send their sons to university or for training in the ministry to Edinburgh. Wealthy Anglican landowners continued like those of their class in the southern provinces to send their sons to English public schools and then to Oxford and Cambridge or Trinity College, Dublin. The original linen industry in east Ulster had introduced steam engines and advanced industrial techniques to the Lagan Valley in the late eighteenth century. When the linen itself began to decline as a commercial proposition a cotton industry took its place. The Lagan Valley had already passed through a crucial first stage of industrialization, and was therefore in a position

ing, altering or subtly redirecting traits already evident in rural society. What it perhaps most clearly demonstrated was that there were two Irelands: one modern, progressive, perfectly in keeping with society in the rest of the United Kingdom; the other isolated, impoverished,

Left: Paul, Cardinal Cullen, 1803-78, Primate of Ireland, 1850-78.

Below: This photograph of the 'Scalan' at Bunlin Bridge in County Donegal was taken in 1867. The hidden places in which Mass was celebrated during the eighteenth century were still frequented in many areas until Catholic Emancipation in 1829. In many cases new stone churches were built on the old site. Here on Lord Leitrim's estate permission was refused and the new church was built a mile away. The Mass celebrated in this picture was organised for historical reasons. The Mass itself was celebrated by the priest under the thatched shed sheltering the altar at the back of the photograph.

Above: International
Exhibition, Dublin 1865.

to expand. Belfast had developed as a port to
facilitate the export of linens and this made it a
suitable location for ancillary industries. When
Lancashire cotton threatened the cotton spin-
ning industry, Belfast and the hinterland suffered, but again recovered by developing a finer
and more specialized linen industry. The northern area around Belfast began to be assimilated
into the industrial economy across the Irish Sea,
and much of its industrial development depended
upon the maintenance of these commercial links
and a sustained image as a suitable location for
capital investment. As the city developed the
areas of its hinterland ceased to look to Dublin as
their commercial capital. Thus a sense of a separate and contained economy emerged, having its
own banks, counting houses and commercial network. This sense of self-contained separateness
was partly a consequence of the removal of the
Irish Parliament, for Dublin was now no longer a
political capital. Sectarianism was a problem in
the northeast in a way that was uncommon in the
rest of the country, merely because there was a
considerable class of poor Protestants competing
with Catholics. In that context sectarianism had
the edge of economic competition and in urban
areas this tension was exacerbated by the com-
pression of newly arrived migrants. The sectarian

tensions of Belfast were similar to those of Liverpool and other northern cities where anti-popery
was frequently a cloak for resentment at the intrusion of the Irish Catholic poor. While religion
may have served as a screen in both cases, it
would be mistaken to underestimate the hatred
and fear it generated.

The liberal egalitarian, revolutionary tradition
of Ulster Presbyterianism, demonstrated in the
United Ireland tradition, survived in pockets of
Antrim and Down, but the prevailing tone of
northern Presbyterianism was that of 'New Light'
fundamentalism which preached a darker,
gloomier vision of predestination, and which did
not view the lax tolerance of the old Presbyterianism with favor. This new Presbyterianism was
liturgically stark and spiritually bleak but it did
have color in the tradition of the dramatic,
highly emotional public speaking that its preachers affected. The style of public speaking found
among preachers in the southern states of North
America has much in common with the tradition
of the Reverend Henry Cooke and the Reverend
(Roaring) Hugh Hanna brought from Scotland
and the north of Ireland. The Reverend Henry
Cooke was one of the early leaders and at great
public rallies he preached the need for an alliance
between the Anglicans and Presbyterians of

Left: 'Her Majesty's visit to the Linen Hall, Belfast,' Etching from the *Illustrated London News*, 18 August 1849.

Ulster, who formed two-thirds of the Protestant population of Ireland in 1861. There were political distinctions between the Church of Ireland and the Presbyterian congregations. Until the 1830s the Presbyterians tended to support Whig or Liberal candidates, while the Anglicans primarily voted Conservative. Anglicans and Presbyterians were further socially divided since those in the professions and the landed gentry tended to be of the former persuasion and merchants, entrepreneurs and substantial tenant farmers of the latter. The working classes were not,

Below: The Queen's Bridge in bustling industrial Belfast with the Belfast and County Down Railway Company steamers, *Slieve Donard* and *Slieve Bearnach*.

however, so neatly divided, and on political issues, particularly after 1886, the two persuasions were virtually indistinguishable. The Orange Order, despite the fire of its early years, lapsed as an organization for most of the nineteenth century, though the property-owning class kept a vigilant eye on potentially independent action from the ground. Northern tenants in general had better relations with their landlords and middlemen than those in the rest of Ireland, since they at least belonged to the same religion, even if they were not part of a shared culture. The tradition of Presbyterian libertarianism which was manifested in the support that certain northern Presbyterian churchmen gave to the issue of Emancipation was less significant in the late nineteenth century when the question of support for or opposition to the Union became the essential basis of political division.

Belfast had been a small, almost exclusively Protestant town of 20,000 in 1800, but by 1850 its population stood at nearly 100,000. More significantly, many of the new immigrants were Catholics from west of the River Bann – the line traditionally seen as dividing the old Catholic Ulster from the new. The most massive expansion of the Belfast economy took place in the post-famine years. In 1852 there was only a single power loom in Belfast; by the following decade there were over 6000. This industry developed at a remarkable pace, assisted by the so-called cotton famine of the American Civil War. But despite these massive advances, linen was a precariously poised product liable to be replaced by the cheaper materials like cotton. The native flax supply was soon insufficient and so the flax was imported from Belgium, Holland and Germany. There were ancillary textile industries in lacework and poplin, but the products which made the city of Derry a commercial center were the shirt and collar industries that developed in the later decades of the century. The wool trade was important but less centralized and less economically crucial. Belfast prided itself on its engineering skills and the shipbuilding trade that developed slowly from the early nineteeth century was central to its development. The first considerable shipbuilders to operate from the port of Belfast were the Ritchie Brothers, who set up there in the late 1790s. They prospered during the Napoleonic Wars and later, under the title of Ritchie and McLaine, built the first steamboat in Ireland. There was a limit to the potential development of the old port and in 1837 structural change on the harbor was begun.

New Harbour Commissioners in 1847

Below: Belfast High Street, 1895.

expanded quay space and further widened the
channel of the Lagan. They reclaimed land to
expand the quay areas and divided the harbor between trade and shipbuilding, allocating a specific area – the Queen's Island – to shipbuilding.
The first significant new shipbuilder was Robert
Hickson, the owner of the existing Belfast Iron
Works. As his manager he appointed Edward
Harland, an apprentice from Scarborough in his
early twenties. Hickson sold his interest to Harland who in 1858 brought in an equally brilliant
draughtsman called Wolff. Their initial orders
came from the Liverpool firm of Bibby's. The firm
of Harland and Wolff was technically innovative,
rapidly expanding into the construction of huge
ocean-going liners. Their third partner, William
Pirrie, joined the firm in the 1870s and eventually
became sole controller. By 1891 the total tonnage
of ships built in Ireland, most of them in Belfast,
was 103,466 tons. At the time of the outbreak of
war in 1914 the figure was 256,547 tons, exclud-
ing Admiralty contracts of which Harland and

Wolff had the lion's share. In 1914 Harland and
Wolff employed 12,000 men and their closest
competitors Workman and Clark employed
10,000. Belfast was the key to the prosperity of
the northeast, and the shipbuilding industry
above all the industries of the Lagan Valley was
the base of this prosperity. It was also to be the
forum for the sectarian politics of the hinterland,
now transformed by an urban setting.

The building grid of Belfast after 1850 is a
coded pattern of sectarian division. In the new
and peripheral west of the city Catholics from the
west of Ulster were packed into an area with the
Falls Road at its core. This was the first interrup-
tion in the otherwise clearly Protestant composition of the city. In the Sandy Row, also to the
west of the city, there were concentrations of
former Orangemen from Armagh. Belfast was
like all Victorian industrialized cities in not being
notable for the religious observance of its inhabitants. Indeed it was a typical Victorian invitation to evangelical fervor to redeem the poor

from their apparent blasphemy. Religious zeal and exhortations to piety were to have more serious consequences than the conversion of souls in Belfast. As Catholics seemed more inclined to vote for Liberal candidates from the mid-century the Presbyterian vote increasingly gravitated, like that of the Anglicans towards the Conservative party. But the Liberals continued right down to the 1868 election to court the now manifestly lost Presbyterian vote, and refused to concentrate on the Catholic electorate, where their only potential strength lay. With the disestablishment of the Church of Ireland by Gladstone's government in 1869 the single issue on which Presbyterians could have looked to Liberals for relief was removed. Their ends were now substantially the same as other northern Unionists.

The term Unionist most clearly emerged during O'Connell's Repeal campaign. It was essentially a reactive term, used to denote those who opposed plans to end the Union of Great Britain and Ireland. The politicization of the Catholic population by O'Connell's twin campaigns of Emancipation and Repeal had clearly established an identifiable public opposition to the union with Great Britain. This opposition took its most dramatic form in the abortive uprising of 'Young Ireland' in 1848. Happening as it did at the height of the famine, having no coherent plan of action, the rebellion of those who followed the romantic nationalist creed of Davis was easily put down. The leaders were deported to Van Diemen's Land, leaving little behind them but the memory of their defiance and the popularization of Irish culture that *The Nation* and their later publication, *United Irishmen*, had effected. Politics in the immediate aftermath of the famine were essentially concerned with the issue of tenants' rights and were moreover increasingly under the direction of conservative forces within the Irish Cath-

Below: Shipbuilding in Belfast, 1910.

olic Church. The notion of an anti-union position was, however, now fundamental to extreme nationalism, and in defiance of it a clearly articulated political unionism emerged.

After the Act of Union the landowning or establishment class were less than enthralled with it. It had been *their* parliament at College Green which the Act had abolished, and their power to carve their own destiny which the Act had terminated. At the time of the passage of Catholic Emancipation many diehards of the old school had been even more disgruntled, feeling that consent to such an erosion in the Erastian basis of the English constitution would never have been permitted by an Irish Parliament. But as the basis of Catholic electoral power widened as a result of the franchise reforms of the nineteenth century, Protestant Ireland began to see what certain of their class had for years proclaimed – that the only defense that they had against the numerical superiority of the majority population was within the larger framework of the English connection. There were many connections between the English and Irish landowning and political classes. Magnates like the Devonshires, Bessboroughs and Lansdownes were connected to the very highest levels of English political and social circles. Even the lesser landlords, through education in England and a social life that sprang from that, were connected by marriage and family relationships with families of equivalent social standing in England. The court of the viceroy was like a mock-up of the English court and was generally the social forum for the lesser nobility and social-climbing Catholics, or the 'Cawstle Cawtholics' as they were later called. English investors had considerable sums in Irish mortgages and under the massive transfers or sales of land effected by the Encumbered Estates Courts after the famine, many had recently purchased further lands in Ireland. At the higher social levels the United Kingdom really was one country, with a steady exchange of social invitations. Thus as the century progressed the Anglo-Irish, for want of a better term, became emotionally committed to the idea of the Union. Moreover they came to look upon it as the best means of ensuring the maintenance of their position in Ireland. Irish Unionism was not an undifferentiated monolith, as publications like the *University Magazine* demonstrate. There were Liberal as well as Conservative unionists and many unionists were aficionados of Irish cultural integrity – indeed much of the romantic nationalism of a cultural or linguistic kind was constructed upon their researches. Most of them would have seen themselves as Irishmen with imperial loyalties, though as novels like the works of Edith Sommerville and Martin Ross suggest they did consider themselves to be implicitly superior to the native population.

As the dependence of the Anglo-Irish on the English government increased so too did their vulnerability. If English principles of English

YOUNG IRELAND IN BUSINESS FOR HIMSELF.

standards were breached by what they expected for the maintenance of their power in Ireland then they could expect to have their need overlooked in deference to the greater need of the self image of the mother of parliaments. In a mirroring process the place of Ireland within the United Kingdom became more important to English politicians as time progressed and it acquired a symbolic significance as an essential component in the core of the Empire. Thus English attitudes towards the Anglo-Irish began to change. They were represented by nationalist opinion as England's garrison in Ireland, and to the British Cabinet this is indeed what they were. But it became gradually apparent as the century progressed that as a garrison or indeed even as a basis of English power they were seriously lacking. Ireland seemed to be in a state of almost continuous rebellion at a fairly localized and unfocussed level. Throughout the century habeas corpus was suspended with disturbing regularity and Coercion Acts were almost continually in force. The London government alternated between blaming the inadequacies of the Irish character for this and blaming the Irish landlords.

Above: This cartoon seems to suggest a predisposition to violence in Paddy and his friends.

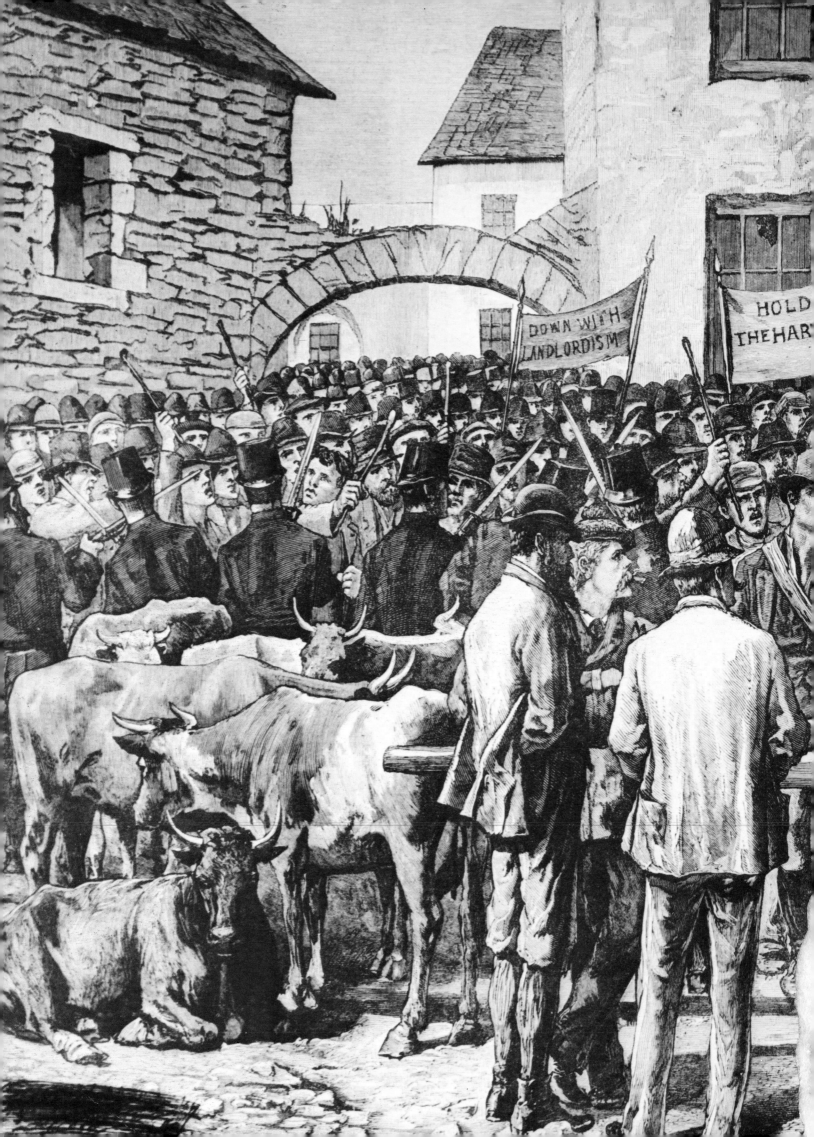

CHAPTER 8

FENIANISM, PARNELLISM AND THE LAND WAR

ONDITIONS improved for the surviving population in the decades after the famine. The very poorest class of laborers had been cut down by starvation, disease and emigration. The census of 1851 revealed that 83 percent of the population still lived on the land. The families of the 570,000 tenant farmers accounted for half of this rural population and the landlords numbered about 10,000, with vast discrepancies in the size and type of their estates. So it seems clear that despite the removal of considerable numbers of laborers and landless men, they still continued to be an important element in rural life.

Over a quarter of the land surface was under cultivation in 1851. The coastal regions of the west remained unproductive and barren, but the bulk of uncultivated land was devoted to raising cattle, and this sector expanded as the century progressed and the British market for Irish livestock increased. However, the dairy industry was a diminishing part of the export trade due to the localized and unsupervized state of production. More importantly, the beef cattle trade did not generate industry in Ireland since it was literally 'live stock' that was exported. Nonetheless, Irish exports were vital.

The size of tenants' farms varied as enormously as those of landlords' estates. In 1861 over half the farms of Irish tenants were under 15 acres. On the other hand, 40 percent of the country was held in tenant farms of 100 acres and over. Over half the

country was owned by less than 1000 great landlords, with 20 per cent of land in the possession of landlords owning from 2-5000 acres. There is therefore great difficulty in speaking of the 'normal' tenant or landlord, and the more substantial tenant farmers were in turn 'landlords' to the small men who held their land from them. Rural towns drew their wealth from the land structure around them. Towns like Tralee in County Kerry served not merely as markets and meeting places, but also as locations for litigation in land disputes, centers of the legal profession in its local and on-circuit forms, and for the offices of landlords' agents as scenes of deferral-pleas on rent. The network of small-town gentility was based around the land, with agents, solicitors, barristers and minor gentry forming the court. The land agent had an ancillary army of minions – process servers, bailiffs, the officers of the Royal Irish Constabulary, whose responsibility it was to enforce the laws on rent, and other minor representatives of authority.

Parliamentary inquiries, like the Devon Commission of the 1840s, had created a public image of Irish rural poverty as vile beyond belief. In certain English liberal circles during the 1850s the treatment of Irish tenants began to assume importance. This concern, activated by reports of travellers and social investigators, was always a minority one. However, it prompted liberal intellectuals like John Stuart Mill to examine the problem. Since rural Irish society was character-

Previous pages: Sheriff's forced sale of cattle during the Land agitation, 1881. The Land League urged that such sales be boycotted.

Below: The contrast between the belligerence of the 1880s and the passivity of the people in the famine of the 1840s was marked. This is a scene from the 1840s, showing cattle being driven to pay rent.

ized by such a high degree of social tension, certain liberal social commentators rejected the standard interpretation of violence as 'endemic' and looked instead to the flaws in the system. There were serious social problems in Great Britain in the second half of the nineteenth century. In the industrial cities there was poverty, disease and exploitation to equal the worst of Irish suffering. But while British industrial misery was seen as the consequence of a complex of social problems, the relative simplicity of Irish social structure seemed to indicate only one culprit, the Irish landlord. This was a view that accorded well with the feelings of many tenants, and one that was in many cases true. The landlord was seen as a random evicter, a drain on the country's resources, an enemy to the people and, in certain liberal circles, a disgrace to his class. This was exacerbated by the sense of guilt felt in certain limited quarters in Britain about the extent and duration of the famine. It in no way reflected majority opinion in any social class in England on the Irish 'situation', which rarely commanded any but the most reluctant attention except in satirical publications where 'Paddy' appeared regularly in menacing or absurd form, depending on the immediate political context. The stereotype of the landlord in this very small liberal and radical perspective was of a man, indeed a class, who had failed to recognize that property had its responsibilities as well as its privileges.

James Fintan Lalor, a political nationalist and radical journalist placed the role of the Irish landlord at the center of political nationalism when he said that the struggle for land would be the engine in the struggle for Irish nationalist goals. From the 1850s on there was a minority who accepted his view and looked to the discontents and miseries of life under the agrarian system as the potential raw materials of popular nationalist support. For while the stereotype of the Irish landlord as a cruel and heartless absentee owes more to fiction than to fact, there was clear evidence that tenant farmers of all classes resented the social pretensions of 'the gentry', saw them as their oppressors and resented their arbitrary powers. Specific local complaints arising from economic conditions created specific demands for redress. Transforming those grievances into political capital was a matter for a minority of nationalist leaders.

Clerically directed Irish MPs played an unimpressive role at Westminster in the 1850s and 1860s. They were significant merely in that they were the first coherent post-O'Connellite Irish party at Westminster. Many of them were Catholic, paid a certain lip service to nationalist aspirations when it seemed politically opportune, and displayed a craven ability to be ruled by Cardinal Paul Cullen the energetic and conservative Catholic Archbishop of Dublin and primate of Ireland. Cullen was horrified by the anti-Catholic nature of liberalism and nationalism in Europe

Left: The earlier parliamentary threat, Repeal.

and saw his prime duty as the preservation of his flock from the pernicious influence of such modern forces. The style of the Young Irelanders had shocked him, he had no sympathy with advanced nationalism and the party that he directed at Westminster, known sardonically as the 'Pope's Brass Band' was devoted exclusively to issues of education, disestablishment and land.

Below: Described as a Fenian banner, this American propaganda is in fact merely loosely nationalist.

Right: Colonel John O'Mahony, described as the 'Head Centre of the Fenian Order' by 'Harper's Weekly' in November 1865.

Cullen was concerned with the material condition of the population, but wished to keep those social concerns outside the exploitative powers of advanced thinkers, who might drive the population away from 'their church' as had happened in Europe. French anti-clericalism was always before his eyes as a dire warning, hence his desire to

'direct' politics himself. Despite electoral reforms the franchise remained economically restrictive and the Catholics who had votes tended to be reasonably affluent and consequently somewhat conservative in their views.

The romantic nationalism espoused by the Young Irelanders had not, however, disappeared. A small group of committed individuals in Paris and the United States developed the notion of a secret oath-bound society committed to the establishment of an Irish Republic by force of arms. Many were former Young Irelanders who had fled after the abortive 1848 rising. James Stephens, Michael Doheny and John O'Mahony first fled to Paris. Stephens was a somewhat eccentric civil engineer from Kilkenny and O'Mahony was from an old and prosperous landowning family in Cork. Both O'Mahony's father and brother had been 'out' in 1798, and the family had a long tradition of political involvement. O'Mahony was a scholar, a linguist and a believer in social-democratic or neo-socialist ideals which he kept to the forefront of the new movement. Doheny left for New York almost immediately after arrival in Paris and in 1854 O'Mahony followed, convinced that little was to be gained by endless exposure to the other failed revolutionaries for whom Paris was an asylum in the 1850s.

The organization of this new movement emerged over a few years from a small beginning. Known in Ireland as the Irish Republican Brotherhood and in the United States as the Fenian Brotherhood and later Clan na Gael, it re-

Right: Allen, Larkin and O'Brien were to become known as the 'Manchester Martyrs.' They were executed for murder following the death of a policeman when a group of Fenians helped two of their arrested leaders to escape from custody in Manchester in September 1867.

flected in its title O'Mahony's preoccupation with the Gaelic past. The Fianna, the ancient mythical warriors, provided one title. The other title meant literally the family or sept of the Gaels. Joseph Deniffe, a Fenian, reveals in his memoirs *A personal narrative of the Irish Revolutionary Brotherhood*, the haphazard and meandering nature of the initial structure. Deniffe, a tailor's cutter, concluded his career in South Anne Street, tailoring for some of Her Majestys most devoted servants while his upstairs rooms acted as the virtual headquarters of the IRB in Dublin. The organization existed in no formal fashion until 1858 although much of the early membership was drawn from the Emmet Monument Association of New York. The meeting which brought the IRB in Ireland into formal existence took place in Maginess Place in Dublin in 1858. From Deniffe's account of recruiting in Dublin it is clear that the bulk of the initial membership in Ireland were Dublin artisans distressed at economic conditions, and many of them were already active in loosely nationalist movements. He speaks of the poet John Locke; of Heffernan Dunne, the nailer; Mr Farrell, a master chimney sweeper; Peter Langan, proprieter of a lumber yard in Lombard Street. The first members in Dublin included Garrett O'Shaughnessy an iron manufacturer, Thomas Clarke Luby, a graduate of Trinity College, Stephens, who had returned

from Paris and Deniffe. At the meeting on St Patrick's Day 1858 the assembled members swore the following oath:

I, A.B. in the presence of Almighty God, do solemnly swear allegiance to the Irish Republic now virtually established, and that I will do my very utmost, at every risk, while life lasts, to defend its independence and integrity; and, finally, that I will yeld implicit obedience in all things, not contrary to the laws of God, to the commands of my superior officers. So help me God. Amen.

The oath clearly demonstrates the extent to which the Fenians were absolutely uncompromising in their opposition to the current political realities. The tiny group of men who spoke of an Irish Republic 'virtually established' were clearly messianic, optimistic and unrealistic. Yet within a few years they had constructed a lucrative Irish-American organisation, were loosely affiliated to a large number of American radical organisations, capable of raising very considerable financial support and running a newspaper, the *Irish People*. They were to become the central organization of the potentially powerful Irish in the United States. They recruited ex-soldiers from both sides of the American Civil War, attempted an invasion of Canada, an insurrection in Ireland and dynamite bombings in England. By the late 1860s the Fenians were a

Above: Fenian bombing at Clerkenwell, London, 1867. The bomb was designed to help imprisoned Fenians escape from the Clerkenwell prison. No escapes were made but 30 people died and the British people were alerted, in Gladstone's words, to 'the vast importance of the Irish controversy.'

Right: Called 'A duel in the dark,' 1868, this cartoon reveals the popular view of police incapacity to deal with Fenianism.

byword in England and a source of fear to English public opinion. The leaders of Fenianism who followed and overlapped with the early founders – Jeremiah O'Donovan Rossa of the Phoenix Society, John Devoy, Charles Kickham and later John O'Leary were not distinguished as organizers. Fenianism was never coherently centrally controlled, as the incompetence of the rising of 1867 demonstrated, but in its subtle development through the towns of Ireland it did create a structure of what the RIC were to call 'known activists' who were to play a role in whatever protest movement was currently in the ascendant. Urban, literate, political activists started the movement but there were Fenians of varying degrees of commitment in all areas of life. They clearly boasted and exaggerated their prowess. Such 'military' or strategic successes as they achieved were frequently despite, rather than because of, organization. Their structure as a secret, oath-bound infiltrationist movement meant that they were more frequently infiltrated by spies and government informers than they infiltrated structures like the British Army. They did have a few men in most places and though the decentralized structure of the movement often militated against any overall strategy, it ensured that the infiltration of one branch would not lead to the collapse of all and did allow Feniansim to permeate almost organically through word of mouth and social contact. In certain circles to be one of 'the lads' or 'the men' or 'the boys' as they were variously known had considerable social cachet. By the 1900s James Joyce was mocking the number of *post hoc* 'Bould Fenian Men.' But there were many others who risked their careers and often their lives to fight for an end that many assumed to be simply unobtainable. In the late 1860s in particular, long prison sentences, exile or execution were the potential rewards for any active Fenian. A campaign of dynamite bombings in Britain led to the creation of the Special Branch of Scotland Yard. Irish Fenians were seen in contemporary demonology as infinitely more dangerous than the stereotyped fear figure, the bomb-waving European anarchist. The Catholic Church feared and condemned the Fenians, seeing their secrecy and proclaimed republicanism as the enemy of all order and control. Bombings in England placed the Fenians in the political limelight. In Ireland

Right: 'The Martyr Church.' Prime Minister Gladstone succeeding in Disestablishing the Irish Church in 1869.

the Amnesty movement made them more than a minority cause. Many Irishmen sympathized with them. Few had faith in their prospects of success, but they were viewed as fundamental to all 'advanced nationalist' postions.

The substantial tenant farmers had dominated Irish politics in the 1850s and 1860s in the clerically controlled 'Irish party.' They were primarily concerned with issues of tenure: fair rent, free sale, fixity of tenure. These demands were to be known as the 'three Fs', demands that were primarily the concerns of the larger tenant farmers, though they were later to have a significance for the smallest class of tenants who were to see this cry as a protection from eviction and an entitlement to security. Initially these demands related to the desire of large tenants to acquire a right in land in which they had made substantial investment by effecting 'improvements' to secure a situation in which they could 'sell' the accumulated financial gain of their investment to an incoming tenant. The tenurial demand was also a response to the general legal revision in the status of land that was precipitated by the large sales that were provided for by legislation in the Encumbered Estates Act. This persisted as an issue through the 1850s and attracted the analytical skills of John Stuart Mill. During this period there was a renewed historical interest in early pre-Christian Ireland. This brought to public attention the old Irish or Brehon law which provided for communal ownership of land. Ironically this highly romantic view of the dim past influenced Mill and provided a strand in his attack upon the Irish land system. Free trade in land, the treatment of land as an ordinary commercial commodity as provided for in the Encumbered Estates Act was seen by English liberals to go against the 'traditions' of land ownership in Ireland. As a mildly contradictory corollary to this the three F's were seen to provide a more 'organic' model of the relations between landlord and tenant, seeing the tenant as more securely grounded in the soil. Such a view had a further appeal in radical circles since it could be represented as a form of compensation for historical wrongs, wrongs for which the landlord class were held to be responsible.

The question of Ireland was clearly a political issue demanding political attention in London in the late 1860s. The chief reason for this was the fact that Fenian bombs were bringing Ireland forcibly to the attention of the British public only two years after rebellion in Ireland. The country seemed reasonably prosperous, agricultural prices were high and there was little agrarian unrest. Gladstone therefore concluded that the problem of Irish discontent was not merely economic, nor was it due to Irish recalcitrance alone. He turned to the political demands of parliamentary representatives. The disestablishment of the Church of Ireland seemed to be one means of placating Irish majority opinion. It was an irony that the single clearest consequence of Fenian violence

Above: A French view of Irish woes, 'L'Irlande: O Dieu, que j'ai si longtemps imploré. . . Seriez-vous Anglais?' (Lord, I have prayed to You for so long. . . . Can You be English?).

VANITY FAIR.   May 3, 1873.

Left: Isaac Butt as seen by 'Vanity Fair,' 3 May 1873. Butt had opposed O'Connell's Repeal movement in the 1840s but became the first parliamentary leader of the home rule movement.

was to be disestablishment, an irrelevance in terms of Fenian strategy, since 'the men' affected to despise all ameliorative measures as diversionary. Gladstone's radical response to the Irish situation was to differentiate him from prevailing nineteenth-century English attitudes to Ireland. He was to base his political actions on the assumption that Irish violence was the consequence of Irish grievance. In addition to the disestablishment of the Anglican Church in Ireland, Gladstone further decided to alleviate the grievances of the tenant farmer in the Land Act of 1870. His final aim, to establish a university for Catholics, was not successful, since the Catholic hierarchy would not agree to support a secular university and Gladstone would in no circumstance grant state funds for a Catholic university.

The fundamental, ostensible, aim of the 1870 Land Act was to ensure that evictions for reasons other than non-payment of rent would be legally regulated. This was a part of the demand for the three Fs, or the Ulster custom, as the demand for security, compensation and free sale was otherwise known. In effect, the Act was a practical irrelevance with terms so ambiguously defined as to render any legal efficacy unlikely. Evictions were not particularly high in the early 1870s, and those who were evicted were usually so poor as to have no capacity to pursue legal redress. Moreover the large tenant farmers who sought the three Fs as a justification for investment found

that holders of leases of over 30 years, the larger tenants, were excluded by the terms of the Act. Since Gladstone had no clear notion of the distinctions between different classes of Irish tenants, this is perhaps not surprising. The Land Act was an irrelevance except in its concession to the principle of a tenant 'interest' in land and the provision of state aid for a limited number of tenants to purchase, if both landlord and tenant were in agreement.

Disestablishment, though providing generously for the Church of Ireland, while terminating its role as the established church of the state, had seriously shaken the confidence of the Protestant community in Ireland. As Cardinal Cullen reported, perhaps gleefully, to Rome: 'The poor Protestants are all very irritated. They never *did* imagine that England would have abandoned their cause.' This was to overstate the significance of the change. Symbolically it was almost as wounding to the Protestant community as the granting of Catholic Emancipation.

Isaac Butt, a Protestant barrister of conservative temperament, acted for Fenian political prisoners in the late 1860s, as he had acted for Young Irelanders in the late 1840s. He acted not out of sympathy with their cause but out of a sense of social justice and a barrister's nose for his brief. In 1869 he became involved in the massive public campaign for an amnesty of Fenian prisoners many of whom had been held since 1865. He proceeded from this new involvement in politics to

Below: The Vandeleur estate at Kilrush, County Clare was one of the so called 'test estates' on which Arthur Balfour determined to defeat the Plan of Campaign, 1887.

FATHER GILLIGAN & THE EVICTED FLANIGAN FAMILY. VANDELEUR ESTATE.

establish the Home Government Association. The movement was devoted to the achievement of a federal arrangement between Ireland and Great Britain, one that would not undermine Ireland's commitment to the Empire but would allow a 'home' government in Dublin. Butt's first meeting was attended by a considerable number of minor landlords, by Irish parliamentary representatives at Westminster, and by a smattering of Fenians drawn through personal affection for Butt and a desire to maintain an eye on new developments. Butt's ideal was a union of landlords and tenants and a local government that would absorb the energies of violent nationalism to develop the economic resources of the country. In 1873, the year in which the Fenian organization was reordered, Butt replaced the original movement with the Home Rule League. Many existing Liberal MPs affiliated themselves to the new organisation. Many did so with a view to electoral survival after the secret ballot franchise reforms of 1872. Though these men were loosely affiliated only on this aim, they were also likely to vote together on other Irish issues. Butt epitomized the views of the bulk of his new affiliates when he rejected a proposal that they should vote together as a party on *all* issues. Such a policy would have represented an ungentlemanly invasion of the Mother of Parliaments, for which institution he felt a profound respect.

In 1874 59 Home Rule members were returned. The Liberal Party in Ireland was effectively electorally eradicated with only 10 anti-home rule Liberals being returned. The remaining 33 seats were Conservative. The newly elected Home Rule members were upper or upper-middle class, although among the landlords, rentiers, merchants, bankers, newspaper magnates, professional men and lawyers there were now two tenant farmers.

Fenians were active in supporting certain home rule candidates. At the 1872 election contest in Kerry a Protestant home ruler was returned with Fenian support in defiance of clerical pressure, getting over three-quarters of the vote in Cahirciveen. The defeated Whig candidate prophesied, 'There will be *very few* priests found at the next general election *to oppose* the extreme party. The will *pretend* to *lead*, in truth being *driven*.' The new electorate was a source of worry to the Catholic Church, the Westminster Government and the authorities at Dublin Castle. As a land agent from County Clare reported to the chief secretary, the younger farmers were 'far more intelligent and independent and educated in the national schools.' The number and membership of farmers' clubs increased during the 1870s and their dissatisfaction with Gladstone's Land Act of 1870 grew rather than diminished with time. Laborers were no more satisfied than tenant farmers with the terms of the Act, since it affected indirectly their security of employment. The compensation clauses of the 1870 legislation did have one consequence, however, they made it easier to acquire credit from bankers and rural gombeenmen, as the money lenders were called. Rural Irish society in the 1870s was prosperous, educated, and politicized.

Butt's electoral successes were not translated into political power in parliament. His polite gentlemanly approach ensured that his demands were ignored and his Association seemed to lack a cutting edge. Joseph Biggar and John O'Connor Power, two ex-Fenian MP's, altered tactics by employing obstruction on the floor of the House of Commons to gain attention. They were despised and excoriated by English MPs and Butt was horrified by their procedural sabotage of the House. In 1875 they were joined by two newly elected MPs of dissimilar backgrounds who were to persist shamelessly with the obstruction technique. Charles Stuart Parnell was the Cam-

bridge-educated son of a Wicklow landowner and
an American mother. For entirely different reasons, his contempt for the Mother of Parliaments equalled that of the Fenians. The other
new man, Frank Hugh O'Donnell was handsome,
educated, intelligent, vain, impossible and ultimately rendered inane by jealousy of Parnell and
an obsession with his own superior and unack-
nowledged skills. However, for the first few years
in parliament he was impressive and useful. In the
face of this assault Butt's leadership ended in circumstances that he found heartbreaking and
unjust. He was replaced by Parnell and the Home
Rule Party under Parnell became the first paid
political party at Westminster, enabling the election of men of all social classes. Within three
years it was a party with a stern whip, a clear mandate and the popular support of nationalist Ireland. It was to ensure that issues relevant to
Ireland occupied relatively more parliamentary
time than any other single issue at Westminster
and ultimately it was to precipitate the greatest
divide in British politics for generations. Its basic
aim was the exertion of sufficient pressure to *force*
attention on Irish issues. Parnell's haughty
leadership imprinted itself on the style of his party
which demanded rather than requested reforms.
The new party's most vital weapons in imposing
this pressure were the votes with which they were
returned and the conviction of British politicians
that the Irish had the power to subvert the British
constitution if they were ignored.

This political development coincided with a
serious economic crisis in Ireland. In 1878 agricultural prices fell dramatically. At the time it
seemed like a temporary setback. In fact it was the
beginning of a prolonged agricultural depression
in the British Isles. In the west of Ireland the drop
in prices was felt acutely since for three years
there had been a poor potato crop. Irish wheat
and barley were affected by the fall in exports, but
it was the internal repercussions of specifically
Irish agricultural failures that created the dimensions of the crisis. The slump in the United States

since 1873 had diminished the number of Irish
emigrants. The usual recourse of emigration
seemed more difficult in 1878 than at any earlier
time. The authorities were worried as such
depressions had produced isolated outbreaks of
violence in the past. The difference in the agitation of the late 1870s was that all through the
country there now existed a small class of men
who no longer saw isolated acts of God as simply
that. They were politicized, nationalist and
unwilling to allow others to tolerate former
suffering.

Tenants were unable to pay their rents in 1878
and in many cases landlords granted voluntary
abatements, as they did in England. Many others
did not. The 'Land War' of 1879-82 – like all
revolutions – is in retrospect a confused period.
There is a temptation to see consecutive events as
showing cause and effect, to accept the subsequent rationalizations of participants who are, as
in all historical situations, unreliable. Further,
there is a temptation to isolate social facts,
usually true, and to pin on one or two of them the
label of 'primary cause.' The reasons advanced for
the development of the Land War have changed
over time but can be summarised as follows: the
iniquity of the landlord system which rendered an
explosion ultimately necessary; the increased
prosperity of the rural population and a consequent unwillingness to tolerate relative decline;
improved communications with the United
States and consequent modernization of Irish
society; the existence of an organized Irish party
at Westminster with the capacity to direct politically an agrarian movement; the personalities of
Parnell and Michael Davitt, the later a former
Fenian who had served years in prison; the political laxity of Gladstone who indicated a capacity
to concede under pressure; and the excessively re-

pressive application of the law by the authorities of Dublin Castle and the Royal Irish Constabulary. Further theories on the course if not the causes of the Land War are: that effectively it was a movement designed to suit the class interests of the substantial tenant farmers who exploited the near-starvation of the wretched paupers of the west to advance their own desired economic ends; or, in direct opposition, the view that the capacity for revolution was derived from the integration of all rural classes in a 'collective action' devoted to the destruction of the landlord interest. Almost all of these hypotheses have some merit though it is unlikely that any one of them contains all of the truth. In reality the Land War was about several quite distinct issues, conducted on different levels. In its course it was more contingent than necessary, more haphazard than it might at first appear. The advantage of the hypotheses listed above is that whether correct or incorrect each of them allows, almost like a beam through the confusion of events, a certain area to be illuminated from which useful conjectures can be developed.

At the time of imminent economic collapse in the west of Ireland Parnell was in the last stage of his political battle with Isaac Butt. Moreover, the majority of Fenians admired Parnell's tactics in parliament. They saw that the Home Rule movement was popular in Ireland. Many like Biggar and O'Connor Power had left the Fenians in order to enter parliament. Though the Irish organization in the United States was a Clan na Gael structure, many of its financial supporters were in favor of any move in Irish affairs that appeared potentially successful. John Devoy saw that if the new parliamentary movement was to succeed in capturing Irish support the Fenians would be wise to step aboard. The move towards raprochement between Fenians and parliamentarians thus became more than a stiff alliance of formal but distant friends.

Evictions for non-payment of rent rose dramatically in late 1878. The position of the tenants was further exacerbated by the amounts that they already owed shopkeepers and local traders. The scale of evictions and the absence of alternative resolutions for the tenants meant that they frequently resorted to outrage and attacks on property. Local traders and journalists on provincial newspapers acted as leaders of local tenants' groups. As William O'Brien, the special western correspondent of the leading Dublin newspaper, the *Freeman's Journal*, noted, there was a 'desperate partnership' between small farmers and shopkeepers. In Mayo in 1879 shopkeepers were owed a total of over £200,000 yet the increase in the number of processes in civil bill courts was slight. Traders were sympathetic to the people's plight, but also realised the futility of legal proceedings. Landlords however did have an alternative. They could evict non-paying tenants and replace them with solvent ones. The violence of 1878 and 1879 was a direct response to evictions or to the re-

HARPER'S WEEKLY.

JOURNAL OF CIVILIZATION.

Vol. XXIV.—No. 1209.]   NEW YORK, SATURDAY, FEBRUARY 28, 1880.   [SINGLE COPIES TEN CENTS. $4.00 PER YEAR IN ADVANCE.

Entered according to Act of Congress, in the Year 1880, by Harper & Brothers, in the Office of the Librarian of Congress, at Washington.

THE *HERALD* OF RELIEF FROM AMERICA.

placement of tenants on farms from which old tenants had been evicted.

The Irish National Land League was set up at a meeting in Dublin on 21 October 1879. Its immediate aims were the protection of the tenant farmers threatened with mass eviction and the eventual achievement of a peasant proprietorship through agreement. Controlled by Parnell and Michael Davitt it revealed in the person of Parnell and the involvement of the Irish parliamentary party that the land issue was clearly linked to the demand for home rule. The connection was not explicit in Land League publications and the interconnection between the two aims – agrarian and constitutional – was one that emerged over time. Parnell was primarily interested in the land question in relation to its potential for mass commitment, though he appreciated the real economic distress of tenants. It was an issue which he could not afford to ignore. A section of the Fenian movement had agreed to some form of assistance being given to the constitutional movement before the land question became a

Above: The appeal for help from America.

Above: A contemporary cartoon on the Monaghan election of 1880.

burning issue. The nature of the agreement between the parties was never clear or unambiguous, though it acquired a spurious certainty in the term the 'New Departure' by which it was known. As the land movement grew in importance in 1879 a section of Irish-American Fenianism, led by John Devoy, acted as if the agreement were explicit and threw the resources, the capital and the frequently unhelpful grand gesture of American might behind the Land League. It was a tacit agreement with inherent capacity for misunderstanding. That it survived and appeared to function for so long was a tribute to the shrewd, careful nature of Parnell's shifting strategies in holding disparate elements together in a coherent fashion. The aim of the movement, apart from the local functions of protection, was the extraction of maximum political concessions from the British goverment on the tenurial issue.

The structure of the Land League spread rapidly through the west and south. The League had a staff of paid organisers and an efficient central office in Dublin. More significantly, it had funds, most of which came from Irish America. In late 1879 and 1880 the number of evictions rose dramatically, as did the number of agrarian outrages. These outrages varied from threatening letters to verbal or physical intimidation to murder. Many of these offenses were outside the control of the League and were locally organized reactions to evictions, old feuds or local rivalries over land. The Liberal government initially saw all violence as the deliberate work of the League. As their evidence for this they cited the public utterances of League officials which they viewed as incitements to violence. Speeches like Parnell's in which he urged tenants to 'keep a firm grip of your homesteads' were represented as direct orders to intimidate and oppress all who interfered with that end. The Liberal Government did however concede that there was near starvation in the west and attempted to build on the earlier work of the Marlborough Relief Committee in relieving distress. The League Distress Fund they saw as merely a mask for financing organized resistance, a financial prop to the 'boycott.'

In Britain the 'Land War', as it was soon known, became a paramount political issue. In Conservative political circles it was represented as the first stage in an attack on the nature of property, a precedent for social revolution. It was argued that to give in to the demands of the League or the Irish Parliamentary Party would be to concede that property had no rights, that debt had no meaning and that those who rejected the law would ultimately be deferred to. This fixed position manifested in votes in the House of Lords stymied any attempts that Gladstone made to accommodate the ostensibly reasonable demands of the League. Before losing office in 1880 the Conservatives had established a commission to inquire into the problems of agriculture in the British Isles. Gladstone on achieving office appointed a separate commission to inquire into the nature of tenurial relations in Ireland. Gladstone saw the problem as one of class relations in Ireland, historically conditioned. The

Conservatives saw it as merely the unwillingness of a stubborn peasantry to acknowledge the economic logic of a market that could not sustain them in their present numbers.

In the Land Act of 1881 the Gladstonian analysis triumphed and tenants were granted a system within which their rights were given weight. A regulatory mediator in the form of the Irish Land Commission was constituted to arbitrate in tenurial disputes. Summary eviction was no longer in theory possible. Agreed rents were set by commission valuers and the untrammelled rights of property were effectively eroded. The majority of tenants was clearly satisfied with the arrangement and accepted the new procedures with alacrity. The leaders of the Land League had been prosecuted, imprisoned and excoriated in the British press, but by 1882 Gladstone saw that he required the political authority of Parnell to ensure the Land Act's success. Parnell saw that the offer required new politics on his part with a retraction of his unpopular 'No Rent' manifesto, lest the majority of tenants follow in a direction that he had failed to lead. These respective needs lay at the heart of the so called 'Kilmainham Treaty' of May 1882 which led to Parnell's release from prison. The ostensible accommodation between Gladstone and Parnell was, however, shattered by the Phoenix Park murders in which the chief secretary for Ireland, Lord Frederick Cavendish and his under-secretary, T.H. Burke were assassinated by a group of neo-Fenians, known as the Invincibles, acting on their own mandate. It is not unlikely that their aim was to abort the new alliance between Irish parliamentarians and Gladstone. Temporarily they succeeded.

Parnell was satisfied that the Land League had

in substance triumphed. Minor details would require resolution in time. The ultimate aim of peasant proprietorship was not utterly abandoned, but the immediate needs of the majority of the tenants had been satisfied. His priority was now the issue of Home Rule. The suppression of the Land League in 1881 was never more than a legal fiction. In 1882 a new organisation, or rather a new title, replaced it – this was the National League. Both were known by supporters and opponents as 'the League' and this accurately reflects the continuity between the two. The primary aim of the new League was to provide electoral machinery for the Irish Parliamentary Party. By 1885, with 85 seats, Parnell held the balance of power in the House of Commons. In this context Gladstone agreed to introduce a measure of Home Rule to Ireland. To his Conservative opponents, and to critics within his own party, this was no more than a cynical exercise for the maintenance of the power which Irish votes could grant him. To those who have read his correspondence and examined the evolution of his thought on Ireland since 1879 it seems clear that he was acting in response to a perceived moral imperative. That Gladstone's moral imperatives

Above: From *The Illustrated London News*, 24 April 1886, 'The Grand Old Magician's Irish Policy,' a satirical parody of Gladstone's approach to the 'Irish Problem.'

Left: Arthur James Balfour (1848-1930), Chief Secretary for Ireland from 1887-1891. Nephew of the Conservative Prime Minister Lord Salisbury he rapidly terminated the Liberal policy of concession in Ireland. On going to Ireland he had said 'I shall be as relentless as Cromwell in enforcing the law, but, at the same time, I shall be as radical as any reformer in redressing grievances, and especially in removing every cause of complaint in regard to land.'

seemed to coincide with alarming frequency with his own immediate political needs is perhaps merely a useful example of the benefits of being a political actor in a pre-Freudian age. A section of Gladstone's own party broke with him – these were radicals led by Joseph Chamberlain and Whig landed aristocrats like the Earl of Devonshire. Home Rule was defeated in the House of Commons by Conservative and dissenting Liberal votes and the political fever that the campaign had created in Ireland was left untreated. The Irish Party were left with a clear choice to support Gladstone indefinitely, consigning all their hopes to a faith in his person, or to negotiate with the Conservatives for the achievement of short term amelioration. They were prepared to countenance the latter option but the situation soon deteriorated into a war of attrition between Tory coercion and nationalist resistance in the form of the 'Plan of Campaign.' This was the strategy for further rent reductions organized by Parnell's lieutenants John Dillon, Timothy Healy and William O'Brien. The dramatic public campaign was orchestrated through the National League newspaper *United Ireland*. Parnell saw the campaign as diversionary, misguided and politically an aside. For those who supported it, however, it was a response to the real needs of tenants, a means of keeping feeling about land at a pitch and an issue through which British Convervatism and Irish landlords could be engaged.

The Tories were unambiguous in their approach to Ireland. In their view Gladstone had conceded too much. The rights of Irish landowners had been eroded and the primary responsibility of the Conservative Government was to ensure that Home Rule, which was the first move in an erosion of British imperial achievements, was killed as a political possibility. The 'Irish problem' was a problem of law and order in Conservative eyes, and having restored order the administration of Arthur Balfour was prepared to concede material reforms to ensure that Ireland became a contented area within the United King-

dom. The Conservatives further believed in a policy of the gradual creation of peasant proprietorship, since this appeared to be the best means of rescuing Irish landowners from the state of impotence to which Liberal legislation had consigned them. Thus, ironically, Conservative legislation began to implement a solution to the land question that radical Irish agrarian reformers had demanded.

During the period when Arthur Balfour was chief secretary for Ireland, relations between Irish parliamentarians and the Dublin Castle administration reached a nadir. This was most clearly demonstrated by a parliamentary special commission set up under the government of Lord Salisbury to investigate the nature of the relationship between 'Parnellism' (as the joint agrarian/Home Rule movement was known) and crime. This investigation clearly reflected the nature of Conservative thinking on political movements in Ireland, that they were, in effect, criminal. The 'prosecution' of Parnell, for that essentially was what the special commission was, collapsed when the central 'evidence' provided by *The Times* newspaper, linking Parnell to the Phoenix Park murders, was revealed as a forgery. The case collapsed, Parnell's supporters were elated, and the prospect of a Liberal return to power seemed imminent. The optimism of 1886 about home rule was revitalized, unionist organizations in the northeast again marshalled their organization for resistance, and it appeared as if the Grand Old Man, as Gladstone was affectionately known in Ireland, was on the point of a final coup in 1890.

The imminence of Home Rule in the minds of nationalists and Liberals at this time is difficult to understand. If Gladstone had managed to carry a Home Rule Bill in the House of Commons there seems little doubt that it would have been massively defeated in the House of Lords. Such considerations did not seem to weigh heavily. The almost messianic view of Gladstone's potential capacities seemed to create in Ireland a public belief that he would find a way.

Right: The Phoenix Park Murders, as seen by the *Illustrated Police News*, 13 May 1882.

In the optimism of 1890, a factor which had been unanticipated and unimagined utterly altered the configurations of Irish politics. Captain William O'Shea, a disgruntled Irish MP who had played a sinister role in the amassing of evidence against Parnell during the investigations of the special commission, sued for divorce from his wife Katharine O'Shea. As co-respondent he cited Charles Stewart Parnell. O'Shea was closely associated with Joseph Chamberlain and it seems likely that his action was politically prompted. A small circle in politics had known of the relationship between Parnell and Katherine O'Shea for a number of years. It seems clear that she bore him a number of children, one of whom died while he was imprisoned in Kilmainham in 1882, and it seems equally clear that her husband had ceased to live with her on any consistent basis for many years. The divorce suit was undefended. Parnell led his supporters to believe that he would be vindicated in an unspecified fashion, and many believed that this was merely another attempt to blacken his name. The Irish Parliamentary Party re-elected him as chairman in the teeth of public speculation, and bishops of the Catholic Church in Ireland shrewdly held their tongues. It was not that they did not intend to throw stones, merely that they did not intend to provide for their future excoriation by throwing the first one. The moral onus was removed from them by Gladstone who, in response to English Nonconformist opinion, made it clear that he could not continue to lead his party on the platform of Home Rule if the Irish Party continued to be led by Parnell. This was the signal for a section of Parnell's own party, led by Tim Healy, to turn on him. Ostensibly their grounds were realistic and pragmatic. For the good of the cause for which he had done so much, Parnell should stand down. Soon the Catholic Church in Ireland was publicly taking the same view.

Parnell fought for his political life in a circuit of by-elections throughout 1891. The division between pro- and anti-Parnellites was to tear apart families, to end friendships and to remain for generations the essential divide in Irish politics between romantics and pragmatists. Opposition to Parnell was not merely pragmatic, however.

Many of his supporters saw 'the priests' as the direct beneficiaries of the split, recovering through it their primary leadership role in Irish society. Under Parnell they had been involved, but not in control. With the collapse of 'Parnellism' they were in the ascendant. In Parnell's last days 'the hillside men,' the old Fenians, were his loyal allies, his arch-defenders. Parnell had been proud, aloof, arrogant, silent and passionate. As a leader his imaginative power as 'the chief' was always as great as his political maneuvering. His utter disregard for English convention and English standards of behavior gave him a mythic stature. That his destruction should be at the dictation of the English nonconformist conscience, executed by Irish Catholic clerical power, was seen as an irony too bitter to be expiated. He died in October 1891 in his early forties. The language of his detractors was to ring through political discussion for decades, the image of quicklime thrown in Parnell's eye to be a recurring representation of his destruction. The octogenarian Liberal leader for whose political powers Parnell had been destroyed, succeeded in passing a Home Rule Bill through the House of Commons in 1893. The Lords refused to pass the measure.

CHAPTER 9
AFTER PARNELL?

I N Irish history the period from 1891 to 1910 is represented as a hiatus, a static time between the fall of Parnell and the final stages of Home Rule negotiations before World War I, an intellectual preamble to 1916. Seen through the prism of the immediate past or the immediate future it is considered a period of imaginative excrescence.

O he'll remember this when he grows up, said Dante hotly – the language he heard against God and religion and the priests in his own home – Let him remember too, cried Mrs Casey to her from across the table, the language with which the priests and the priests' pawns broke Parnell's heart and hounded him into the grave. Let him remember that too when he grows up.

James Joyce evoking memories of a Dublin childhood in the late 1890s in A *Portrait of the Artist as a Young Man.*

The reality of these years is rather more varied than a purely cultural analysis would seem to suggest. According to William Butler Yeats' retrospective analysis 'men's minds turned from politics' after the sordid spectacle of the Parnellite battle. There was a period of remarkable cultural activity in these two decades but it seems clear that despite the subsequent significance of

cultural debate initiated during these years, and the subsequent political significance of cultural alignments, 'culture' was not the sole forum of activity. Politically the period was devoid of glamor. Culturally it was vibrant.

The Conservative administration after 1893 granted Ireland substantial material investment. The Conservative policy of state-assisted land purchase was hastened by new legislation and in the Wyndham Act of 1903 the final basis for a mass transfer of landed property was effected. Thus by the 1910s the majority of Irish farmers were owner-occupiers. Landowners were bought out on generous terms and in general retained a demesne and home farm together with the 'big house.' This final settlement was precipitated by the violent protests of the poorest class of tenants from the west of Ireland under the leadership of William O'Brien a former lieutenant of Parnell. There was little public agitation elsewhere as the reasons for agrarian crime receded. Under the Local Government Act of 1898 the control of local government was democratised and within a few years local politics at all levels were in the hands of Catholic nationalists. The Irish Parliamentary Party reunited on the issue of the rights of western tenants and old adversaries submitted to the compromise leadership of Parnell's loyal supporter John Redmond. Literature cannot be seen as directly representing reality, but James Joyce, when trying to capture the mood of Dublin in the 1900s searched for a means of conveying a sense of the scrupulous meanness and paralysis that he saw at the heart of society. The angry young men who had followed Parnell with passionate fervor in the 1880s were now old, respectable and established. Parliamentary nationalism had itself become a respectable verity and a class of *nouveau riche* and politically ambitious merchants, lawyers and ranchers seemed to control the power and rhetoric of nationalist feeling. Dublin was a city of indescribable misery with housing conditions that could not be equalled in western Europe. In general the proprietors of large slum establishments were Catholic, nationalist and rhetorically committed to 'the cause.' William Martin Murphy, the employers' leader in the industrial lockout of 1913 and proprietor of the *Independent* newspaper, was an impeccable parliamentary nationalist. Nationalism had become a well-worn route to political advancement, an automatic 'assumed' criterion of Irishness, in short a counter-establishment establishment. Certain middle-class Dublin boys were encouraged to see themselves as the natural leaders of a new independent state. The Irish Party hoped for a Liberal electoral victory and the Home Rule settlement that was presumed to flow directly from it. As brokers at Westminster, the Irish Party remained a potent force. They skilfully campaigned for grants, drains, buildings and expansion: their actions manifestly altered standards of living. On issues like the Boer War they took a vociferous anti-

Below: The poet and dramatist William Butler Yeats, 1865-1939. Much of Yeats' work was concerned with developing Irish literary traditions.

English line and in the Centenary Celebrations to commemorate the rising of 1798 they kept control of proceedings.

At the height of the land agitation in the 1880s the Gaelic Athletic Association was founded. it was an organization committed to the 'revival' of formal interest in traditional Irish games like hurling and the improvised form of football which was described as Gaelic. The GAA was essentially a modern movement, imitating the standardizing of games like football and cricket. It had specifically nationalist connotations from the beginning, banning the participation of those who played any non-Gaelic games, a ploy that was initially intended to exclude British soldiers stationed in garrison towns across the country. Many Fenians became members of the GAA and a radical nationalist tone underlay it from the beginning. Much of the formulaic ritual surrounding the game was deliberately 'traditional,' and the Irish language was encouraged at all levels of the organization. The association spread slowly at first, but by the mid 1890s it had a nationwide organization, a huge membership and a resolutely combative, not to say militaristic air. Like all nationalist organizations it was divided by the Parnellite split in the early 1890s.

In 1893 a rather different national organization was established. The Gaelic League was founded as a cultural protest against the extinction of the Irish Language. In a paper delivered before the Irish National Literary Society in Dublin on 25 November 1892 Douglas Hyde, a scholar and linguist, spoke of 'The necessity for de-anglicizing Ireland.' He was a Protestant Unionist, who had

little interest in political independence. His feeling for Ireland was determined by culture to which he saw the Irish language as the essential key. If the key language died, he claimed in a romantic vein, so too would the distinctive way of life that was Irish. Without language Ireland was no more than a cheap derivation of England, a cosmopolitan cultural wasteland of pale imita-

Left: Grave of Yeats, Drumcliff Churchyard, County Sligo.

Under bare Ben Bulben's head
In Drumcliff churchyard
Yeats is laid
An ancestor was rector there
Long years ago, a church
stands near,
By the road an ancient cross.
No marble, no conventional
phrase;
On limestone quarried near
the spot
By his command these words
are cut;
Cast a cold eye
On Life, on Death.
Horsemen, pass by.

Left: Visiting the houses of the dead after street riots in Belfast in August 1907.

tion. Branches of the Gaelic League were supported particularly by Anglo-Irish intellectuals. While intellectually significant, the organization remained small and select until the early 1900s when it became fashionable among radical schoolteachers, journalists, political nationalists and GAA enthusiasts. As the membership changed so too did its political tone. It became a forum for 'advanced' nationalists, a cell structure for nationalist contacts and a suitable base for Irish Republican Brotherhood infiltration.

The increased political significance of the Gaelic League was also a direct response to the more belligerent and plebeian exhortation than the need to 'de-anglicize' emanating from the scathing pen of D.P. Moran in the columns of his newspaper *The Leader*. Moran is perhaps the most significant figure in the formation of that confused mesh of prejudice, conviction and culture that is the twentieth-century Irish sense of national identity. He spoke in the same terms as Hyde. He clearly relished writing in the English language which he affected to despise. He would not have viewed Hyde as a suitable fellow-campaigner, since his idea of nationality was racial as well as cultural. The profound interest in Irish culture manifested by the old 'Ascendancy' he saw as merely the desire to wield power translated into cultural form. The literature in English written in Ireland and referred to as Anglo-Irish, he saw as a cultural usurpation, a belief many Gaelic League members shared. Yeats, in responding to attacks on the writing of an Irish literature in the English language in a society in which the vast majority of people spoke only English, said, 'Gaelic is my national tongue, but it is not my

mother tongue'. Yeats chose to engage with the cultural politics of his time. More accurately, he sought to mold them. His contemporary failures were compensated for by his historiographical re-ordering, so that for many scholars of the period it seems that Ireland is no more than a piece of wax for the forging of the poetic identity of William Butler Yeats. Joyce found contemporary Irish politics nauseating, absurd and distasteful. As a bourgeois Catholic he ought to have pursued the political goals of his contemporaries, Tom Kettle and Sheehy Skeffington, but to him their nationalist posturings were absurd, their cultural aspirations laughable and their eternal war with the cultural oppressor tedious. Joyce was not afflicted by the semantic cultural insecurities of his contemporaries. He saw no tension between his scrupulous attention to his native place and his celebration of the English language. If anything his sense of a Gaelic linguistic past merely endowed him with the audacity to subvert the English language.

Joyce was however an exception to all rules. Cultural ferment in Ireland was essentially a reflection of desires to escape insecurity about self, class and nation and more obliquely the pursuit of power.

At the fringes of cultural politics were small parties and neo-radical groups, many of whose members overlapped with the GAA and the Gaelic League. Sinn Féin was a small political party founded by a journalist, Arthur Griffith. It was intended to challenge the hegemony of the Irish Party. Its policies were largely concerned with economic development, with an escape from the tedious repetition of nationalist dogma,

Right: Anti Home Rule demonstration, Coleraine, September 1912. Men from district Orange Lodges marching to Manor House Grounds.

a stance that was reflected in the Sinn Féin newspaper, *The United Irishman*. Dublin politics was a vibrant mess of publications, small political parties of brief duration, debating clubs, linguistic self-improvement classes and faddists. Some of the greatest cranks were 'improving' Anglo-Irish patriots like Horace Plunkett who combined the roles of government adviser on an assortment of matters, with agricultural improvement, schemes for the regeneration of the Irish character and diffuse cultural scavenging. This level of political and literary life is captured by George Moore in his trilogy *Ave, Salve, Vale*. Here all of the leading figures of the Irish cultural renaissance come together against a backdrop of vegetarians, theosophists and spiritualists. Culture was a serious political weapon. When the Abbey Theatre, founded by Yeats and Lady Gregory put on John Millington Synge's play, *The Playboy of the Western World*, the opening was marked by riots of protest against the slur on Irish peasant culture that was felt to be implicit in its approach. Cultural dignity was all.

Individual members of the Irish Party were involved in the Gaelic League. On the surface the party was healthy and politically vigilant. Certain of the local party branches in Dublin were connected with the new movements through young members, many of whom were from the new National University of Ireland. The party appeared to have a talented younger generation moving in to replace the old leaders and with the triumph of the Liberals in the general election of 1906 it seemed that Home Rule was

again 'in the realm of practical politics.' In reality the Liberal majority was so great that they did not require the support of Irish nationalists. A new generation of Liberal politicians resented the damage that the Irish cause had already done to the Liberal Party and proposed to proceed with social reforms and ignore the Irish demands for as long as was politically possible. The government of Asquith clashed with the House of Lords when the Lords refused to pass Liberal legislation, culminating in the defeat of the radical budget of 1909. After a general election in 1910 on this issue the Liberals became dependent on Irish support. In an exercise in political nerve the government introduced a Parliament Bill limiting the powers of the House of Lords. The government forced the Lords to pass the bill by threatening to create sufficient peerages to pass it anyway if the House as constituted refused. Since the statutory legislative vetoing power of the Lords had in the past been the stumbling block to the passage of Home Rule legislation, the Irish Party were utterly confident of success. Under the new arrangement any bill twice passed by the Commons with successive rejections by the Lords could not be vetoed a third time. The first bill was introduced in April 1912 and passed through all Commons stages by January 1913. It was rejected by the Lords. It again passed through the Commons and was again rejected by the Lords in July 1913. In theory if the Home Rule bill once more passed through the House of Commons it could no longer be refused by the House of Lords and would necessarily become law.

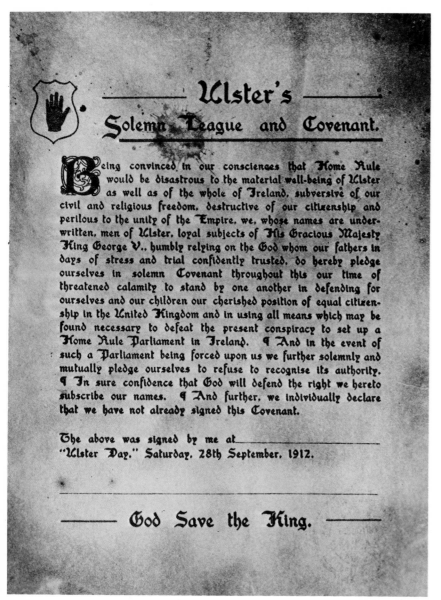

Ulster's Solemn League and Covenant.

Being convinced in our consciences that Home Rule would be disastrous to the material well-being of Ulster as well as of the whole of Ireland, subversive of our civil and religious freedom, destructive of our citizenship and perilous to the unity of the Empire, we, whose names are underwritten, men of Ulster, loyal subjects of His Gracious Majesty King George V., humbly relying on the God whom our fathers in days of stress and trial confidently trusted, do hereby pledge ourselves in solemn Covenant throughout this our time of threatened calamity to stand by one another in defending for ourselves and our children our cherished position of equal citizenship in the United Kingdom and in using all means which may be found necessary to defeat the present conspiracy to set up a Home Rule Parliament in Ireland. ¶ And in the event of such a Parliament being forced upon us we further solemnly and mutually pledge ourselves to refuse to recognise its authority. ¶ In sure confidence that God will defend the right we hereto subscribe our names. ¶ And further, we individually declare that we have not already signed this Covenant.

The above was signed by me at_____
"Ulster Day." Saturday, 28th September, 1912.

_____

God Save the King.

Above: The Solemn League and Covenant, the Ulster Protestants state their opposition to Home Rule.

Irish Unionism had not diminished as a political force, and it continued to retain the passionate commitment of the majority of British Conservatives who viewed the proposed concession of Home Rule to Ireland as an act of national treachery on the part of the Liberal Government. The government was committed to such a concession, but the commitment was based on expediency and political necessity rather than on loyalty or sympathy. The Irish Party under Redmond placed their trust utterly in Asquith since without a radical unconstitutional departure they had no alternative strategy. This was a dangerous game since it allowed Redmond little or no room to maneuver. If he rejected a Liberal compromise on the original agreement his only sanction was to bring the government down and restore the Conservatives, thus postponing Home Rule yet again. He lacked the nerve for such a course, particularly since in his mind timing was now of the essence. The Irish Party could not again tell the Irish people to carry the torch for yet another undetermined period. Thus the campaign of Irish Unionists for the defeat of the Home Rule cause was tactically neatly positioned. The Unionist leader was Sir Edward Carson, a southern Irish unionist. For Carson the maintenance of the Union was 'the guiding star of my political life.' He centered his campaign for the defeat of Home Rule in Ulster where the Orange Order, the tradition of loyalism, the 'Home Role as Rome Rule' campaign played by British Conservatives in the past, provided a stout base for resistance. Southern Irish Unionism was no less deeply felt, but its forces were scattered, community tensions were not high, and there was no developed working class to sustain an Orange Order. Carson had no specific love for Ulster as such. His organization of resistance in Ulster was merely intended to make Home Rule for all Ireland impossible. Yet at the very earliest stage of negotiations between Asquith and Irish Unionist representatives it was clear that the possibility of partition was discussed. Most of these early discussions centered on the most appropriate size for the excluded 'Ulster.' It could not be so large as the province of Ulster since such a unit would lead eventually to an internal nationalist majority. It could not, however, be so small as to be economically unviable. Transposition of population was suggested, the prospect of aspiring toward an exclusively Unionist Ulster discussed. All such discussion was desultory since it was hoped that in some unspecified fashion Ulster would remain, with the rest of Ireland, within the United Kingdom.

Redmond had difficulty in taking Ulster resistance seriously. Like most nationalists he believed that this was yet another British Conservative plot to destroy Home Rule. He did not believe in Ulster fears, nor did he understand the depth of their willingness to resist.

James Craig, the other Unionist leader was unlike Carson. He was quintessentially an Ulsterman; a founder member of the Ulster Unionist Council and an advocate of less intimacy with southern Unionist organizations. At a rally in the grounds of Craig's House just outside Belfast, in 1911 Carson said, 'in the event of a Home Rule Bill passing . . . [we are] to become responsible for the Protestant province of Ulster.' Andrew Bonar Law, leader of the Conservative Party speaking to a rally of 100,000 at the time of the introduction of the 1912 Bill reminded them of their besieged ancestors in Derry in 1688:

Once again you hold the pass for the Empire. You are a besieged city . . . The government by their parliament act have erected a boom against you, a boom to cut you off from the help of the British people.

At a reception in Blenheim Palace attended by Bonar Law, F.E. Smith, and Carson, Bonar Law, the leader of His Majesty's Opposition, said of Ulster Protestants:

If an attempt were made to deprive these men of their birth right – as part of a corrupt parliamentary bargain – they would be justified in resisting such an attempt by all means in their power, including force . . . I can imagine no length of resistance to which Ulster can go in which I should not be prepared to support them,

THE ★IRISH ★VOLUNTEER ★

oglác na h-eireann ★★★

Vol. 1. No. 2.   Saturday, February, 14th, 1914.   Price, 1d.

nificent spirit of brotherhood prevails everywhere and in a few months Ireland will be able to boast of a national movement as great as that of '82, and without the social limitations of that Volunteer army.

Step Together

As the movement includes all sections of patriotic Irishmen, those in the ranks should see to it that everything possible is done to weld the units of the various movements in the Volunteers into a solid entity however they may differ cuis de its ranks. To this effect the drill hall's should be open to all members of the Volunteers even though the halls belong to social or political bodies. If Gaelic Leaguers drill in one hall, Foresters in another, Hibernians in another, a distinct loss is suffered, for an army knows no political differences, and training in water-tight compartments is inclined to carry into the Volunteer movement differences of aim and policy which it is essential to exclude as rigidly as may be. Stand together, step together should be above and beyond all the motto of the Volunteers.

In the Capital

In the capital the organisation is going

Standarised Drill

In the provinces Volunteer corps are asking "Is our drill the same as the Dublin drill?" and there is some uneasiness in the matter. The instructors are drawn from different ranks with different terms of service and there is a feeling that a big effort should be made to standardise the drill so that for general movements which will include corps from more than one or two counties the standard of efficiency will be maintained. It would give more confidence to the provincial corps also and from the very first assure the unity so essential to an army.

Spread the Light

Many hundreds were unable to get a

Old Regime Ends.

"If Home Rule is killed Ireland will be absolutely ungovernable under the old regime."—John E. Redmond, M.P.

The Press and the Irish Volunteer

"The Irish Volunteer."—Altogether the publication is bright and interesting, and will undoubtedly become most popu-

From the

and in which, in my belief, they would not be supported by the overwhelming majority of the British people.

By September 1912 tension in Ulster was at fever pitch, and in this atmosphere hundreds of thousands signed the pledge known as the Solemn League and Covenant. They pledged themselves to oppose the king's government, and to use all necessary means 'to defeat the present conspiracy to set up a Home Rule parliament in Ireland. And in the event of such a parliament being forced upon us we further solemnly and mutually pledge ourselves to refuse to recognise its authority.' More significantly, these threats were backed by military force. In January 1913 the Ulster Unionist Council decided to form their amateur groups of drilling supporters into a coherent force – the Ulster Volunteer Force. This force of 100,000 armed men was to be supervised by a former Indian Army General, Sir George Richardson. Advice was forthcoming from all levels of the British Army, including Lord Roberts, and the general attitude of the establishment in Britain is best understood when it is appreciated that even the King, whom the

Unionists threatened with rebellion, was on their side. In March 1914 at the height of debate on Ulster it became known that 57 British Army officers stationed at the Curragh in Kildare, acting on the mistaken assumption that Asquith's Government was ordering them to proceed

Above: Journal of the Irish Volunteers.

Below: Advertising Volunteer uniforms in Redmond's own constituency, July 1914.

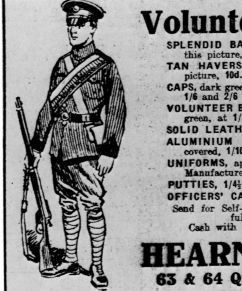

Volunteer Outfits

SPLENDID BANDOLIERS, exact as on this picture, 1/11 each.
TAN HAVERSACKS, exact as on this picture, 10d. each.
CAPS, dark green, exact as on this picture, 1/6 and 2/6 each.
VOLUNTEER BOER SHAPE HATS, dark green, at 1/10 and 2/6 each.
SOLID LEATHER BELTS, 1/3 each.
ALUMINIUM WATER BOTTLES, felt covered, 1/10 each.
UNIFORMS, approved design only, Irish Manufacture, 25/- each.
PUTTIES, 1/4½ per pair.
OFFICERS' CAPS, HAVERSACKS, Etc.
Send for Self-Measurement Forms and full Price List.
Cash with Order. Postage extra.

HEARNE & Co., Ltd.
63 & 64 Quay, WATERFORD.

against the Ulster Volunteer Force, refused to obey such orders. Asquith was left in no doubt as to the unwillingness of the army to proceed against the Ulster men should it prove necessary to do so. He made a show of punishing certain officers, but took the message. From Redmond's point of view it was a devastating one. In 1914 when large shipments of arms were illegally imported at Larne to arm the UVF the police looked on like 'benevolent spectators.' The Home Rule Bill was accompanied by an amendment when finally enacted in September 1914. Home Rule was not to come into operation until the war ended and until special legislation had been enacted for Ulster. Redmond impotently agreed to this, assuming that the measure, though distasteful, was temporary. So did most people in the rest of Ireland, though it is difficult to reconcile this belief with the uncompromising stand of the Unionists. Southern Unionists felt utterly betrayed, cast to the lions, and from this point on began to consider making their own separate accommodations with the proposed future situation.

Perhaps the best explanation of the attitude of nationalist Ireland to the question of partition is to say that they did not understand northern unionism. They saw it as a form of meaningless bigotry and partition as primarily a British exploitation of this bigotry for the purpose of destroying, yet again, the ideal of Home Rule. Unconstitutional methods had triumphed for the Ulster Unionists, and the public opinion of the rest of Ireland, which had in the past won all concessions in this fashion was outraged. It was felt

acceptable for nationalists to win by unconstitutional means since they had no desire to maintain allegiance to the British consitution. Redmond and his party were, by 1914, steeped in constitutionalism after having spent over 30 years at Westminster. Redmond saw no way of proceeding other than by the standards of the gentleman that he had become.

The Irish Volunteers were founded in November 1913 as a counter to the Ulster Volunteers. They were not conceived as a force to fight the Ulster Volunteers, whose style they both admired and emulated. In the Gaelic League newspaper *An Claidheamh Soluis* Eoin MacNeill published an article entitled 'The North Began.' This article was written at the invitation of The O'Rahilly, the editor of the paper and an associate of Arthur Griffith. MacNeill was a respected and well-known Gaelic intellectual and scholar and a moderate nationalist politically. The Ulster Volunteers, he claimed, had taken a vital step towards automomy in which all nationalists should rejoice. From this confused analysis emerged the Irish Volunteers. The IRB had been reorganizing secretly for a few years. Through the Dungannon Clubs, Bulmer Hobson and Henry McCullough had restored the morale, if not the structure, of the movement. In the Clubs' newspaper *The Republic* they preached the old extreme separatist gospel. They recruited talented young men who were active in less extreme nationalist movements like Sean MacDermott who worked as a national organizer for Griffith's Sinn Féin. They purged the old IRB Supreme Council with the assistance of the old but radical Fenian

Right: Expression of feeling on Redmond's commitment to offer the Irish Volunteers for the European war, *Irish Worker.*

The Coming of the Irish Judas and his Paymaster.

Thomas Clarke who had served over 15 years penal servitude before going to the United States, working with John Devoy, and returning to Ireland. They also drew in P.S. O'Hegarty, a brilliant journalist and Major John MacBride, the husband of Yeats' lifelong love, Maud Gonne. The new organization published a newspaper *Irish Freedom* which was suppressed by the authorities in 1914, and acted as the controlling influence in Countess Markievicz's military youth movement *Na Fianna Eireann*. When MacNeill proposed instituting the Volunteers The O'Rahilly met him and proferred organizational assistance The 'provisional committee' had representatives from all shades of nationalist opinion but from the beginning the IRB was in control in a way that the other participants failed to appreciate.

As the Volunteer movement grew from the first mass meeting in Dublin arms became essential. In providing arms the key figures were Sir Roger Casement and Erskine Childers, the 'London Committee,' who travelled to Germany for arms in early 1914. But when a cache of arms arrived at Howth on 26 July 1914 in the yacht *Asgard* which was met by marching Volunteers, British troops fired on the crowd as they returned to the city. This debacle, in which three civilians were killed, brought feeling in Dublin to a high point. There was, however, a crisis in the Volunteers as parliamentary leaders like Redmond and John Dillon, who had tried to control the new movement, put pressure on MacNeill to hand over complete control to them as the future government. This placed MacNeill in a serious dilemma, since if he did so the IRB men would move out taking with them the very considerable arms supplies that he knew to be on the point of importation. Redmond required control of the force if he was to have any final authority in controlling the new state. He published an ultimatum in the newspapers demanding that 25 parliamentarians be placed on the provisional committee. MacNeill and his allies were horrified but had no choice other than to acquiesce publicly with seeming good grace. Hobson supported MacNeill in this decision and in return Clarke and MacDermott never spoke to him again. His willingness to compromise led to the end of his career at the heart of the IRB.

By September 1914 there were 180,000 Volunteers. On the outbreak of war, with a partition-style Home Rule Bill reaching the statute books, Redmond professed his loyalty to the British empire, and the willingness of the Volunteers to fight in return for the settlement that they would receive when the war was over. The Ulster Volunteers similarly pledged loyalty. Most nationalists supported Redmond and hundreds of thousands of Irishmen fought voluntarily in World War I, confident that their struggle was in Ireland's best interests. The poorer classes of course joined because it was a job, an adventure, an opportunity for a new life. The Volunteers split into those who followed Redmond and those

hard-core revolutionaries who would not fight for Britain on any terms. They believed that settlement after the war would be no less unsatisfactory than before. In the light of the maxim that 'England's difficulty is Ireland's opportunity' they planned an uprising. All remaining radicals in Dublin were soon drawn in to the IRB. Even James Connolly, the labor leader and controller of the tiny Citizen's Army decided to place nationalist ends before those of socialism.

The Commander in Chief MacNeill was a 'front' in the last stages of planning preceding the rising of 1916. When he learned that a rising was planned for the morning of Easter Sunday 1916 he issued a countermanding order, since he believed that there was no realistic prospect of success and that his men would simply be led like lambs to the slaughter. A counter-countermanding order was issued. The rebels seized the General Post Office

Above: Erskine Childers, 1870-1922. Childers helped procure arms for the Irish Volunteers in 1914 but opposed the treaty with Britain in 1921-22. He was executed by the Irish government, under an emergency law, for possessing an illegal firearm. Ironically the pistol had been given to him by Michael Collins.

WILL YOU ANSWER THE CALL?

NOW
IS THE TIME,

AND THE PLACE IS THE
NEAREST RECRUITING OFFICE.

in Sackville Street and various other strategic buildings around the center of Dublin. In the General Post Office one of the most significant leaders was the messianic barrister, Gaelic League enthusiast and writer, Pàdraig Pearse. The Irish Republic was declared to be established by proclamation. The language of the proclamation is in the style of Pearse's earlier writings, though possibly Thomas MacDonagh assisted in its composition. This document was to be of critical importance in determining the nature of subsequent nationalist self-definition. The 'tradition' of Irish nationalism was declared to be canonical, stretching back unbroken through time. Further, that tradition was declared to be republican. The 'differences' within the island, a reference to northern Unionists, were declared to be 'carefully fostered by an alien government.'

Below: An incident in the attack by the 36th (Ulster) Division at the beginning of the Battle of the Somme, 1916. After a painting by J.P. Beadle.

Right: The ruins of the General Post Office in Dublin after the Easter Rising of 1916.

Nationalism is represented as an immanent absolute, romantically 'hidden' during certain periods, but awaiting rebirth. The language is emotional and organic in a nineteenth century fashion. Pearse, MacDermott or Mac Diarmada, MacDonagh and Plunkett were poets, writers and intellectuals. They spoke in a messianic language of blood sacrifice that was not atypical in Europe during the Great War. Pearse spoke of national freedom in the following terms:

Like a divine religion national freedom bears the marks of unity, of sanctity, of catholicity, of apostolic succession. Of unity for it contemplates the nation as one; of sanctity, for it is holy in itself and in those who serve it; of catholicity, for it embraces all the men and women of the nation; of apostolic succession, for it, or the aspiration after it, passes down from generation to generation from the nation's fathers.

Below: Sir Roger Casement, 1864-1916. Casement helped arrange the arms shipment to Howth in 1914. Casement arranged a further shipment to arm the 1916 Rising but the arms were intercepted and Casement separately arrested and executed.

Joseph Plunkett wrote a poem, an address to Ireland in the manner of the eighteenth century *aisling*. Its title 'The Little Black Rose Shall Be Red At Last' conveys the notion of a national redemption through blood sacrifice which motivated the leaders of 1916:

Because we share our sorrows and our joys
And all your dear and intimate thoughts are mine
We shall not fear the trumpets and the noise
Of battle, for we know our dreams divine,
And when my heart is pillowed on your heart
The ebb and flowing of their passionate flood
Shall beat in concord love through every part
Of brain and body – when at last the blood
O'er leaps the final barrier to find
Only one source wherein to spend its strength
And we two lovers, long but one in mind
And soul, are made one flesh at length;
Praise God if this my blood fulfils the doom
When you, dark rose, shall redden into bloom.

In the poem *The Fool* Pearse answered the accusations of those 'wise men' who doubted the sanity of meaning of his messianic vision:

O wise men, riddle me this: what if the dream come true?
What if the dream come true and if millions unborn shall dwell
In the house that I shaped in my heart, the noble house of my thoughts?
Lord I have staked my soul, I have staked the lives of my kin
On the truth of Thy dreadful word. Do not remember my failures
But remember this my faith.

In all, about 3000 men and women were killed in the fighting in Dublin. In Galway Liam Mellowes led a smaller rising. Sir Roger Casement was captured at Banna Strand in County Kerry in an attempt to import arms from Germany and subsequently hanged for treason. In Dublin Eamon de Valera commanded one center of resistance at Bolands' Mill. In the GPO Michael Collins fought beside Pearse and Connolly. Many of the participants were under 30 years of age, members of a network of nationalist associations and, from a British point of view, unimportant politically. They were to become the future leaders of nationalist resistance. The rising was not utterly militarily incompetent. The rebels held out for over a week. Heavy casualties were inflicted on the British Army and the center of Dublin was devastated. The population of Dublin, most of whom were living indirectly on the pay warrants of the British Army, in view of the number of Dublin working-class men serving in the trenches, saw the rebels as misguided lunatics. There was little public support for the 'Shinners', as the rebels were soon known, because of the mistaken analysis of Dublin Castle that it was a Sinn Féin uprising. The administration at Dublin Castle had a complex and efficient intelligence network detailing all 'known activists' throughout the country. Outraged by the rebellion they decided to root out revolutionary nationalism for once and for all. They initiated a policy of executions which were proceeded within an apparently laconic fashion. Every day the story of another execution leaked out 'like a trickle of blood from under a door.' The desultory, slow, steady nature of the decisions to execute caused public revulsion far greater than one decision to execute all the leaders would have done. From apathy, public opinion turned to outrage. In addition to the executions, the government proceeded to round up and intern in camps in England thousands of suspects. Speaking the Irish language was sufficient qualification for seizure. As John Dillon despairingly commented, the government 'seemed bent on manufacturing Sinn Féiners.' On 3 May Pearse, Clarke and MacDonagh were executed. On the following day Plunkett, Edward Daly, Michael O'Hanrahan and William Pearse. On the 5th Major John MacBride. Three days later Eamonn Ceannt, Michael Mallin, Con Colbert and Seán Heuston. On 12 May, James Connolly and Seán MacDermott. The nature and timing of the executions speeded the swing in public opinion on to the side of the rebels but it seems clear that there was a considerable basis of sympathy for the ideals of the rebellion.

The political base of the Irish Party was seriously compromised. It became embroiled in new and meticulous negotiations on Home Rule with Lloyd George as its public support slowly ebbed away. Sinn Féin, the organization which the authorities saw as being the source of the rebellion became the political skeleton within which a new movement was structured. Redmond, desperate to secure an immediate Home Rule parliament in the face of changing political circumstances, conceded the principle of the

exclusion of six rather than four counties, confident that as soon as northern Unionists saw Home Rule working, they would, for unspecified reasons, 'come in.' Southern Unionists and Conservatives in the Cabinet were opposed to a rushed wartime settlement. Southern landowners such as Lord Lansdowne and the earl of Midleton were particularly vociferous on this point and utterly rejected such summary abandonment. The 1916 negotiations were abortive but significant in that Redmond had made further concessions which were to form the basis of the final settlement. Publicly the Irish Parliamentary Party never recovered from the stigma of their failed negotiations. As the headline in the *Clare Champion* announced, 'Betrayed. Home Rule Proposal Smashed Up. Disgraceful Trickery and Deception.' Redmond's bargaining position was further eroded at the end of 1916 when the Liberal and Conservative Parties formed a coalition government, an arrangement which made the divisive issue of Ireland all the more likely to be ignored or compromised. Conservatives slightly tailored their commitment to Unionism, but the Liberals under Lloyd George ceased to hold any great interest in the plight of Redmond's beleaguered party. Unable to deliver, his party was pushed to the side. Despite subsequent negotiations the status of northern Unionism was subsequently decided by fiat.

Above: Thomas J. Clarke, an old Fenian, and one of the leaders of the 1916 rebellion. Clarke was one of the first group to be executed along with Pádraig Pearse and Thomas MacDonagh.

CHAPTER 10
THE FIGHT FOR FREEDOM

IN early 1917 Lloyd George in a gesture of reconciliation released the interned prisoners from Frongoch and other camps in Britain. These men were rapturously welcomed back to Ireland. As Redmond and the constitutionalists met in the sessions of an Irish Convention convened by Lloyd George as a 'talking shop' in Trinity College, Dublin, Sinn Féin was reorganized by the returned prisoners. Of nine parliamentary by-elections fought between February 1917 and June 1918 Sinn Féin won six. Lloyd George's government ceased to follow events in Ireland as the war became their sole focus, particularly after the entry of the United States. The gestures of the releases and the convention had been motivated by a desire to appease American criticism of the executions of 1916. Eamon de Valera, one of the 1916 leaders, had been spared execution because of his American citizenship. In June 1917 de Valera, standing on the platform of the proclamation of 1916, was elected to parliament as the member for East Clare. He was elected President of the restructured Sinn Féin. In the summer of 1917 the Dublin Castle administration began a desultory harrassment of the realigned Sinn Féin and Volunteer supporters, banning meetings, prohibiting the wearing of uniforms and arresting leaders. In September 1917 one of these men, Thomas Ashe, died on hunger strike. At his funeral Michael Collins gave an oration: 'Nothing additional remains to be said. The volley which we have just heard is the only speech which it is proper to make above the grave of a dead Fenian.' This was the first public acknowledgment of the role that the IRB continued to play. In the re-ordered Sinn Féin, in the remnants of the Volunteers who were to be restructured as the Irish Republican Army, IRB men were numerous. They retained their own separate secret organization up to 1921 and after, and Collins, the leader of military operations in the following struggle with the British forces was a leading IRB man. By late 1917 Collins had reorganized the IRB. He also rose rapidly within the hierarchy of the Volunteers.

Elections were fought under the banner title of Sinn Féin but what precisely Sinn Féin was seemed unclear. It certainly no longer stood for the old moderate dual-monarchy arrangement that Griffith's original party had supported. In effect it was no more than an umbrella title for an emerging movement that adhered to the vague principles of 1916. Within the Volunteers and Sinn Féin there were forces opposed to and suspicious of the IRB. Their argument was that in an open movement gradually pursuing public support through the ballot there was no role for a secret, oath-bound society. The Irish people now had the means to express their will publicly and there was no need for a secret élite to choose what was 'best for the Irish people.'

Public opinion continued to flow in the direction of the Volunteers and Sinn Féin. The leadership of both organizations was united in the person of Eamon de Valera and the declared policy of Sinn Féin was 'securing the international recognition of Ireland as an independent Irish republic.'

Previous pages: The Anglo Irish War, the destruction of the Custom House in Dublin May 1921. The Custom House was seized by over 120 men of the Dublin Brigade of the IRA. Although they succeeded in destroying British administrative records held in the building, all were captured or killed making the event a serious defeat for the IRA.

Right: De Valera is greeted by a welcoming crowd on his return to Ireland, July 1921, after the preliminary treaty negotiations with the British.

In April 1918 Lloyd George announced his intention to introduce conscription to Ireland. This intention acted as the catalyst for the solidifying of anti-government feeling. The Irish Party opposed conscription, but the real energy behind the campaign of public resistance was supplied by Sinn Féin. The imposition of conscription, both Sinn Féin and the Volunteers claimed, would be an act of war against the Irish people and would be met by war:

If England decides on this atrocity, then we, on our part, must decide that we shall acknowledge no limit and no scruple . . . Thus the man who serves on an exemption tribunal, the doctor who treats soldiers or examines conscripts, the man who voluntarily surrenders when called for, the man who in any shape or form applies for an exemption, the man who drives a police car or assists in the transport of army supplies, all these having assisted the enemy must be shot or otherwise destroyed with the least possible delay.

This is an extreme statement of resistance and does not reflect the thinking of the Catholic Church, who nonetheless rejected conscription utterly. The war ended, conscription was not introduced, but the language and intent of Sinn Féin grew more intransigent.

In the postwar general election of December 1918 the old Irish Party was decimated. Seventy-three seats went to Sinn Féin, 26 to the Unionists and a mere seven to the Irish Party. Many of the Sinn Féiners elected were in prison at the time of polling. Sinn Féin had been elected on a four-point program: first, withdrawal from Westminster; second, 'making use of any and every means available to render impotent the power of England to hold Ireland in subjugation by military force or otherwise'; third, the establishment of a native parliament as 'the supreme national authority'; and finally, an appeal to the Peace Conference in Paris 'for the establishment of Ireland as an independent nation.'

The constituent assembly Dáil Eireann met on 21 January 1919. It was composed entirely of Sinn Féin members. Thirty-six of the elected representatives were in prison. The party had used the structure of British-controlled elections to acquire its mandate, and had then deemed itself to have withdrawn from the English body politic. Henceforth the official administration in Ireland was spoken of as an enemy occupation, and the public pronouncements emanating from the Dáil adopted the tone of a government established from time immemorial confronting an enemy usurper. In republican rhetoric this was the reality of the situation and in time the population of the country supported such an interpretation. The Republic proclaimed in 1916 was ratified by the Dáil and the Dáil further proclaimed itself to be the sole law-making body. The central demand of the Dáil was 'the evacuation of our country by the English garrison.' Ulster Unionists were undismayed by the withdrawal of nationalist representation from Westminster since it gave

them a monopoly of influence in the cabinet committee, under the chairmanship of Walter Long, which was constituted to consider the Home Rule settlement. London treated the constitution of the Dáil as a temporary aberration and used this diversion of nationalist and republican energies to proceed with a final settlement.

The verbal protests of Dáil Eireann spilled over into a Volunteer-initiated guerrilla war against British forces in 1919. This was the beginning of two years of armed struggle. This struggle was directed by Michael Collins who created an IRA General Headquarters Staff in March 1918. In February 1919 he masterminded the springing of de Valera and others from Lincoln jail. His reputation for daring and courage grew. He was soon a legendary figure. Throughout 1919 de Valera was absent on an American tour and much of the power for directing events was in Collins' hands. He continued to attract the antagonism of individuals like Cathal Brugha, hostile to the secret IRB influence, but most internal differences were suppressed in view of his superb skills as a military commander. There were those within the Dáil who had hoped that the battle against Britain could be won without firing a single shot, and they were reluctant followers in the sporadic cam-

Above: Sinn Féiners held at point of revolver by Black and Tans, 23 November 1920.

Right: Barricades outside Dublin City Hall, 22 January 1921.

Right: Barricades outside Dublin City Hall, 22 January 1921.

paign waged by 'the Army,' as the IRA was known. Relations between the Dáil and the Army were not clearly defined, and in effect the Army acted alone under the command of its own headquarters. The national role of Sinn Féin revolved around the organization of constituency branches and the administration of Dáil Courts which served as an alternative legal system. By late 1919 the guerrilla war was in full flight with daily battles, attacks by 'flying columns,' and, always, the slow disappearance back into a community that supported the fighters. Dáil Eireann was suppressed, and soon a serious attack on the guerillas was mounted.

The Royal Irish Constabulary was the chief target of the Army, or 'the rebels,' as Dublin Castle called them. They were the force which supplied Dublin Castle with its intelligence network and without them control was unfocussed. Not merely did Collins destroy the intelligence system throughout the country but he also succeeded in penetrating the headquarters of 'G' Division of the Dublin Metropolitan Police, the central intelligence unit. He therefore had access to all government intelligence. The other 'professional' arm of his campaign was the 'Squad,' of handpicked men chosen to kill police agents, informers and detectives. The other chief

Right: An armored car halted at the site of an IRA ambush, County Tipperary 1921.

weapon of the movement was the social ostracism of the families of all RIC men. The RIC was a force composed of Irishmen, except at senior officer level and the sanctions of their own community proved effective over time. Lloyd George moved in a new force to support the police and the army. These were the Auxiliary officers and a force known as the 'Black and Tans' from the colors of their uniform. They were recently demobilized soldiers and officers who had fought in the trenches. Let loose upon a civilian population they ran amok. Midnight searches for arms, curfews, areas proclaimed under DORA, as the Defence of the Realm Act was known, characterized the new tougher regime. Attacks on soldiers were avenged by the burnings of towns like Balbriggan and Cork. The shooting of 'G' men in their beds by Collins' 'Squad' was avenged by indiscriminate shootings on a crowd at a match in Croke Park, the central GAA football ground. Terror and murder prevailed. The Catholic Church condemned acts of violence by the rebels, but protested even more strongly at official atrocities. Lloyd George was aware of the international outrage that the activities of the Crown forces evoked. There appeared to be an officially sanctioned policy of random reprisals on the civilian population, with the intention of provoking a public resistance to the guerrilla campaign. By 1921 the situation seemed deadlocked. Lloyd George had proclaimed 'we have murder by the throat' but there was little evidence to support his claim. The Crown forces, no matter how large or how well equipped seemed incapable of breaking an infinitely smaller group of active rebels who enjoyed the support of the community.

While 'the war' was at its height the Government of Ireland Act was passed. This provided in effect, though it involved an actual vote by the Unionists, for the partition of the island into two areas, each to have its own parliament. It provided for a Council of Ireland and for the possibility of rapid reunification by consent. Elections were held for both parliaments in May 1921. The return of de Valera from the United States after the arrest of Arthur Griffith, the acting Dáil President, in late 1920 had altered the balance between the military and political wings of the rebel forces. De Valera did not like or understand war, and shared the reservations of the Catholic hierarchy as to whether it was indeed just or 'proper.' Collins was not disposed to fight indefinitely, so from early 1921 there was a propensity to negotiate should the occasion seem right. Craig and de Valera met before the elections of 1921 but there was no common ground. Sinn Féin participated in the elections despite their repudiation of all 'alien governmental structures' and the Second Dáil sat in Dublin as before. In composition it was urban lower middle class and young, a reasonable representation of the men who had conducted the struggle. The members chose not to sit in the offically constituted parliament designated by the Government of Ireland Act. In the newly constituted state of Northern Ireland those elected took their seats at Stormont. At the opening of the new parliament of Northern Ireland on 22 June 1921 King George V appealed for conciliation. Three days later de Valera received a letter from Lloyd George proposing peace talks. This was a remarkable about-turn by a prime minister who had earlier protested

that he would never negotiate with 'murderers, thugs and gun-men.' A truce was declared on 11 July 1921. According to Lord Beaverbrook, de Valera met Craig immediately before his first meeting with Lloyd George. 'Are you going to see Lloyd George alone?' Craig asked him. 'Yes,' said de Valera. 'Are you mad? Take a witness. Lloyd George will give any account of the interview that comes into his mind or that suits him.'

In December a negotiating team led by Griffith and Collins went to London. Their status as negotiators was unclear to begin with, with the question of the limits of their power unclarified. It was apparent that Lloyd George would not agree to a republic or to complete independence. It was in addition clear that renegotiating the status of the already constituted state of Northern Ireland would be no simple matter. The negotiators further realized that there was no public appetite in Ireland for continuing the war. While Lloyd George might not be capable of defeating the guerrilla forces should hostilities be resumed, he clearly had the resources of one of the most powerful states in the world with which to fight indefinitely. The threat of the resumption of 'immediate and terrible war' hung over the negotiations. The treaty as signed provided for the continuation of partition subject to the revisions of a boundary commission which seemed likely to award portions of Northern Ireland to the South. The assumption was that in such reduced contours, the state of Northern Ireland would not be capable of survival. The southern 26 counties were to be excluded from the terms of the Government of Ireland Act. The 26 counties were to be known as the Irish Free State and to have dominion status on the Canadian model.

The Irish Free State was to have its own armed forces, revenues, laws and, in certain degree, external relations. Britain retained military and naval bases for strategic reasons, unlimited powers in such bases in times of war and a supervisory role in the constitution of the new Free State. All elected politicians were to take an oath of allegiance and the Crown was to retain a governor general as its representative. After signing the Treaty Collins said, 'early this morning I signed my death warrant.'

Public reaction to the treaty in Ireland was one of immense relief. As far as most people were concerned what was good enough for Michael Collins was good enough for them. De Valera however recalled, as did members of the cabinet, that the negotiators had been specifically directed to consult the cabinet in Dublin before signing a treaty. The debate on the treaty in the Dáil was bitter and long. Collins argued that the treaty gave Ireland the freedom to achieve freedom, that it granted the independence that had been sought for so long. He pointed out that the history of Ireland was not a story of continuous armed resistance, but rather a 'history of peaceful penetration. . . It has not been a struggle for the ideal of freedom for 750 years symbolized in the name Republic. It has been a story of slow, steady economic encroach by England . . . Nobody notices, but that is the thing that has destroyed our Gaelic civilization.' De Valera proposed in place of the treaty a 'Document No. 2' which provided for a form of external association with the British Commonwealth, whereby the king would be granted recognition as head of the Commonwealth and there would be no oath of allegiance. For de Valera the oath was the crucial issue. Symbolically it seemed too great a renunciation of recent achievements. To betray the republic by compromise was perhaps essential – but to return to proclaiming loyalty to the king seemed unthinkable. The Dáil voted for the Treaty by 64 votes to 57 – De Valera – in tears, resigned as president of the Irish Republic and head of the government. His words on leaving the Dáil were:

The Irish people established a republic . . . Therefore, until such time as the Irish people in regular manner disestablish it, this republic goes on. Whatever arrangements are made [the Dáil] is the supreme sovereign body in the nation; this is the body to which the nation looks for its supreme government, and it must remain that – no matter who is the executive . . . until the Irish people had disestablished it.

The treaty split every organization in the country. The IRA divided for reasons more intransigent than those of de Valera. A section believed that any compromise was by definition a betrayal. As the divide slipped toward civil war de Valera continued to use inflammatory language, but though his initial rejection may have lent constitutional gravity to the split, he was excluded from the military campaign of the anti-treaty side. The IRA was now split into the new Free State Army under the control of the newly constituted Provisional Government of the Irish Free State with Michael Collins as chairman, and what now came to be known as the Republican Army or the 'Irregulars' under no specific civilian control. The Provisional Government of Collins was answerable only to the British Government. They labored under the threat of the resumption of British rule if they failed to control the new state – in effect this meant if they failed to suppress the republican rebellion. In early 1922 an attempt at negotiations was made between the two sides. Collins in particular felt closer to many of his opponents than to his new allies. Very soon it seemed as if establishment Ireland, which had played no role in the struggle to date, was moving in behind the Treatyites. The Catholic Church threw its full weight behind the Provisional Government, and in the general election of June 1922 the Treatyites won a clear majority of 58 to 36 seats. Collins became increasingly dissatisfied with the treaty as he witnessed, powerless, the pogroms against Catholics in Belfast. When Field Marshal Sir Henry Wilson, a security adviser to the Northern government, was murdered, the British government concluded that the killing was the work of the Irregulars who had seized the Four Courts in Dublin. Collins was given an ultimatum – to attack them, or to prepare for the re-entry of British forces. With the shelling of the Four Courts the civil war really began. Six weeks

later Arthur Griffith, who had taken over as president of the Executive Council died suddenly at the age of 51. Shortly afterward Collins, now commander in chief of the Free State Army, was killed by a bullet in the head at an ambush in Beal na mBláth in Cork. He was just 32. He had been attempting to meet Liam Lynch, the Irregulars' leader, to halt the war. Even before June, differences between Collins and the rest of the Free State cabinet had become apparent. He was closer to his former allies and present enemies than he was to men like William T. Cosgrave who now took over Griffith's role, or the dour Ernest Blythe, or the cold and impeccable Kevin O'Higgins. The death of Collins removed any possibility of the aversion of civil war.

The Free State Government restored order scrupulously, meticulously and coldly. In a 12-month period the National Army executed 77 Irregulars. Some were shot without trial in exemplary retaliations. The government campaign succeeded. Law and order was restored, a new administration was constituted, the Irish Free State took over from the former United Kingdom province. Republicans, as treaty opponents were all called, refused to sit in the newly constituted Dáil and retained the fiction of being the 'true' Dáil in apostolic succession to the Second Dáil, which had been the Dáil of the Republic. Many Republicans remained in internment camps, many fled to the United States, but all agreed in denying recognition to the institutions of a state that they felt had been erected on the betrayed body of the republic.

Above: Young boys sing nationalist songs among a crowd outside Mountjoy prison in Dublin, 1921, on the day of the execution of an IRA man.

CHAPTER 11

TWO IRISH STATES, 1922-69

Tʜᴇ pro-treaty party in 1922 was reconstituted as the Cumann na nGaedheal party. De Valera's anti-treaty party retained the name Sinn Féin. The retention by de Valera's party of the old name, under which nationalists had fought reflected the Republicans' claim to be the true inheritors of the tradition of 1916. According to their analysis the men in power were British lackeys, traitors who had betrayed the republic, compromisers of an incorruptible ideal and policemen of the retained British connection. To the pro-treaty party the Republicans were self-deluding hypocrites, more attached to the rhetoric of independence than the reality of maintaining an independent state which was the maximum that could have been extracted through negotiation. By agreeing to negotiate in the first place they claimed de Valera had displayed a willingness to compromise, and now excoriated them for the best compromise that could realistically have been extracted. The bitterness and loathing that the civil war engendered cannot be exaggerated. Instead of merely seeing one another as having different routes to a shared goal, both sides lashed out furiously, each seeing the other side as treacherous, duplicitous and insincere. The civil war was the greatest tragedy of twentieth-century Ireland, as men who had shared their strength to fight a common enemy unleashed that strength on one another. The pro-treaty party won, if either side in such an internecine conflict can be represented as winning, and in their victory ensured that democratic forms and structures would be the basis for subsequent constitutional development. The Republicans retained their self-image as incorruptible true patriots, but the first independent Irish state was constructed by their opponents.

Under the leadership of the former Dublin municipal politician William T. Cosgrave, the new government displayed a willingness to take extreme measures to clamp down on any threat that the Republicans posed to the state. These included executions, internment and a ruthless restructuring of the Army. They saw dangers to a democratic state as emanating not merely from the Republicans, but also from militaristic army men on their own side who had never recognized the principle of the subordination of military to civilian power. This threat from within their own ranks was finally resolved by the subordination of the military in an army crisis in 1924. When the military threat posed by Republicans was seen to be resolved the government proceeded to reduce the size and power of the Free State Army.

Sinn Féin boycotted the Dáil, though they continued to accept the principle of standing for election. For the first years after independence constitutional opposition was provided by the Labour Party and a handful of Independents. Despite these constitutional anomalies the state functioned democratically under the constitution of 1922 which had been subjected to the vetoing power of the British Government. The legislature was a two-tiered structure with a Dáil and Senate, the Senate providing a regulatory role not dissimilar to that of the House of Lords. The Upper House, as the Senate was known, was heavily representative of the former Unionist community in the 26 counties, and was designed to serve as a watchdog on their constitutional rights which were explicitly enshrined in the constitution. Politicians were extremely conscious of the 'Home Rule, Rome Rule' taunts of Unionists in the past and nervously tried to demonstrate the inaccuracy of such predictions. The transfer of

Previous pages: Eamon de Valera, 1882-1970.

Below: Unionist workers drive Belfast nationalists down York Street, Belfast, 2 September 1920.

Below right: Signatures on the treaty of December 1921.

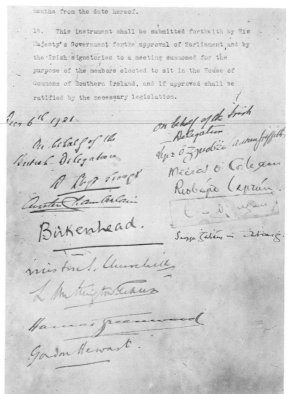

Left: Kevin O'Higgins, 1892-1927, seen in February 1923. O'Higgins was minister for Home Affairs in William Cosgrave's Free State government and helped suppress the anti-treaty republicans before his own assassination in 1927.

power in the civil service and judiciary was apparently smooth. Many of the former 'senior men' stayed on to supervise a period of transition. New departments were structured out of the bones of the old boards through which Dublin Castle had administered the country. The structure of the judiciary remained substantially unchanged though, as in the civil service, a new élite moved in, usually amicably, to assume old roles. The Free State Government proceeded gradually, courteously and cautiously. They were above all concerned to demonstrate the capacity of the Irish to govern themselves, and this desire served as a brake on any extreme or radical experimentation. Their aim was a smooth and peaceful transfer of power and in this they succeeded.

From the beginning cultural nationalism, which had formed the views of the new generation of politicians, was recognized as central to nationalist feeling. Since Republicans seemed to have appropriated all of the obvious impedimenta of romantic nationalism the government, under the influence of the Irish language enthusiast Ernest Blythe, pursued one clear nationalist goal – the restoration of the Irish language. Thus, in the first decade of independence education policy was largely dominated by this one issue. The attempt at revival was sincere, though limited, and the introduction of the Irish language into schools and government departments was not accompanied by any clear public commitment to actually speak the language.

The creation of the state of Northern Ireland had come about while the remaining parts of Ireland were absorbed in a guerrilla war. What was happening in the north seemed remote. It was assumed that when the war in the south was won the matter would, in some unspecified fashion, be resolved. After the signing of the treaty the issue of the status of Northern Ireland was not central to the civil war divide, since it was assumed that the Boundary Commission which was provided for in the terms of the treaty would 'settle the issue.' The South's Provisional Government was appraised of events in Northern Ireland by the Northern Advisory Committee composed of poli-

Below: Eamon Duggan, Arthur Griffith and Michael Collins (left to right), at a Sinn Féin meeting.

Above: Cumann na nGaedheal election posters in Ennis, County Clare, 1923. Although Cumann na nGaedheal won the election, their anti-treaty opponents succeeded in gaining about one third of the elected candidates.

tically active northern nationalists and Catholic clerics, and in the months before the death of Michael Collins the plight of northern Catholics who were apparently being massacred in the ghettoes of Belfast and Derry, was politically to the fore. Collins met Craig on the issue, but a pact that they reached broke down on Craig's unwillingness or inability to control his own supporters. One of the few areas in which the treaty split was initially insignificant was in relation to that part of the IRA who 'conducted operations' in the new northern state. They continued to act as an undivided force, harassing and undermining the new northern government. It is possible that Collins, in the months before his death, considered increasing military support to northern nationalists in direct contravention of the treaty terms. After his death however, the remaining cabinet ministers demonstrated clearly that they were not willing to risk a repudiation of the treaty settlement by Britain for the sake of assisting northern Irish Catholics, however serious their plight. In principle, northern nationalist leaders agreed with them. To jeopardize the existence of the first independent Irish state for any group of nationalists was agreed to be indefensible. The Dublin government therefore ceased all arms supplies and turned its attention to the less contentious

issue of Catholic education in northern Ireland, which the northern bishops saw as the most grave and immediate threat. Realists above all, both government and hierarchy recognized that the northern state did in fact exist, and that the best accommodation within it for the nationalist population was the paramount issue. Moreover, both parties agreed that the Boundary Commission provided for in the treaty would deal with the fundamental issue of partition. There were considerable numbers of northern nationalists who took a quite different view, but they continued to act alone in attacking the new state from within.

The outcome of the negotiations of the Boundary Commission in 1924 was devastating to southern public opinion. Instead of conceding vast tracts of territory to the Irish Free State as had been predicted – baselessly – the Commission report, as leaked to a London morning newspaper proposed to remove a few patches of territory from the south. The Dublin Government was shocked and cornered. The greatest institutional hope for the reintegration of the island, in which all faith had been blindly placed had, proved empty. As a reasonable mode of extrication, they agreed to accept the existing situation.

The southern government had established the new Irish Free State by a scrupulous embracing of constitutional principles. The only constitutional route to a reintegrated Ireland was now closed to them. Unless they had repudiated the constitutional basis on which they had acted to date they had no choice but to accept the status quo. This they did quickly and in a fashion best calculated to cause them minimum internal damage. Public opinion in the south saw the Commission as having been controlled by the British who were now committed to the maintenance of the state that they had constructed, as duplicitous, treacherous and determined to 'ruin' the ideal of Irish independence which lay at the heart of Irish nationalist aspiration. Northern Irish Catholics were stunned, frightened and disbelieving. The constitutional route to unity had been closed, the southern government had already displayed its unwillingness to attempt to achieve it by force. Yet, at least in the ideal, the public desire for re-unification was so great that a belief in re-unification 'somehow' remained fundamental to the political life of the Free State. In this belief it was convenient to forget the existence of the Protestant population who emphatically did not want to 'come in,' and imaginatively to see the north as lost territory or the home of exiled nationalists. Northern Irish Protestants could then be represented as merely deluded dupes of British machinations. Before the outcome of the sessions of the Boundary Commission nationalists elected to the Northern Ireland parliament had turned to the Dublin Government for instructions as to how to proceed – should they enter or not? After the sitting of the Commission and Dublin's acquiescence in the status quo they

were uncertain on the best course of action. They gave allegiance to a southern parliament, unwilling or unable to sustain the burden of that allegiance. They had boycotted the institutions of the state of Northern Ireland in deference to their allegiance to the Free State, yet the Free State now seemed in effect to be willing to recognize the constitutional existence of Northern Ireland. De Valera seized upon the Boundary Commission as yet another example of how the Free State Government had departed from nationalist ideals. He lamented their betrayal of 'our north-

Above: Waiting for poor relief, Dublin, February, 1921.

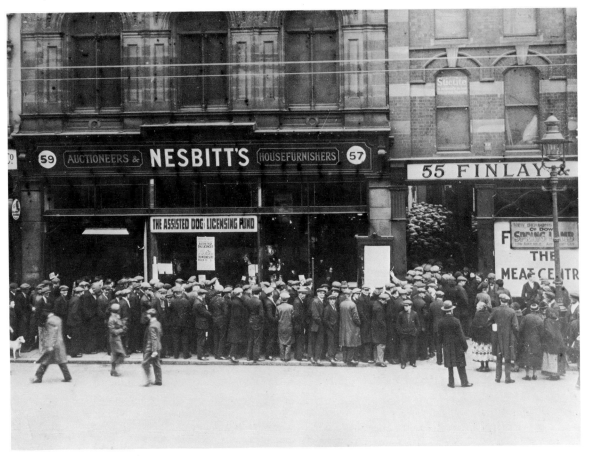

Left: Queue for assisted dog licensing fund, Belfast.

Above: Immigrants sighting Canada.

1927, made the government unwilling to tolerate any continued ambiguity on the question of constitutionalism. Provision was made whereby members could not be elected to parliament unless they declared their willingness to take up their seats. By the elaborate fiction of treating the oath of allegiance which was taken before assuming a seat in the Dáil as an empty formula, de Valera led his party into the Dáil. Many were said to have revolvers about their person, but they nonetheless took their seats in the prescribed manner. Only four years after the conclusion of a bloody civil war the protagonists faced one another across a constitutional assembly. In 1932 de Valera's party won a constitutional majority.. Cumann na nGaedheal demonstrated their democratic commitment by conceding power in the prescribed constitutional fashion. On assuming power de Valera behaved in a constitutional manner. He continued with the policy of steady disentanglement from the British connection begun by his predecessors. He removed the oath of allegiance and ceased payment of land annuities as had been his election platform. By 1931 the Free State had achieved the appearance of political sovereignty through the Commonwealth though that reality was diminished by the provisions for times of war. During the 1930s, de Valera further diminished the role of the British Government in the internal affairs of the Free State by undermining the role of the governor general. The core of de Valera's policy was demonstrated on the issue of land annuities, agreed payments under the treaty, which the British Government claimed to be owed for monies advanced in the land transfers made at the turn of the century. This issue appealed to de Valera as a means of appearing to repudiate the treaty in a manner that was apparently constitutional. This confrontation with the British Government was popular with his own supporters, who rejoiced in a public show of defiance. In

ern brothers,' yet failed to provide any clear indication of how the situation ought to have been treated.

In 1926 de Valera broke with the more intransigent members of Sinn Féin who still wished to maintain a policy of denying constitutional recognition to either of the states established on Irish soil. De Valera saw clearly that the Free State was a constitutional reality, and that all future politics would be conducted within the forum of the state. This was a measure of the Free State Government's success. In 1926 he formed his own party, Fianna Fáil (Soldiers of Destiny), which contested elections in the following year. The assassination of Kevin O'Higgins, one of the most formidable of the Free State's ministers in

Right: Immigrants in the Registration Room, Ellis Island, New York, 1912. Ellis Island was one of the main receiving points for entry to the United States.

Left: British propaganda photograph from the end of World War II captioned 'Behind the crisis with Eire . . . the Northern Ireland bases we must protect.' This refers to an exchange of speeches by de Valera and British Prime Minister Churchill in which Churchill criticised Eire's neutrality and denial of British access to former naval bases in Southern Ireland.

defense of this position an economic war of respective tariff impositions was fought, which inflicted grievous economic loss on Irish farmers. De Valera negotiated with the Dominions Office on the issue, and acquired the habit of negotiating with British ministers. On his election in 1932 the British press and most government ministers had represented him as a fanatical and dangerous revolutionary. By the mid-1930s he had however won a reputation as a skilled if long-winded negotiator. He had demonstrated his capacity to display the limits of his tolerance to his former allies in Sinn Féin by outlawing the IRA their military wing, in 1936.

His constitution of 1937 was merely a final public pronouncement of his success in the achievement of 'a republic in fact,' if not in name, which was his declared ambition in 1932. He had already availed himself of the abdication crisis of 1936 to rush two bills through the Houses of Parliament to 'delete from the constitution all mention of the king and of the representative of the crown' and 'to make provision by ordinary law for the exercise by the king of certain functions in external matters as and when so advised by the Executive Council [the Free State cabinet].'

De Valera had come to power on the issue of repudiating the treaty in a constitutional fashion. He had presented his party to the electorate as superior nationalists, as more truly 'Irish' than the Cumann na nGaedheal party. He had concentrated his political skills after achieving power on successive further dismantlings of the treaty. By 1937 he had diminished the office of governor general, removed the king to the fringes of the constitution and rejected the agreement that the Free State was bound to honor 'debts' for Irish land. In return the population had paid an economic price. They had also enjoyed the 'victories' that de Valera had won for them, and seemed to accept his self-representation as more truly nationalist than his opponents. The achievements of the first Cumann na nGaedheal government were forgotten in the litany of nationalist 'sins' they were alleged to have committed, and in some unspecified fashion it seemed as if they were 'responsible' for permitting partition to harden into permanence. The price that the Free State paid during the economic war (96 percent of Irish exports went to Britain) was represented as the price that had to be paid for true independence.

The Irish economy had been shattered in 1922. The Free State Government had the added burden of rebuilding a country in which much of the infrastructure had been destroyed by war. The revolutionary language of the rebels did not extend to any social radicalism in the new state. Conventional economic verities ruled and the only evidence of radicalism was confined to concluding the creation of a class of small agrarian proprietors who were notoriously conservative after appeasement by land. Budgets were balanced, health services remained unchanged in their provisions, if not their structures. Economically the old system was preserved in all particulars. Emigration continued at its old rate from the mid 1920s onward, and by the mid 1930s had escalated to a positive rush from the country's shores. De Valera had an image of Ireland that was rural, isolated and still. In reality the new state was stagnant.

The Cumann na nGaedheal Government had passed legislation for the censorship of films and books, had refused to provide facilities for divorce and had generally presumed that Catholic moral values were universally accepted. Since the Church of Ireland and other Protestant communities in the south were conservative in the extreme, there was little public opposition from them on such issues. There was, however, opposition from intellectuals in both communities who were horrified by what they saw as the complacent insularity of the new state.

De Valera's constitution of 1937 enshrined the moral values of the new society in permanent form. Morally, the constitution was conserva-

Above: World War II
bombing in Belfast.

tive, but not atypical for its time. It was more radical in its claims to sovereignty. The constitution did not refer to the national territory as the Irish Free State but as Ireland or Eire. The first official language of this state was declared to be Irish. The national territory was proclaimed to be 'the whole island of Ireland, its islands and the territorial seas,' but the actual existence of the state of Northern Ireland was recognized, obliquely, in the statement that 'pending the reintegration of the national territory' the laws of the state would apply only to that area currently administered by Dublin. The constitution was a careful and comprehensive document. It has proved adequate for 50 years. In the matter of the 'national territory,' however, it reveals a willingness to deal with reality as it ought to have been rather than reality as it was. The constitution was passed by a majority in the legislature and by an electoral majority in the country. No clause of the constitution was to be altered in the future except by a referendum of the people. The British Government accepted the new situation. De Valera had been cautious in his dismantling of the treaty. He had taken care to enlist the sympathy of other Commonwealth countries, and had given the appearance of a scrupulous constitutionalism in all matters. That he had used the Abdication crisis in an ungentlemanly fashion was resented, but the intrinsic embarrassment of the situation ensured that the British government would not publicly confront him on the issue. In the constitution he had carefully not proclaimed a republic, which would have forced the British Government into confrontation. His final act in the dismantling of the treaty was to secure the return of the treaty ports from Neville Chamberlain in 1938. This return, which seemed a moderate concession to Chamberlain in 1938, was vital to de Valera's view of Irish sovereignty. In his eyes Ireland was not a truly sovereign state until such time as the

government was free to pursue an independent foreign policy. This the agreement of 1938 provided for. Henceforth the British Government had no automatic right to make use of Irish bases in times of war.

That situation was soon put to the test, and in 1939 de Valera decided on a highly popular policy of official neutrality. This was not a new penchant for isolationism. In the very first years of the Free State the army had revealed a desire to protect Irish neutrality in times of war. The difference was that in 1939 this was a practical possibility and not merely an aspiration. In practice, as recently released documents demonstrate, de Valera's neutrality was heavily loaded in favor of the Allies. At the time there was no obvious public sign of this, as, for neutrality to be observed, it was essential that it appeared to be scrupulously enforced. De Valera interned former colleagues in the IRA, now an illegal organization, who indicated an intention to aid German attacks on Britain. The new state was closed to the world during the war years, but there was a sense of shared pride in the actual pursuit of an independent foreign policy which was seen to be a final proof of independence. There was widespread public support for the avoidance of a war in which it was felt that Ireland would have been no more than a pawn. To the British and Americans however, particularly the former, Irish neutrality was inexcusable, a deliberate stab in the back, motivated by no desire other than a will to spite the British. Northern Ireland by contrast was an exemplary ally, providing vital bases for transAtlantic supplies, placing every facility at the disposal of the Allies and contributing in every way at the highest level. When Belfast was bombed, de Valera immediately sent a fleet of ambulances to assist in the relief effort, but after the war it was his offer of condolences to the German ambassador on the death of Adolf Hitler that was most clearly remembered. De Valera was a man who did things by the book, and as far as he was concerned such an action was demanded by the protocol of neutrality. During the war Churchill forwarded a telegram seeking Irish entry into the war which included the phrase 'A nation once again?' This was presumed to be an oblique commitment to reunification in return for assistance in the war effort. De Valera declined the offer. Irish neutrality rankled Churchill. In his victory speech Churchill, congratulating the Allies for their forbearance in respecting Irish neutrality, commented that without the Irish ports the war had been won, while the Dublin Government was left to 'frolic with the Germans and later with the Japanese representatives to their heart's content.' De Valera in a public broadcast replied that if British necessity were admitted as a moral imperative 'no small nation adjoining a great power could ever hope . . . to go its way in peace.' He further congratulated Churchill on having failed to add 'another horrid chapter to the already bloodstained record of relations between the two islands.' Irish public opinion was thrilled by de Valera's response. His public standing had never been so high, and there was a widespread public belief that in some obscure way the state had come of age as a result of the experience of the war years.

There was however one serious outcome of the policy. As a result of the loyalty of Northern Ireland during these years Churchill recognized that new bonds between Northern Ireland and the rest of the United Kingdom had been forged: 'The bonds of affection between Great Britain and Northern Ireland have been tempered by fire and are now I firmly believe unbreakable.' Even Craig had believed in the 1930s that the state of Northern Ireland could not be maintained indefinitely. If the policy of neutrality had represented a coming-of-age for the southern sense of independence, it had even more clearly lent to Northern Ireland a sense of statehood. The increased British commitment to its maintenance was central to that revised perception.

Though de Valera's popularity was at a high point immediately after the war it was also, like Churchill's, at a zenith from which it was to fall. As a wartime leader de Valera had been superb but on returning to political 'normalcy' the population of Eire, as the British persisted in calling the state (disliking the claim to the whole island felt to be implicit in the title Ireland), was faced by economic realities. The economy was stagnant, antiquated and arid. Emigration was constant at approximately 100,000 in a five-year period. Rural lifestyles had changed scarcely at all in the two decades since the achievement of independence. After 16 years of uninterrupted Fianna Fáil rule the electorate rejected them in the election of 1948.

The Cumann na nGaedheal party had fallen into disarray after the election of 1932 in which they had lost power. During that election the

Above: IRA bombing in London, 25 June 1939. Although de Valera had declared the IRA illegal in 1936, they continued their campaign against partition.

existence of an alleged communist plot to overtake the state had been much vaunted. The scare was based on the activities of an IRA group Saor Eire who had turned to radical socialism as an alternative to arid abstentionism. The threat posed was never very serious, but the Cumann na nGaedheal government reacted hysterically nonetheless. The reaction was similar to red scares all over Europe in these years. Associated with this fear of communism, with which it was felt Fianna Fáil might collude on achieving power, was the expectation that de Valera would summarily dismiss Free State Army officers. In fact he did not do so, but the Army Comrades Association which had been founded to guard against such an eventuality remained active during 1933. Called the Blueshirts, the comrades were a rather innocuous Irish version of embryonic fascist movements in Europe. It is doubtful if the ideological similarity can be pushed beyond a shared propensity for strutting around in uniform and a dislike of communism. The leader of this movement was a former army officer Eoin O'Duffy. In 1933 Cumann na nGaedheal united with the small Centre Party and the Blueshirts to form a new party Fine Gael under the leadership of O'Duffy.

O'Duffy was soon revealed to be an inflated embarrassment and within a couple of years the leadership of the new party was placed back in the hands of Cosgrave. It was an embarrassment from which the new Fine Gael party only slowly disentangled itself. Since there was no ideological divide in Irish politics, since the treaty alone was the source of division, it was impossible for Fine Gael to find a handle with which to defeat Fianna Fáil as the party displayed such skill in dismantling the treaty. They could scarcely campaign on the ground of wishing to retain the treaty intact. Nor were they capable of transforming the terms of debate on to social or economic issues since

CHAPTER 12

A TROUBLED TIME

Previous pages: Stormont Castle, seat of the government of Northern Ireland until its abolition by the British in 1972.

Below: Loyalist supporters prepare to attack the People's Democracy marchers at Burntollet Bridge, January 1969. Police did little to protect the marchers and the repercussions of the event helped widen the divide between the communities in the north.

FROM its foundation Northern Ireland had defined itself as a state under siege. Under siege from the state on its borders and under siege by the minority within the state of Northern Ireland who wished to overturn it and become a part of the 'Irish nation.' In its early days, in the face of IRA threats, it acquired London's permission to constitute its own subsidiary militia to defend the state and assist the Royal Ulster Constabulary in maintaining order. In 1922 and 1923 sectarian rioting in certain areas soon degenerated into a systematic campaign against the Catholic community. This was motivated by a desire to avenge the attacks that the IRA was seen to be mounting against the new state. Despite the protests of Dublin the forces of law and order did not seem able or willing to protect the Catholic nationalist community. The 'B Specials,' as the most significant section of the auxiliary militia were called, were seen by the Catholic community as a force deliberately constructed for their persecution. In the early years, before the Boundary Commission, northern nationalists placed the new state at arm's length. They refused to acknowledge its authority, boycotted its assemblies and generally behaved as if it was an unsavory temporary reality. Thus all the institutions of the state became by default Unionist or Protestant. Catholics felt persecuted within the state and because of their lack of allegiance the Protestant majority developed an interest in maintaining them in their position of impotence. Proportional representation, which had been placed at the center of the rules governing the

constitutional ordering of the state, was abolished in 1929, thus permanently ensuring Protestant majority rule. The population of Northern Ireland in 1922 was 1,256,000, with a ratio of Protestants to Catholics of two to one. In the parliament of Northern Ireland, out of a total of 52 seats, the Unionists never held less than 34 seats before 1968. Northern Ireland also sent 12 MPs to the British House of Commons, the majority of whom have always been members of the Unionist parties.

The internal politics of Northern Ireland in the years preceding 1968 were dominated by the divisions between the two communities. Economic pressure acted upon sectarian tensions at period of recession. Riots in Belfast and Derry which died down in the mid-1920s flared again in the recession of the mid-1930s. The Unionist party was uninterruptedly in power from the foundation of the state in 1920.

Northern Ireland appeared to be a society without an agreed consensus as to its right to exist. For Northern Unionists their state was a proud achievement. The Catholic community was seen as a fifth column within the state, anxious to bring about its destruction. It is from this perspective that discriminatory legislation against the Catholic community must be understood. The preservation of a separate Catholic educational structure ensured that two communities were educated with different values and different allegiances. The Nationalist Party was as monolithic a representation of Catholic opinion as the Unionist Party was of Protestant opinion.

Left: A Civil Rights demonstration rally in Trafalgar Square, London 1968.

The Nationalist Party was a constitutional party. Its declared aim was the reunification of Ireland. Its policy of parliamentary abstention was not consisent, and after the confirmation of the status of Northern Ireland in the mid 1920s representatives entered the Northern Ireland Parliament. Withdrawal was however a protest response that was frequently evoked in the face of what nationalists viewed as extreme political provocation. Financial relations between London and Belfast dominated the political thinking of Craig, the Northern Ireland prime minister throughout the 1930s. In the face of massive unemployment Craig was forced to confront pressure from Progressive Unionists dissatisfied with economic conditions. But as de Valera in the southern state distracted attention from economic problems by focussing upon issues of sovereignty, so Craig in the north deflected economic criticisms of his administration by focussing attention on the threats posed to the constitutional status of Northern Ireland. Rifts in Unionist ranks were soon closed by evoking this specter, and the homogeneity of Unionism in these years is best understood as a cleaving together induced by shared fears. As in the southern state, constitutional preoccupations militated against the evolution of class-based politics. There were exceptions, as the Northern Ireland Labour Party demonstrated, but any renewal of insecurity, as at the time of the declaration of the Republic in 1949 resulted in a return to the political fold.

It is not possible as yet to analyze politically developments either north or south since the late 1960s. Certain observations can, however, be made. In the changes that have taken place since the late 1960s certain outlines seem clear. The initial pressure that provoked the civil rights agitation of the late 1960s was an unwillingness on the part of Catholics to continue to accept what they believed to be second-class citizenship. While traditional Catholic resistance to such disabilities had taken the form of sporadic support for IRA campaigns to destroy the state of Northern Ireland, the protestors of 1968 were different in means and intent. They were the first educated

Below: Bernadette Devlin MP, 28 February 1972. Bernadette Devlin was a young radical leader of the People's Democracy movement when she was elected to Westminster in 1969. In 1970 she was convicted and imprisoned for making petrol bombs during the troubles in Derry in 1969. She lost her parliamentary seat in 1974 but, now Mrs McAliskey, she remains active in politics.

Above: The Reverend Ian Paisley.

Above right: Captain Terence O'Neill, Prime Minister of Northern Ireland, discussing the crucial February 1969 election with the press, 26 February 1969.

Below: A British soldier in Belfast, March 1971.

generation of Catholics born within the state of Northern Ireland. They lacked their parents' blind faith in the willingness of the south to 're-scue' them in some unspecified fashion. Thus the marches of students in the People's Democracy and Northern Ireland Civil Rights movements of 1968 and 1969 were primarily concerned with the achievement of specific rights within the state of Northern Ireland. Moderate unionists like Terence O'Neill had been moving toward a 'lib-eralization' of the state in the mid-1960s, but such attempts activated the fundamentalist, uncom-promising wing of Unionism as manifested in the street-preaching rabble-rousing of the Reverend Ian Paisley. Unionism had relied upon the bogey of constitutional threats to ensure electoral domi-nation since the foundation of the state and now found that the working classes were not prepared to depart from deeply held convictions. It is from this tension that the present divide within Unionism comes. The Democratic Unionist Party of the Reverend Ian Paisley represents the most fundamental working-class roots of Union-ism. That he attracts middle-class support is unsurprising. Though not taken literally by such support, he is the best possible negotiator for Unionism.

The British Government had displayed limited interest in the state of Northern Ireland since its inception. The systematic dismantling of the constitutional protections provided for Catholics was ignored by Westminster. In the words of a senior Northern Ireland civil servant:

History teaches very simplified lessons. The relevant 'lesson' learnt from Irish history by Great Britain derives from a long drawn-out defeat. The residual 'lesson,' learnt much too well, was that Ireland entails trouble of an unintelligible kind and that the whole island is politically hostile. The attitude tends to be applied to Northern Ireland as much as to the Republic.

Thus when in 1969 the Northern Ireland 'prob-lem' burst upon the television screens of the world, the British Government's attitude was one of irritation and annoyance. Since the mid-1960s Harold Wilson had felt confident that O'Neill was proceeding to end discrimination against

Left: Masked youths stone a security force position in Belfast.

Below: A British soldier with a young child in Northern Ireland.

Catholics in jobs, housing, in the gerrymandering of constituencies and in the existence of plural voting. Official British policy was to 'press' the Unionist Government for reforms. When the issue of Catholic disabilities received the forced attention of the British Government through the actions of the police in 'restraining' the civil rights marches, it was, unfortunately, on the administration of law and order that attention focussed. While reforms in any area were electorally difficult for the Unionist party to sell to their supporters, reforms in the area of the administration of justice were seen to go to the very roots of the state's stability. Thus the events of 1969 were soon seen by the Unionist community as yet another assault on the very existence of the state of Northern Ireland. By construing events in that way, by withdrawing electoral support from Unionist politicians who attempted to compromise, the Unionist community sealed its own institutional fate. The state which had been 'closed' since its foundation was exposed to the world through the media and Unionists became increasingly defensive as their reasons for denying Catholics fundamental rights were represented as untenable. The British Government had ignored internal events in Northern Ireland for so long because world attention was not focussed upon them, but the decision to send in British troops to 'defend' the Catholic ghettoes from attack in 1969 marked their reluctant involvement.

Southern opinion was at a high pitch in the period before troops were sent in. The Taoiseach Jack Lynch made a speech in which he said that the south would not 'stand idly by' and watch the

Right: Irish Taoiseach Jack Lynch, 7 September 1971. Lynch succeeded Sean Lemass as leader of Fianna Fail in 1966 and was Taoiseach from then until 1973 and again later in the 1970s.

Catholic population be attacked. Refugee camps were set up along the border with Northern Ireland, and in a consequence of the hysteria of these years two government ministers were sacked and faced criminal charges for conspiring to import arms for the Catholic community in Northern Ireland. Initially the British Government supported the northern Unionists in advising the southern government to desist from interfering in the internal affairs of a foreign state. The rhetoric of this position was to an extent betrayed by isolated gestures which indicated a willingness to recognize that the republic did have some greater degree of involvement, if only because of the existence of a shared border.

Below: Brian Faulkner, former prime minister of northern Ireland, October 1972. Faulkner was prime minister from March 1971 until Stormont was suspended in 1972 and in 1973 helped work out the short-lived Sunningdale agreement.

The views of the Catholic community on the IRA in the years of the late 1960s were clearly revealed by the daubed imprint on the walls of a Belfast ghetto 'I Ran Away.' The IRA had been a negligible factor in the early stages of middle-class or student protest. But as the debate focussed around the 'No Go' areas of Derry and Belfast in 1970 the songs of protest shifted from international civil-rights airs like 'We shall overcome' and 1960s' peace songs to republican songs. The old Nationalist Party effectively collapsed to be replaced by the 'new politics' of the Social Democratic and Labour Party. The entry of British troops had been accompanied by a reform package which was intended to appease Catholic discontent. So great were the changes proposed, however, that they went to the very foundations of the Unionist Party. Successive Unionist leaders lost support as they accepted the need to reform, O'Neill to be replaced by James Chichester Clark, and Clark in turn to be replaced by the reputedly 'hard-line' Brian Faulkner.

The reforms forced on the Ulster Government that were to prove most crucial were those of the police and 'B' Specials. Their dismemberment or restructuring was seen by the Protestant working classes as a final betrayal by their own Unionist government. From this discontent the Democratic Unionist Party, through superb local organization, developed. Sectarian riots in Belfast in 1970, the expulsion of Protestants from Catholic estates and the first clear confrontation between the British Army and the Catholic community escalated tensions. The reform package of the previous year did not appear to have 'worked,' though it was certainly proceeding, and the British Government took the view that it had done all in its power. As James Callaghan said to a Labour Party audience in 1970, 'Some problems you can't solve, you have to live with. This is one I think we have to live with.' Such an attitude dominated thinking on Northern Ireland for the following 15 years, or at least until 1981. The 'problem' was seen to be impossible and since such analyses have a tendency to become self-fulfilling prophecies, the problem did indeed become more intractable. The speed with which paramilitary associations grew in both communities bewildered politicians. Class provided a fatal barrier to understanding, since much of the political action seemed to be concentrated in working-class ghettoes. The speed with which the young returned to apparently outworn extreme positions and reforged them seemed amenable to analysis in terms of high unemployment, acclimitisation to violence and any one of a number of institutional factors. The consequences of such revised self definitions were rather harder to come to terms with.

Insofar as the IRA still existed, it split in late 1969. The 'Officials,' the majority section at the time of the split colluded in the civil rights analysis and saw the crisis as one primarily concerned

Left: A meeting of sympathy for the Northern Ireland Peace Movement, 1976. Although the Peace Movement attracted world attention, it did not prove to have any lasting effects despite the appearance of considerable support.

with reforms within the Northern Irish state. The 'Provisionals' on the other hand saw the crisis as an opportunity to use the weaknesses in Unionism to press for the destruction of the state of Northern Ireland. They further emphasized the extent to which the British Government sympathy for the nationalist community appeared to have been shortlived, and suggested that the imminent return of a Tory government in Britain would make this even more true. Chichester Clark's government attempted to woo back Protestant supporters by increased law and order measures against the civil rights movement and by an apparent unwillingness to control Orange marches and processions. In July 1970 there was fierce rioting in Belfast. Five hundred Catholics were driven out of the shipyards. Catholics no longer turned to the British Army for protection and in this instance they were protected by what was to emerge as the Provisional IRA. This was precisely the scenario that the Provos' analysis had required, enabling a strategy of recasting the debate in terms of the oppression of a community by 'imperialist' forces. By casting the British army in the role of oppressor, a recasting facilitated by some of the army's actions, the situation could be reconstructed imaginatively, and ultimately politically, as a straightforward colonial situation. It was against this recasting that the Social Democratic and Labour Party claimed to stand. They sought equal rights within the state of Northern Ireland, though they aspired to a united Ireland in the long term. They recognized that such an end could not be achieved without the consent of the Protestant population of the north, and opposed attempts to bring it about by force.

The Conservative Government of Edward Heath substantially followed the policies laid down by their Labour predecessors. This, in effect, allowed Chichester Clark to proceed in his own fashion. In the summer of 1970 the Provos pursued a bombing campaign, in disregard of the tougher security legislation introduced earlier in the year. Internment was introduced in August 1971. Paisley's departure from the realm of orthodox Unionist politics was confirmed by his opposition to the move and by his clamor for direct rule from Westminster and the abolition of Stormont, the Ulster Parliament. In this, his demands coincided with those of the Provisional IRA. Heath suspended the Stormont Parliament in March 1972, initially for a one-year period. Under direct rule William Whitelaw became Secretary of State for Northern Ireland and the province was administered from the Northern Ireland Office. The Provisional IRA attempted to present direct rule as their victory, though the real reasons for Heath's decision were rather more complex. Moreover the IRA campaign was proving increasingly unpopular within the Catholic community, and outside their ghetto strongholds it was clear that the Catholic community was more willing to listen to the voice of the SDLP.

From the beginning of the 'Troubles' the Dublin Government had presented itself as an external guardian of the rights of the Catholic community. In effect, up to 1972 this meant a re-iteration of the statement that the injustice of partition lay at the roots of violence. In the south certain individuals, notably Conor Cruise O'Brien who had returned to Ireland to join the Irish Labour Party, attempted to disturb what

Far left: Teenage IRA supporters in West Belfast.

Left: A demonstration in support of the nationalist hunger strikers, 1981.

they saw as southern ambiguity on the issue of partition. On the one hand the southern government condemned violence as a means of ending partition and clamped down on the IRA in the south. On the other hand, it reiterated its commitment to unity as the only real solution to the problem, thus it was claimed, lending moral authority to the ends if not the means of violent nationalists. Jack Lynch's government encouraged the SDLP to negotiate with Whitelaw and was horrified by the British government's willingness to talk to the Provisionals after their much-vaunted 'truce' of 1972. In 'Towards a new Ireland' the SDLP declared their policy. They sought a British declaration to withdraw from Northern Ireland, a provincial 'power sharing executive' of Nationalists and Unionists, and the whole to be subordinated to a British-Irish condominium. In the British Government green paper published in October 1973 it was stated that 'whatever arrangements are made for the future of Northern Ireland must take into account the Province's relationship with the Republic of Ireland.' Since the republic had been officially designated as a foreign country with no imaginable claim to internal interference in the affairs of Northern Ireland this was treated as a major advance. The replacement of the Lynch government with a coalition of Fine Gael and Labour deputies, including Conor Cruise O'Brien, resulted in a diminished emphasis on the partition issue, and concentrated more clearly on the need to effect a reasonable accommodation for the Catholic community in the state of Northern Ireland.

The 1973 Sunningdale Agreement between the government of Edward Heath and the coalition government of Liam Cosgrave aimed at power-sharing between the two communities in the north and a degree of cross border co-operation in the proposed Council of Ireland. Ulster

Unionists saw the southern government as acting in concert with the SDLP, quite accurately. The coalition government had been less insistent on the 'Irish dimension' in the settlement than the SDLP but could not afford to be seen to be less nationalist than the SDLP. The Sunningdale Agreement collapsed due to the fall of Heath's government and the Labour government's lack of will to attempt to enforce it in the face of massive Unionist mobilization against it in the 'Front' that organized the Ulster Workers' Strike. The

Below: Republican wall mural at the entrance to Derry's Catholic Bogside district formerly the entry point to 'Free Derry.'

Above: Triumph of the Ulster Workers' Strike, 28 May 1974. Celebrating the fall of the power sharing executive set up by the Sunningdale Agreement.

Below: The signing of the Anglo-Irish Agreement, the most significant agreement in Anglo-Irish relations since the Treaty of 1921.

paramilitary elements in Unionism moved to the fore, as did politicians like James Craig, Ian Paisley and John Taylor. The story of developments in the Unionist world of paramilitaries is no less complex than developments in the nationalist community and cannot be attempted in so brief a survey as this.

While Sunningdale failed, it was significant in that it officially acknowledged for the first time the role of the Republic of Ireland in relation to the problem of Northern Ireland. Henceforth, despite occasional repudiation from the extreme wing of the Conservative Party, the claims of the southern government to some say in the overall strategy governing the northern situation were admitted, though reluctantly by most British politicians.

In 1983-84 in the New Ireland Forum nationalists from north and south attempted to reconsider the basis of their shared aspirations. The features in southern Irish society that made it particularly unattractive to northern Unionists were examined, in particular the role of the Catholic Church in influencing the nature of the law in relation to matters of sexual morality. The Forum had been conceived as a means of rescuing the SDLP from possible political extinction after the hunger strikes of 1981. It was a 'talking shop' in which constitutional nationalists, in broad agreement on most fundamentals, examined possible accommodations to the realities as opposed to the mythologies of nationalist aims. In many respects the Forum Report was a predicatable compendium of nationalist verities. It reiterated the standard nationalist explanation that partition was imposed by the British government, while failing to emphasize the extent to which a separate northern Unionist community had existed before partition. It did, however, represent a new departure in nationalist thinking in one respect – it acknowledged officially the existence of a separate sense of identity in the Unionist population of the northeast based upon its Protestantism, sense of Britishness and economic links to Britain. While such recognition might appear to be merely the statement of the obvious, in terms of Irish nationalism it represented a real departure. For while in the past Irish nationalists had been implicitly aware of such realities they were unwilling actually publicly to admit or confront them. For so long as the republic could claim that partition was the result of divisions artificially fostered by the British government, politicians could refuse to recognize or come to terms with the very real presence of over one million northern Unionists who emphatically did not feel Irish. Such an admission was an acknowledgment of the status quo up to 1920. The Forum did not confront the changes in the Northern Irish nationalists' sense of self since the inception of the state of Northern Ireland. The northern Irish nationalists were represented as remaining frozen within their sense of Irish identity, as if 50 years in a new state had wrought no transformation. This concentration on conflicting identities was the most significant contribution of the Forum Report to the nature of the debate. Another contribution was an explicit statement of three possible acceptable options as the basis for a solution. Only one of these was the reunification option, though all contained an implicit longterm aspiration to that end. Though most southern politicians had agreed in private for many years that immediate reunification was not a possibility, translating that implicit belief into a public pronouncement represented a significant shift.

The Anglo-Irish Agreement of November 1985 was significant in that it was an international treaty on the future of Northern Ireland between the governments of Dublin and London. It adopted one feature of the Forum Report – its preoccupation with the concept of conflicting identities and its willingness to structure future solutions around those identities. It was as spokesperson and watchdog of the rights of Northern Irish nationalists that the Dublin Government was to have a say in the administration of Northern Ireland. The creation of an Irish Government secretariat in Northern Ireland represented the most fundamental shift in Anglo-Irish relations since the treaty of 1921. The agreement provided for an intergovernmental conference to meet at intervals; at this the Irish Government would be able to place its views on the degree of success with which it felt the nationalists were being accommodated. The Dublin Government further retained the right to register complaints if it felt that the administration of justice was falling below standards of impartiality. The agreement is complex but from the northern Unionist point of view it seemed clear on one point, that the republic of Ireland had been given a say in the internal affairs of Northern Ireland. It further seemed to suggest that unless Unionists were prepared to enter into a power-sharing arrangement with Nationalists, to which they remained utterly opposed, then that degree of southern involve-

ment would increase rather than diminish. The aims of Northern Irish Unionists were to destroy the agreement or to render it unworkable.

To the northern Unionists it seemed as if their future had been decided without their consent. According to the British Government, their claim to be a part of the United Kingdom meant that the British Government was their government and therefore it was their duty, if they were in truth loyalists as they claimed, to accept the agreement made on their behalf. Ironically it is perhaps the loyalist sense of identity that is most in need of institutional protection since, apparently betrayed by the British connection to which they give allegiance, they attempt to accommodate the changed nature of that identity. Perhaps the most unfortunate aspect of recent developments in Northern Ireland is the official fossilizing of identities at a time when, if anything is fluid, it is the sense of identity of both communities in Northern Ireland and that of the community of the Republic of Ireland.

Above: Ulster Says No Rally, the Unionist response to the Anglo-Irish Agreement, 3 March 1986.

INDEX

Page numbers in *italics* refer to illustrations

SELECT BIBLIOGRAPHY

Terence Brown *Ireland, a Social and Cultural History, 1922-1979* (Dublin, 1981)

LP Curtis *Anglo Saxons and Celts* (New York, 1968)

George Dangerfield *The Damnable Question* (Quartet, 1976)

Brian de Breffny (ed) *The Irish World – The history and cultural achievements of the Irish people* (Thames and Hudson, 1977)

Liam de Paor *The Peoples of Ireland, from Pre-history to Modern Times* (Hutchinson, 1986)

Ronan Fanning *Independent Ireland* (Helicon, 1983)

FSL Lyons *Ireland Since the Famine* (Fontana, 1971)

Oliver Mac Donagh *States of Mind: A study of Anglo-Irish conflict 1780-1980* (G Allen and Unwin, 1983)

Joel Mokyr *Why Ireland Starved: A quantitative and analytical history of the Irish economy, 1800-1950* (G Allen and Unwin, 1983)

Kenneth Neill *An Illustrated History of the Irish People* (Dublin, 1979)

Conor Cruise O'Brien *A Concise History of Ireland* (Thames and Hudson, 1972)

Patrick O'Farrell *Ireland's English Question: Anglo-Irish relations 1534-1970* (London, 1971)

Thomas Pakenham *The Year of Liberty, the story of the Great Irish Rebellion of 1798* (London, 1969)

Charles Townshend *Political Violence in Ireland, Government and Resistance since 1848* (Oxford, 1983)

Maureen Wall *The penal laws, 1691-1760* (Dundalk, 1961)

ACKNOWLEDGMENTS

The Publisher would like to thank Donald Sommerville who edited the book, Martin Bristow who designed it, Melanie Earnshaw who did the picture research and Ron Watson who compiled the index. We would also like to thank the following picture agencies, institutions and individuals for supplying illustrations on the pages notes:

BBC Hulton Picture Library: pages 47 (below), 76 (top), 85, 86, 89, 92, 97 (top), 99 (top), 103, 105 (both), 106, 108, 113, 117 (top), 121 (top), 123 (both), 124, 125, 126, 128-129, 132 (both), 134 (below), 135 (both), 138 (both), 139, 143 (both), 144-145, 146, 147 (below), 148, 149, 150, 151 (both), 152, 153, 156 (both), 157, 158-159, 160, 161, 162 (both), 164, 165, 166-167, 168 (both), 169 (both), 171 (top), 172 (both), 173, 181 (top), 182 (below), 184 (both), 188 (top)

BBC Hulton/Bettmann Archive: pages 118, 120

Belfast Telegraph: page 180

The Board of Trinity College Dublin: pages 1, 17 (below), 22 (top left), 45

James Brindley: page 38 (below)

The British Library: pages 31 (top), 46, 56

Peter Clayton: pages 23 (inset right), 27 (inset right), 47 (inset right), 54 (inset right)

Commissioners of Public Works in Ireland: pages 12, 13 (top), 20 (2 below), 24-25, 53 (top), 70, 73 (below)

E T Archive: pages 43 (top), 54, 84, 87, 94, 97 (below), 131 (below), 154

John Freeman: pages 10, 15, 21, 22 (below), 23 (below), 30 (both), 75, 178-179

Michael Gibbons: pages 34-35

John Green: pages 11 (below), 14 (top)

The Irish Tourist Board: pages 12, 13 (below), 16, 20 (top), 65 (top), 71, 74 (right), 147 (top), endpapers

Leeds City Art Galleries: page 79

Dave MacLeod: page 17 (top)

The Mansell Collection: pages 28, 44 (both), 52, 55 (below), 59 (top right), 60, 61 (both), 68, 93 (below), 107, 109, 115, 117 (below), 119, 127, 130, 131 (top), 134 (top), 137

Monaghan County Museum Collection: pages 74 (left), 140 (top)

National Gallery of Ireland, Dublin: pages 3, 27, 58, 62-63, 66-67, 69, 78, 82-83, 90-91, 95, 112

National Library of Ireland: pages 4-5, 26, 47 (top 2), 57, 64, 77, 80, 88, 93 (top), 98, 99 (below), 102, 104, 110, 111, 114, 116, 121 (below), 136, 150, 155 (top)

National Museum of Ireland: pages 14 (2 below), 19, 23 (top), 37 (top), 76 (below)

National Portrait Gallery, London: pages 38 (top), 39, 43 (below), 51, 55 (top), 81

Pacemaker Press: pages 182 (top right), 188 (below), 189

Royal Irish Academy: page 18

Mick Sharp: pages 8-9, 11 (top)

Roger Stalley, Trinity College Dublin: pages 29, 32 (both), 33, 36, 40, 41, 53 (below)

Homer Sykes: pages 59 (below left), 65 (below), 182 (left), 183 (both), 186, 187 (left)

TPS/Central Press: pages 163, 170, 181 (below)

TPS/Fox Photos: page 175

TPS/Keystone: page 185

Ulster Folk and Transport Museum: 72, 73 (top)

Ulster Museum, Belfast: pages 42 (top), 48-49, 50, 96, 100-101, 155 (below), 171 (below), 174

Dr R J A Wilson: page 22 (top right)